Sally Kettle

Growing up in Northampton, Sally Kettle lived about as far away from the ocean as you can possibly get, which is surprising as she now speaks and writes about her adventures at sea.

After completing a theatre degree at Brighton University she decided a 'normal' job was not for her, so she set out to row an ocean with her then-partner, Marcus, in October 2003. When circumstances took a turn for the worst she ended up making the Atlantic crossing with her mother, Sarah.

Eighteen months later Sally set out to break another record as skipper of a women's four before tragedy struck and her crew had to struggle for survival in some of the harshest Atlantic Ocean conditions ever recorded.

She has tales enough to tell of freak waves, unrelenting storms and encounters one would rather not have on a boat, but it is her experiences of people that provide inspiration and insight for all.

Sally now lives in Kingston upon Thames with her fiancé, Clint, and her dog, Burt.

www.myspace.com/sallysoddatsea

'I knew we were in trouble the moment our knickers, which are pegged to the mast, started flapping in completely the wrong direction'

SALLY KETTLE

Sally's Odd at Sea

Linda

Enjoy!

Sally x

First published in Great Britain in 2007 by Orana Publishing Limited
www.oranapublishing.com.

A CIP catalogue record for this book is available from the British Library.

ISBN: 978-0-9550751-5-5

Cover design and typesetting by Reluctant Hero
www.reluctanthero.co.uk

Printed and bound in the United Kingdom by Mackays of Chatham

All pictures © Sally Kettle except page i biog picture © Rhys Frampton; picture page 4 top © Claire Mills; picture page 4 bottom © Stephen Kettle (Snr); picture page 6 © Dan Byles; picture page 7 top © Stephen Kettle (Snr); picture page 8 bottom © Steve Kettle (Jnr).

Contents

Part One

ONE

Biking and Bonding

IN THE SUMMER of 2002 Tommo and I had an argument, which wasn't unusual. We'd been seeing each other for three years, but to all intents and purposes the relationship had reached its sell-by date six months before. We managed to fool ourselves into thinking it was still fresh and admittedly we had somehow kept the love light burning. To me, Tommo still looked delicious as he padded around his flat in 'the fluffsters', a gorgeous pair of grey fleecy trousers, and he would leave me in giggles when he launched into his silly 'dirty old man dance'. He would also whittle like an old woman when I lounged all over him 'like a big daft dog' on his rather-too-comfortable sofa, engrossed in his TV. Unfortunately, like siblings on a long car journey, we'd bicker and snipe, to the distraction of our friends and family. Tommo is the only person I know who can wind me up from calm to killer in less than sixty seconds. His ability to annoy me, woo me and make me laugh made me crazy! Perhaps that's why it worked … ish.

That summer we had spent weeks planning a cycling trip to France. It would be our very first holiday together. As Tommo lived on the seafront, just two minutes from the beach, we decided we'd cycle from there, along the coast road to Newhaven, catch a ferry to Dieppe and then make it up as we went along. Because we were skint but adventurous we decided we would camp our way along the northern coast of France. Tommo hadn't been under canvas since he was a kid, so to acclimatise him we bought a tent and pitched it in his front room. We cunningly used some cushions and a carefully placed dining table to erect the four-man tent with in-built gazebo. It was perfect for the two of us and the bikes; it also had enough room in which to cook. So, with tent up and light fading I made some mince and mashed potato and we sat eating it in the dark with only our head torches to guide us. Tommo's neighbours stared in through the windows laughing as we made tea from a Thermos and hopped to the loo in our dayglo sleeping bags. We had achieved a certain sort of peace, a peace that only exists in a makeshift home where we didn't argue over what was on the telly.

~

LURED BY THE naive idea that life would be more exciting by
the seaside – a throwback from my childhood holidays in
Bournemouth, where boys were better looking, ice-cream
came on tap and bonfire parties were the norm – I had moved
from Northampton to study theatre at Brighton University. To
ensure my safe and punctual arrival at lectures and workshops,
where we learnt to be trees, arms flaying as we discovered our
inner selves (isn't that what theatre students do?), my Mum gave
me her blue 'shopper'. It was a fabulous 'sit-up-and-beg' bike,
complete with white basket; the sparkly blue paint was peeling
away from the frame revealing the rusty metal beneath. It was
so ancient I remember sitting on the back of it as a five year
old in a black plastic baby seat. With Brighton's network of
cycling lanes it was the best way to get around, although it was
so heavy I could barely get it upstairs. The gears were so mature
I was at serious risk of a hernia trying to make it up any hills.
Several bikes, boyfriends and a degree later, I met Tommo after
gatecrashing his birthday party wearing a very naughty smile
and a dreadful red wig.

I won't tell you what he said to lure me into his arms, but my
Granny would have blushed. Even though I thought he was a
bit of a weirdo with awful hair (a mop of big brown curls) and
really bad glasses, thick rimmed in tortoiseshell, I was round at
his house within the week. I have to reassure you at this point
that I'm not normally that easy! Tommo was rather shocked
that he had managed to bag a bird in her twenties. He was ten
years my senior, and with the aforementioned looks he did have

to work his maturity, intellect and dry wit. As a writer, he was well read, sensitive and emotional; he wore old-man slippers and a cable-knit cardigan. He had a goldfish tank so dirty you couldn't actually see the fish (he told me he was trying to recreate their natural environment) and, to my dismay, also possessed an obsession with tea making. If I didn't make his mug to his stringent tea-making rules then the whole lot went down the drain.

- Warm the pot
- Scorch the leaves
- Leave until you're able to stand the spoon in it
- Add the milk after pouring the tea

But, strangely, I grew to love all these idiosyncrasies and I knew that being with Tommo would help me become a better person. I began to listen to Radio 4 and learn the names of the all the Cabinet MPs, but most importantly I began to be emotionally honest with myself and with him. Perhaps I was growing up?

~

TOMMO LOVED CYCLING and bombed through the town centre traffic on his red hybrid as I pottered along on my girl's bike in a fluorescent jacket and plaited pigtails. I would pull a face whenever he tried to convince me to cycle to friends' parties. Why couldn't we go by taxi like normal people? He never really understood that a creased forehead, greasy ankles and sweaty armpits did not compliment my party outfit, so as a compromise we would walk there and I would grab a 'backy' back. We would swerve through the darkened streets, me in high heels, slightly inebriated, giggling and complaining that my backside was killing me, Tommo panting as he peddled hard, desperate to get me home before we both fell off the ailing bike. After a pint of cider and a glass or two of whisky I didn't seem to care that my skirt was flapping about and my knickers were on show for all to see.

Tommo's enthusiasm for two-wheeled transportation became infectious and I soon joined him by falling in love with the cornucopia of gadgets that went with the sport. Having installed the appropriate pedals he bought me a pair of cleated shoes, I borrowed his Campagnolo shirt and off we went for our week exploring the highways and byways of northern France, eating pains aux chocolat and arguing over the melted chocolate we had in our morning porridge. We had stupidly bought the wrong porridge oats; they were horribly gritty, requiring an overnight soak. Because we had no milk and neither of us felt brave enough to tackle the goats in the fields nearby, we had to use water. Also, the gas stove we had just wasn't subtle enough, so after half an hour over a roaring flame we had created a gluey wallpaper paste, which could only be saved by the insertion of several chunks of Dairy Milk.

It was a blissful week of wrong turns, which took us into unexpected sleepy seaside villages. We bought paella from enormous sizzling pans at morning markets and found the shark that had been advertised on posters in every town we visited. It was sitting on a truck in Fécamp, life-sized and very plastic. We amused ourselves for at least half an hour, taking photographs of our heads jammed between the bloody plastic teeth, pulling faces of anguished horror. Tommo was much better at it than me.

My bike was a complete wreck and disaster struck on several occasions. In fact, Tommo threatened to throw it from the ferry on the way home. The gears didn't work, the chain kept slipping and eventually broke, as did the pannier rack, but we managed to get it to a bike shop where we persuaded them to weld it all back together again. We returned to England with some very smelly heart-shaped cheese and a couple of bottles of Dieppe's finest cider. As we lounged on the very comfortable sofa deciding what to watch, we congratulated ourselves — against all the laws of emotional physics we had become a really good team.

So, a couple of weeks later, with all this bonding and biking experience under our belts, I decided to pop the inevitable question. I had been saving it up for a while, and although it may not have been the right time and certainly it wasn't usual for a woman to ask, I threw all caution to the wind and went for it anyway.

Tommo could only say no, right?

TWO

Popping the Question

'CAN WE CYCLE from Land's End to John o'Groats?'

'No.'

I didn't get it. I was certain I had asked him before and he'd given me the thumbs up, so why not? We had just returned from France having had a fantastic experience and I had run the London Marathon earlier in the year, so surely I was fit enough to keep up?

Tommo has epilepsy and some of the medication he takes affects his memory, so I was willing to believe he'd forgotten that we'd discussed it before, but after much debate the real reason why he decided I couldn't go finally came out.

'I'm going with Hend. We talked about it ages ago, so you can't come.'

Duncan 'Hend' Henderson, an actor with a powerful, rugby-player physique and dashing good looks (setting many a heart aflutter, including my own), had been Tommo's best friend for five years. They regularly played poker together and spent many an evening screaming at the television whilst watching the footy. They couldn't have had a more stag relationship: in fact I'm convinced they only talked about breasts and Leeds United, although Tommo denies it.

It seemed Hend and his girlfriend, Joanna, were expecting their first baby, so between the two of them they had plotted a final 'big boys and their toys' holiday and I wasn't invited. As you can imagine, I wasn't impressed. Tommo explained at length that this would be their opportunity to celebrate the end of Hend's life. Yes, it was that dramatic. The arrival of this bundle of joy was to herald the end of freedom and life as he knew it, so Tommo and Hend intended to trawl through the British countryside honouring the wishes of a dying man.

There was absolutely no way to compete. Although Tommo couldn't organise his way out of the bathroom, no amount of 'I'll drive the support vehicle' or 'We can cycle back the other way' was going to convince him to go with me. I even suggested I go with my Dad, meeting Tommo and Hend in B & Bs along the way, but he still wasn't having it. Distinctly put out, I huffed and puffed for about half an hour.

'Why don't we row the Atlantic?' Tommo said, nonchalantly.

Where the hell did that come from?

I couldn't believe it: he was trying to appease, patronise and taunt me all at the same time. He knew I got seasick in the bath, he would run the water so hot I'd flush pink with the intensity of the heat and after I had tentatively lowered myself into the bubbles he would swish the water until I felt sick. Apart from the inevitable nausea, neither of us had any seagoing experience, let alone any knowledge of the Atlantic Ocean. I had never even stepped on a yacht. Although we lived by the sea and often popped down for a swim during the summer months, that was about the extent of our combined experience. I was certain no amount of breaststroke in the grey murky waters along Brighton's seafront would prepare us to row an ocean.

'Don't be so stupid,' I spat back. 'You can't row across an ocean, that's ridiculous!'

Of course, I knew you could, theoretically, but actually … ? I curled up into a little ball, grabbing all the covers, and pretended to go to sleep, leaving Tommo to gloat over his small and somewhat insignificant victory. I began to imagine a little wooden boat bobbing amongst the waves – you know the type I mean? 'Come in, *Mother Hubbard*, your time is up.' My heart began racing. I was annoyed and upset. I felt resentful that Tommo had thrown this proposal at me and for some reason I was completely overreacting.

~

HAVING HAD SOME time to think about it, I have now discovered the root of my anger, one which isn't based on the relationship I had with Tommo but on the relationship I had with myself. It took me many months and many miles to understand fully. I mean, you don't just row the Atlantic Ocean on a whim – do you?

Let me explain … For many years I struggled with desperately low self-esteem. I loathed my body. Everything about it made me unhappy. I was too thick round the middle, my legs were stocky, my hair untameable, and not just on my head! My skin was plagued by acne, especially on my cheeks and back, it erupted at every given opportunity. The more important the event/party/date, the greater the number of unsightly boils. So wearing anything that exposed too much dimply, spotty flesh was an absolute no no. I cringed at every photograph, this blobby body sporting a toothy grin with a forehead that was so enormous it reflected the sun like a satellite dish.

To compound the issue I spent a considerable proportion of my teenage years battling an eating disorder that reduced me to surviving on one yoghurt a day. Ten years later I ran the London Marathon, to take control of my body and my life.

I did 'get skinny' preparing for the marathon. For someone who could barely make it to the end of the street before doubling over with a stitch, I forced myself into a punishing training schedule. I went to the gym every morning for an hour and running three times a week. I also joined a running club, which met every Sunday at 9.00 am come rain or shine. Members ran along the seafront and into the Downs, individuals choosing distances varying from half to full marathons cross country. Having trained myself up to a seven-miler I dragged myself out of bed on a particularly miserable day and trudged down the road to Brighton prom. Having felt apprehensive about how my backside looked in my new clingy black leggings I proceeded to whinge and complain my way through an agonising thirteen miles up hill and down dale.

The following weekend I begrudgingly trundled down to the

seafront for the start of another Sunday run. I'm not sure how it happened, but I was talked into attempting the eighteen-mile circuit. Once you start jogging across the Downs, you get to a point where you can't turn back. I was even advised to take my mobile phone just in case I got stuck in a cow pat with no means of escape. I didn't want to be left at the back pulling my legs out of methane-emitting muck, so I kept running. It was horrendous and I whimpered pathetically the entire way round. Keep going. No, stop. Keep going. Go on, stop … you know you want to. Chinese water torture would have been welcome by the time I stumbled to the Meeting Place Cafe. As tears sploshed into my cup of tea a warm flame of self-confidence began to spark in my belly … or was that heartburn from drinking too quickly? Either way, I felt I was making a difference and beginning to regain control of my life.

The following day I couldn't walk. I rolled out of bed, heaved myself up using a couple of chairs and threw myself down the stairs fast enough so as not to notice how much pain my legs were causing me. Hurting but encouraged by my running prowess I set out on a gentle seven-miler through the streets of Brighton only to knacker my knee running down a hill on the way home. My dreams of being the next Zola Budd went out of the window and I had to stop running for the last two months leading up to the marathon. I gallantly attempted the Hastings Half, but ended up in a St John Ambulance before I even got halfway.

But two months later and a stone lighter I made it round the streets of London dressed as Lara Croft in five hours, fifteen minutes and sixteen seconds. With dangerous quantities of Deep Heat and the determination not to ask for help, I managed to run all the way round. This included a sprint into a pub toilet at the nineteen-mile mark, having underestimated just how long I could hold it having passed the portaloos at mile eighteen.

I achieved the goal, I felt more confident, capable and fitter than ever before, but to my utter irritation the nagging insecurity crept up on me. I had accomplished something incredible – over just six months I had gone from a wheezing jog to the end of my street to running twenty-six miles through London non-stop. Having lost the weight, how the hell was I going to stay thin?

In many ways I based my decision to row on the fact that it would be an excellent way to keep trim. I went to work the following day feeling slightly the worse for wear having spent the entire night visualising a small boat in the middle of the ocean, being whipped about amongst the waves, with me, weather beaten but skinny, on its deck.

~

WHEN I LEFT university with the near-mandatory student debts, I started work as an assistant in a valuation firm in the centre of Brighton. The job was entirely traditional in so far as the surveyors were male and their secretaries female. Because of this, I spent most of my time working with a group of five women with an average age of about fifty.

The Girls were fantastic: never in my life have I had so

much childbirth expertise available in one room. I loved their company, I could talk to them about the blokes I fancied, the recipes I'd tried the night before, in fact anything and everything that affected my life. I was hanging out with my favourite aunts who were ready to offer advice and counsel whenever I asked.

Six months into my new job, with the help of my boss and a little financial jiggery-pokery, I was able to take my first steps on the property ladder and into the smallest studio flat in Brighton. Bijou is slightly too big a word to describe the property, maybe bijouette is better. I didn't care: for the very first time I had a home I could call my own. All seventeen-by-twelve feet of it.

As the office was just around the corner I often made the most of the morning by staying in bed until 8.50 before washing, dressing and diving out of the door, arriving just on time at 8.59. If I stayed at Tommo's I would have to be out of the house by 8.30, a highly inconvenient arrangement.

But it didn't take long before I knew all there was to know about the limited life of flat roofs and the intricacies of building regulations and, although I enjoyed my time there, ultimately it wasn't a career move and everyone in the office knew it.

The morning after our night-time altercation I discreetly spent much of my working day trawling the Internet trying to find information on ocean rowing. Between phone calls, report typing and keeping my eye on the boss, I typed a couple of well-chosen words (i.e. 'ocean' and 'rowing') into a decent search engine and amazingly a list of several thousand entries popped up. It seemed Tommo hadn't been entirely spontaneous in his suggestion. I should have known that he would have read about it somewhere. To my utter amazement it didn't take me long to discover that several people had been across oceans before, either alone or in pairs, conquering both the Atlantic and Pacific. I could not believe it. Surely nobody in his or her right mind would actually jump in a wooden boat and head off across an ocean?

During my sneaky research I discovered there was the aptly named Ocean Rowing Society (ORS), which archived every ocean row ever attempted. The wealth of information was too much to take in, and I carefully avoided the lost at sea statistics. I also found a company called Challenge Business, of yacht-racing fame, which ran biennial rowing races across the Atlantic. My heart thumped in my throat: reading through the Challenge Business site I found the details of the next race and a call for entrants. Leaving from La Gomera in the Canaries, the double-handed teams would race to Barbados, starting in October 2003. It was just over a year and a half away.

I began to sweat with a heady mix of excitement and anxiety. Obviously there would be no spaces left in the race and we certainly would not pass any athletic criteria. My head was whirling with the image of Tommo and me running on a treadmill with pegs on our noses, wires suckered on to our chests, breathing into a tumble drier hose. But for the briefest of moments it crossed my mind that this could be it – Tommo and I could actually row an ocean.

I'm usually quite confident on the phone, but my voice trembled as I rang Teresa Evans, race project manager.

~

'TOMMO'S ASKED ME to row the Atlantic! What do you think?'
I dropped into conversation whilst dishing out cups of tea.
There was a resounding 'You are joking, aren't you?' from the
gobsmacked Girls. I relayed the events of the previous evening,
embellishing it ever so slightly – 'Tommo was horrible, he said
lots of hurtful things' – and making sure I laid it on thick for
the ultimate sympathy vote. Sue, a beautiful woman in her
sixties with Audrey Hepburn bone structure and pearly white
hair (which she occasionally dyed bright red), sat opposite me
with a puzzled look on her face. She knew Tommo and I didn't
have the perfect relationship, as I had spent many an afternoon
whinging about it to her.

'I know if you put your mind to it, Sally, you'll do it, but with
Tommo? What are you thinking!? And why the hell would you
want to row the Atlantic?'

'Um …' Good point, I thought. 'Well, Tommo did come up
with the idea, other people have done it before, I think we can
do it, and I'd like to give it go.'

Sandy asked if I could do something a little less dangerous.
Maybe a sponsored walk?

'Nope, we're going to row the Atlantic, I've already spoken
to the race organisers, there's a meeting next Saturday in
Southampton and as long as we pay the entry fee we're in!'

Having professed our intention to the five women I thought
I'd better call Tommo and tell him our decision. 'You are serious
about this rowing thing, aren't you?' I asked aggressively.

'Yes,' he replied, laughing. He could tell I was still upset from the night before. The truth is I was over it, but like most women I wanted to ensure he didn't get off the hook lightly!

'Well, I've looked it up, there's a race next October, I've already spoken to the organisers and there's a meeting next Saturday in Southampton. So as long as we pay the entry fee we're in! Oh, and by the way you owe me £75, I've already put a cheque in the post to secure our place.'

THREE

'Check'

THE DAYS PASSED by slowly, our apprehension growing. Tommo and I spent a ridiculous amount of time discussing the pros and cons of our forthcoming adventure. We also promised that we would not discuss our decision with anyone else. We were not 100 per cent committed yet, so bragging about it to all and sundry would not be wise. But hey, I'm only human, and by the Saturday morning I had blabbed to practically everyone I knew. The only people I hadn't told were my family, but why put them through the stress and strain of their wayward child deciding to launch herself off the coast of Africa never to be seen again? Anyway, Mum would go ballistic.

First things first: the money situation. Tommo was claiming

benefits because of his epilepsy and I was earning just a little bit more than minimum wage. So, although we weren't poor, if we pooled our money together at the end of the month we'd just be able to buy a couple of Belgian buns and two mugs of tea, maybe even have a trip to the cinema if we found buried pennies in the cracks of the sofa.

We needed to value the project, so we thought the best way to do this was to think of the row as a camping trip at sea. Instead of hills and cows it would be waves and whales. We'd need to buy a boat, equip it, pack it with lots of food, pay for the training courses, get the flights sorted and organise some accommodation. Easy. Anyway, if the worst came to the worst we could pack the boat with value baked beans: at 9p a can we'd save shedloads of money.

If we entered the race it was stipulated that we would need an Atlantic class ocean rowing boat, a twenty-four-foot plywood craft that came in kit form. The £9,000 laser-cut jigsaw looked like a model aircraft you buy from the newsagent, except it was bigger, you couldn't make it in your bedroom and it would take more than an afternoon to build. I scoured the Challenge Business and ORS websites to find second-hand boats and equipment for sale. As you can imagine, the last thing we wanted to do was glue together our only means of survival.

At our guesstimate of £50,000 the basic cost of the project would amount to much more than my studio flat by the seaside. We certainly wouldn't be able to pay for it with a mortgage, let alone convince any self-respecting bank manager to lend us the money. We decided we'd find out how other people had raised the money when we got to Ocean Village in Southampton and put it out of our minds. Challenge Business needed teams to get to the start of the race, so they must have some idea as to how to do it.

Check.

We looked closely at the website pictures of the boats and crews. They were all men, big men, with bodies that rippled more than the surrounding water. We quickly decided we were not going to race. There was absolutely no way we could compete. Tommo called us the 'token spacky disabled girl team'. The likelihood was that we would be physically inferior to every other team in the race. Let's face it: we were going to come last! Not knowing how long it would take to row an ocean, we resigned ourselves to it taking several months. Thinking positively, we had over a year to train – we would be honed to perfection. We weren't going to win, but damn it we were going to look good losing!

Check.

We couldn't row.

'How hard can that be?'

Check.

We were frightened, but we adopted the policy 'If it scares you, it's worth doing,' a statement we'd probably regret. In fact I spent many evenings curled up under my patchwork blanket thinking everything from *What the hell have I got into?* and *Why did I go and tell everyone?* to the practically hysterical *WE'RE GOING TO DRRROOOWWNNNNNNN!* We hadn't even been to the first meeting and I was already sick to the stomach at the idea of rowing across an ocean that was seven miles deep. Can you blame me?

Tommo tried, with limited success, to reassure the both of us. Everything would be ok, he said; if not, there was probably nothing we could do about it. Great! It looked like I would have to live with the vivid nightmares of failure, debt and drowning (in that order).

But then again, 'If it scares you it's worth doing' … right? Check.

~

I FOUND MYSELF talking about the rowing to a guy called Tony Plank. I'd met him on several occasions during my marathon training. Aside from the Sunday runs I would go to a Tuesday evening training session at Withdean Stadium, a small, tired-looking field surrounded by hard seating and empty hot dog stands. The fit fifty year old, dressed in tracky bottoms and kagoul, would stand at the edge of the track calling split times from a stopwatch. The Brighton athletics team was based there and shared the ground with the recently promoted Seagulls. During the months leading up to the London Marathon participants quadrupled in numbers. The regular runners would pound the brick-red track, the guys oozing testosterone with each lap, the girls with long gazelle-like legs sprinting gracefully under the glare of the overhead floodlights. The charity runners in baggy T-shirts and new trainers would herd together for protection as we plodded for an excruciating hour and a half, fartlekking[1] ourselves to a peak of physical fitness.

---

[1] Fartlek (vb): to alternate between fast and slow running in one session, done as training work for marathons and other long-distance races.

I hated the sessions. They brought back hideous memories of cross country running at school. All my classmates would have been sitting on the grass for a good ten minutes before I struggled in with Kay, my best friend at the time. Our faces like thunder, we would jog to the finish line, our feet barely leaving the floor, Kay's pale skin crimson, my long hair sweaty and sticking to my forehead. It seemed not much had changed – I still came in last, the other runners encouraging me from the sidelines. Dying with embarrassment, I reassured myself that I was built for comfort, not for speed, and at least I finished the sessions and was still able to get my weary lead-lined legs up to the bar for a swift half.

At one session I cornered Tony just before we went into the pub. I did have method in my madness for spilling the beans to yet another complete stranger. I had it in my head that Tony would know a little bit about sponsorship, as he had been running for years and had told me how he'd run from London to Brighton, a sixty-mile jaunt over the South Downs. If he didn't know about raising money for stupid sporting ventures, who would?

I told him everything: the argument with Tommo, my research on the Internet, the phone call with Challenge Business and the up-and-coming meeting. We knew it was going to cost a packet and any advice on how to get the money together would be greatly appreciated. He listened quietly. Was it a good sign? He asked me if I could row.

'No.'

'Right. I've been coaching coastal rowing for thirty-five years just down the road at Shoreham. Get yourself down there and I'll teach you to row in no time at all! Is it sweep oar or sculling?'

'I don't know.'

'Well … we can do both, no problem. Come down next Thursday and I'll sort you both out!'

The Plank, fitness and rowing coach extraordinaire, had succumbed to the Kettle charm.

~

WE JUMPED INTO Tony's car. His girlfriend Bev sat in the front; Tommo and I, the bickering siblings, were stuffed in the back. Off we drove to Southampton. It was hot and humid, but we emerged practically frozen to death after two hours in the air-conditioned car. Tony looked sporty in a pair of mid-length 'breathable' trousers and a suitably cringeworthy 'Rowers do it … back-to-front' T-shirt whilst Tommo and I dressed typically 'Brighton'. I wore hipster trousers, high-heel boots, tight black top and silver necklace with my long curly hair in tresses; Tommo was in turn-up trousers and dandy shirt. He has a penchant for over-elaborate shirts bought from charity shops the length and breadth of the country. His collection was well into the hundreds. Either way, we did not look like your typical ocean rowers, which was confirmed the moment we stepped into the marquee Challenge Business had prepared beside the seventy-foot super yachts moored in the marina. It was a swathe of beige cargo pants and shorts, polo shirts and deck shoes.

As Tony and Bev strolled off for a drink, I hissed at Tommo through a fixed smile. 'Look like we know what we're doing.' We split up, a two-pronged attack, to work the room. I overheard Tommo's charming soft Yorkshire accent: 'Are you a rower? Good, so am I! I've never actually rowed, so I haven't got a bloody clue what I'm doing! Have you?'

I made a beeline for the biscuits. A couple of other women were standing near the custard creams, so I thought a quick introduction followed by a brief comment on the sandwich selection would break the ice. 'Are you rowers?'

'No we're the girlfriends of them two over there!' They pointed to two be-deck-shoed guys who happened to be talking to Tommo. They were grinning broadly and Tommo was gesticulating wildly. I sensed they weren't talking about rowing.

'Oh, right!' came my reply. 'Are there any girls taking part in the race?'

'No!'

'Oh! So it's just me, then?'

Fantastic, I thought. One girl and all these men, men soon to be in a similar shape to those in the photos I so carefully studied. Had I died and gone to heaven?

When the call came for us to take our seats I dragged Tommo right to the very front. I wanted to be sure we got down as much information as possible. So, whipping out a large pad and a pen I turned to a crisp new page. Tommo fished out a matchbox-sized notepad and a blunt pencil. We asked Tony and Bev to be an extra pair of ears. Once we'd covered all the bases we'd be poised, a coiled spring, ready for action. No snippet of information or advice was going to be given without our having captured it on paper.

Teresa Evans took centre stage. I couldn't help but think she looked incredibly young. The average age of the audience was about thirty-five – Teresa looked fifteen. She was actually in her mid-twenties, but being small, blonde and slightly nervous she didn't initially fill me with confidence, although I sensed she would be ready to fight anyone who thought she was either too inexperienced or too immature to handle the race. Maybe I was expecting an ex-commando or weather-beaten yachty type. Teresa had, in fact, been the project manager for the Atlantic rowing races in 1997 and 2001.

She in turn introduced Matthew, technical manager for the race, and the infamous Chay Blyth, who I'd never heard of before my sneaky web searching revealed that he had rowed with John Ridgeway in an open dory from the USA to Ireland in 1966.

The meeting proceeded as you would expect. Bound booklets were given out and the laptop experienced technical difficulties, resulting in several people crowding round the machine.

'Have you turned it off and on again?'

'Which button did you press?'

'Oh! Have I just lost it?'

A throng of equally perplexed individuals fought for the kudos of actually fixing the bloody thing. When the cantankerous machine finally sprung into life Teresa, with a sigh of relief, began to talk through a series of bullet-pointed pages:

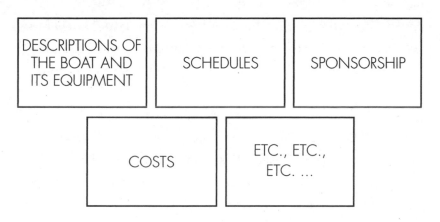

Tommo and I scribbled furiously. Teresa then told us all the slides were in the bound booklet. Tommo scribbled profanities and I suppressed giggles.

Well, it all seemed pretty straightforward, really. You find some sponsors, build a boat or buy a second-hand one, train, learn to navigate by the stars and off you go. There were a few obligatory courses, namely first aid, sea survival and astro-navigation, but everything was laid out in black and white in the booklet. 'Please make a cheque out for the first race entry fee instalment as soon as possible. Thank you!'

It was exactly what we'd expected.

We were also told about the importance of nominating a skipper, for woe betide those who didn't sort it before they went. Oh, and didn't we laugh at the poor souls in Chay's series of anecdotes. The mid-ocean feuds, best friends never talking again, misery on the open seas as rowers lost it, deciding to swim home rather than face another day with their crewmates. But for a bit of backbone and a skipper the stress of living in a twenty-four-foot rowing boat for four months would never have got to them! Tommo passed me a piece of paper ... *YOU'RE SKIPPER.* I turned to him and smiled. 'Thank you,' I mouthed back.

Chay Blyth had stood throughout the meeting with a look on his face like a kid in a classroom desperate to stick his hand up and ask to go to the toilet. His pursed lips and twitching facial muscles did nothing to disguise the fact that he wanted to butt in and say something. In fact, he couldn't hold himself back and did interrupt on several occasions, in his thick Scottish accent with its melodious lilt. I found him amazing: I'd never come across anyone so blunt and tactless, who was also able to put 'bloody' into practically every sentence spoken.

Teresa was talking through the slide entitled 'Sponsorship' and he strolled to the front of the room and motioned for all of us to look at the Bajan team, saying something along the lines of 'Take a look at this bloody lot, they have their bloody sponsorship sorted out and they have flown the whole bloody team across especially for this bloody meeting. The rest of you bloody lot will have to get a move on if you're going to get to the start of this bloody race!'

Tommo and I craned our necks to take a look at the bloody team from Barbados, Phil and Nils. They grinned. They were both in blue polo shirts embroidered with flying fish and the logo 'Team Rowing Home', beige cargo shorts, deck shoes and white socks – they were the epitome of ocean rowers. Shane (the team manager, we found out later) waved enthusiastically from the back, sporting a huge toothy grin. They looked like a lot of fun and I made a note to remind myself to speak to them after the meeting. *TALK TO BLOODY BAJANS.* Anyway, we needed information, and with my charm offensive at the ready I prepared myself to go spy in their camp.

It was early evening by the time the meeting proper was over. A barbecue had been set up. The sun was still warm and Tommo and I took the opportunity to have a look round. We shopped for a super yacht, deciding which one we'd buy if we won the lottery. I even wondered if I'd ever get to stand, let alone sail, on one.

We made our way back to the front entrance and the barbecue, but we found ourselves staring at an Atlantic class ocean rowing boat. It must have been towed into position during our meeting. Compared to the yachts, it looked so impossibly small. This dinky blue and white boat sat on a trailer no longer than your average caravan. We trotted the length of it, stroking the sides. The paintwork was chipped and worn, but the general condition of the hull was fantastic, in our unprofessional opinion! A couple of taps here, a knock there … oh yes, she was seaworthy alright!

Faded stickers bearing company names were still clinging to the sides, some peeling at the corners, others with letters missing. We both chuckled nervously: perhaps the very same thoughts were going through our minds? If the boat was in such great condition after a crossing, then maybe it wasn't as bad as we'd imagined. I was expecting the *Mary Rose* just pulled up from the ocean floor, nothing but barnacles and big holes. This boat was dirty, leaves and grit were caught in the cracks and crevasses, but otherwise you wouldn't have known it had travelled 3,000 miles over 111 days of ocean battery.

Other rowers were beginning to join us. Equally nervous laughs twittered through the crowd as, in turn, each team climbed tentatively on to the boat and disappeared into the cabin. The waiting crowd made water noises and rocked the boat for authenticity so when those on board reappeared they looked slightly dishevelled and disconcerted. Our turn: Tommo and I heaved ourselves over the side, carefully placing our feet to avoid the hatch covers fitted to the floor of the deck. In just two strides we were able to walk the entire length of the boat. With rowing runners down the centre of the deck, the only space to put your feet was either astride them or along a flat narrow stretch on either side. We peeped into a small hatch at the front – it was empty, triangular in shape, mirroring the pointed stern. It had a sickly smell of damp and varnish. A store for food and equipment? A place to stuff Tommo when he'd been particularly annoying, maybe? We climbed into a larger hatch at the other end of the boat.

The sleeping cabin was literally a crawl space with enough room for the two of us to slide on to the mattresses which lined the floor. It also smelt damp and fishy. It was cosy to say the least and Tommo pulled a face when I went all girly, grabbing him round the waist: 'Oh baby, look! It's so snuggly!'

'Get off! There won't be none of that, I'm telling you now!' he teased.

The walls had been painted white, cargo netting ran along the sides and a large electrical panel covered in knobs, switches and lights had been mounted by the entrance hatch. Tommo lay there, I lay there. This would be our bedroom in the middle of the ocean. We also climbed out of the cabin looking rather disconcerted.

The summer smell of barbecue was beginning to waft through the air as we made our way back through the marquee. Tables had been set up with slabs of cooked steaks, sausages and chicken. It was a vegetarian's nightmare! Chay had announced during the meeting that there would be the opportunity to meet previous ocean rowers invited along for the evening soirée, it would give us an opportunity to grill them on their adventure and perhaps they could see just how green behind the ears we were.

As the marquee began to fill, Tommo and I, the two girls I had met over a custard cream and their boyfriends, Adam and Paul, ventured into battle, alcohol in hand. Our mission: to extract as much information as possible, from as many rowers as possible, in as little time as possible. We had to do all this before Tony and Bev became too bored to stay and we'd have to leave for the long journey home.

I left Tommo to scope out potential victims amongst the growing crowd. I sidled up to Phil and hit him with a seductive 'How's it going?' Still grinning and in his laid-back Caribbean drawl he proceeded to tell me how fantastic it all was.

1   Their boat was being built in Barbados as we spoke
2   He would be the first black man to row an ocean, groundbreaking to say the least
3   They would be the first Bajan team to row an ocean
4   They had practically every large company in Barbados sponsoring them
5   On their return they were guaranteed to become national heroes

5a Oh, and their families were here too, paid for by
   sponsorship

So everything was working out brilliantly. I told him:

1 We didn't have a boat
2 We didn't have any money
3 We didn't have any sponsors
4 We didn't know how to row
5 Tommo had epilepsy and we weren't going to win
5a My family lived in Northampton and we couldn't
   afford the petrol money for them to come and join us

A fair trade, I thought. He said it didn't matter, there was still
plenty of time and did I want a glass of Mount Gay rum?
Shane's ears must have pricked because within seconds a glass
of caramel-coloured liquid landed in my hand. Shane, the
unofficial ambassador for Bajan rum, had several cases of the
stuff he'd hoped to shift that evening. Not wanting to upset
the balance of international relations, I drank it in one great
gulp, coughed for several seconds, thanked them and staggered
off to find Tommo. The information so gamely tendered by
Phil wasn't quite as motivating as I'd hoped. Maybe Tommo had
found some rowers in a similar position to us.

   I was stopped by a lady in her fifties. A younger man stood
beside her, he was in his twenties. Again, deck shoes and beige. I
could have been mistaken, but there was definitely a mischievous
glint in his eye.

   'Are you a rower?' the woman asked.

'Yes, the only girl taking part this year.'

'I'm Jan and this is my son Daniel, but people call us Jan and Dan, the mother-and-son team. We were in the first race in 1997. Our boat was called *Carpe Diem*. We made it across in 101 days, we had the most amazing time …'

And that was it. For a good three-quarters of an hour I became completely absorbed in their story. I didn't even notice when Tommo came and stood beside me, slipping his arm round my waist in that 'you're mine' kind of way that boys do when their girlfriends are around other men.

Jan had so much enthusiasm it oozed from every pore. She was fifty-three and Dan twenty-three when they, through a series of unfortunate circumstances, ended up setting to sea together. Jan had cared for her late husband, Keith, who died of cancer and Dan's rowing partner had dropped out only months before the race. Jan saw the opportunity to change her life and do something utterly fantastic and challenging, far from the emotional rollercoaster of the terminal illness of a loved one. They didn't race but decided to have as much fun as possible, and it seems they did. She told us they laughed all the way across. They decorated the boat on Christmas Day, they talked about their lives, their shared experiences when Dan was growing up at home and the time they had spent apart after Dan had left for university and then joined the army. They shared their memories of Keith. Their food was delicious: they didn't pack the boat full of baked beans but army rations Dan had secured through contacts at work. They told us the huge waves were amazing and once in a blue moon they actually surfed down them! Their arrival in Barbados was incredible and the whole trip was the most fantastic experience of their entire lives. They were just so happy that they were able to share it with each other. Dan piped up from time to time to emphasise particular points, adding sizes and dimensions, describing equipment and telling us how much his mother whinged when her hands and backside began to hurt. Brutal descriptions of blistered palms and boil-infested bottoms did nothing to curtail Tommo's and my growing excitement. Jan was infectious.

We had so many questions, and we fired them incessantly.

Q Were you frightened?
A Sometimes, but not really. The boat was too good!

Q How did you get sponsorship?
A It was hard, but you just have to keep writing letters and talking to people.

Q Did you get lots of press?
A Yes, loads. Sally, you're pretty, so that will help! (Cool, I thought!)

Q How big were the waves?
A Some were as big as a house! (Not so cool.)

Q Did you really get boils?
A Yes! And they were huge! (Again, not really a plus point ...)

Q Did you know how to row before you went?

A No, but it's not that difficult to learn.

Q What kind of food did you take?

A Army rations, and they were brilliant! You just add hot water. They did get a bit boring after a while, though.

Q Did you get seasick?

A Not really. Dan was ill the first few days, but we think that was food poisoning. It did mean that I had to do all the rowing!

Q What was the weather like?

A Very hot. We came back with incredible all-over tans. (The mind boggles!)

Q Most importantly, did you lose any weight?

A We lost two stone, but we put on a load of weight before we went. You should do that, or you'll come back emaciated. (Good, I thought.)

Both Jan and Dan seemed happy to talk to us about their adventure and we were ready to listen. They handled our questions with patience, although I was sure they had heard them all before. It had been four years since their journey but they spoke about it as if they had only returned the week before.

It was dark outside, the time was already 11.00 pm and although we could have stayed to the wee small hours Tony came over and asked if it was ok to go. Jan said we could call her at any time if we needed help or advice and Dan gave us his number with the same promise. We left inspired. If a woman of fifty-three can do it then so could we.

FOUR

The Beginnings of Epic
Challenge for Epilepsy

TOMMO HAD BEEN on the mailing list for the Fund for Epilepsy for several years. I think he probably only glanced half-heartedly through the monthly newsletter. He hated all that 'living with epilepsy shit' and had tried several self-help meetings but found them tedious.

He'd spent most of his life hiding from the condition, playing at being normal, but in many ways it completely controlled him. Committing to a year of physical and mental hard work was going to be tough for both of us, but especially for him. The medication he took affected not only his memory but also his mood; any disruption in his routine, like too little sleep, would leave him shaky and worried that a seizure would strike at any time. He couldn't get up early, look at computer screens, drink alcohol or sit under fluorescent lights; by law he wasn't able to drive a car or operate machinery, basically everything a man of his age would do every day. So perhaps it's not surprising that the statistics cite more deaths from epilepsy in young men between the ages of fifteen and thirty: psychologically they find it more difficult to cope with the lifestyle restrictions, especially as their peers continue to lead a 'normal' life. Although Tommo was thirty-six and seemingly out of the danger zone, he still felt the isolation of the condition all too keenly.

Tommo had suggested the Fund when I was looking for someone to run for in the London Marathon, and because it was based in his home town of Halifax it had made sense to call and ask if they wanted to send me some sponsor forms and a couple of badges to add to my Lara Croft outfit. When we got home from the meeting in Southampton he asked me if I would be happy to contact the charity again. We both felt there was plenty of scope for raising a lot of money and we could generate a lot of media attention for the charity. As the saying goes, 'There's no such thing as bad publicity,' but as long as we didn't die I'm sure the papers would love the potential for calamity! With the absurdity of the challenge and some hard work Tommo and I were sure we could encourage people to dig deep and pass us some pennies. Anyway, we both felt it would enrich the project if we were able to make a difference to other people's lives as well as our own.

Before calling the charity we both considered the likelihood that it would condemn the project. We were sure that many would consider it foolhardy for a person so limited by his condition to place himself in such a dangerous position. The race would be more than challenging for a healthy individual, but the risks would be far greater for someone who could fall ill at any time. We had to convince the Fund that it was certainly not a decision we had taken lightly. It was highly likely that Tommo would find the trip punishing and would have seizures but, if asked, I was prepared to argue that it was Tommo's right to go. If he said he could do it, he could do it, and if the worst happened somehow we would cope together.

However, with hindsight there were definitely times when I knew Tommo wasn't capable of the challenge both emotionally and physically.

August

I called the Fund for Epilepsy only a couple of days after the Southampton meeting.

'Hi there, my name's Sally. I ran a marathon for you and I'm going to row across the Atlantic next year with my boyfriend. He has epilepsy, so we thought we'd raise money for you. About £1,000,000 … is that ok?'

Why stay in the foothills when you can climb mountains? After a pregnant pause the reply came: 'You're going to have to talk to Jane.'

Jane and Malcolm Sykes had set up the charity in 1991 after their son, Charles, died when he had an epileptic seizure in his sleep. They were determined to raise enough money through the Charles Sykes Memorial Trust to be able to fund a permanent post in Epileptology at King's College Hospital. Jane ran the office and, whilst he worked for a family-run wool mill in town, Malcolm was often wheeled out for cake sales and other fund-raising events. Jane mentioned that after ten years she and her husband were taking retirement and this would be a fantastic project to get their teeth into before they went off to pasture: 'Go out with a bang, so to speak.'

After a long and absorbing conversation, Jane and I made arrangements for us all to meet up. She had given a tentative yes, but I think she wanted to make sure we weren't psychopaths, dangerous thrill seekers or thieves.

Even at this early stage I was so impressed by Jane's bravery and vision to consider taking on the ocean rowing project – it would certainly send the pulses of the charity trustees racing. The possibility of raising £1,000,000 was an opportunity not to be missed and it would be more than adequate to fund the hospital post. She may well have thought it to be the perfect end to a long but rewarding ten years.

~

I IMMEDIATELY GOT a set of business cards made up with 'Sally Kettle: Ocean Rower' emblazoned on the front. I then dished them out to friends and family in an attempt to convince both them and myself of my authenticity. If we were going to raise £1,050,000 over the next year and a half I would have to look the part. The essential rowing skills would most certainly come later.

So, with headed paper in the printer, I began preparing for our first meeting with Jane and Malcolm. I spent hours drafting a project plan, detailing everything Tommo and I had discussed, from the choice of boat and the extensive list of equipment to a media plan and fund-raising ideas. At the time it really helped to break down the enormous project into manageable chunks. When you see it written down on a piece of paper it doesn't seem quite so impossible. Looking back at it now nothing could have prepared any of us for the sheer scale of the project and the costs it would undoubtedly incur both financially and emotionally. For two years it became about the rowing, for the rowing or because of the rowing. If I thought chasing a page full of £5 sponsors after a ten-kilometre fun run was hard, this was going to be a hell of a lot harder.

We met Jane and Malcolm for the first time at an Italian restaurant in Brighton one warm and sunny Sunday afternoon. I had spoken to Jane on several occasions over the phone and was excited but apprehensive about meeting.

'See the West Pier?'

'Which one's the West Pier?'

'The one that looks like it's going to fall into the sea.'

'Oh yes.'

'Walk towards it …'

'Is it supposed to be on our left or on our right?'

'I don't know. Where are you?'

'There're lots of white buildings on our left and sea on our right.'

'Yep, keep going, there's a restaurant on the seafront side, lots of windows. Smells of pizza.'

'Is that on our left or on our right?'

The down-to-earth fifty-something couple settled into their seats beside us and as we ordered food Tommo and Jane hit it off straight away. Tommo paraded his deprecating dry wit as they spoke about his mother, Josephine, who Jane had met on several occasions. Inevitably the conversation moved on to epilepsy and clearly Jane was able to sympathise as they talked emotionally about its limiting effect on Tommo's everyday life. Charles would have been the same age as Tommo, which, I have no doubt, played on Jane's mind.

Malcolm was a charming silver fox. He had a cheeky glint in his eyes and a lovely gentle smile. I instantly warmed to him in his white socks, walking boots and shorts (enormous calf muscles! – from fell walking, he explained). We talked about our lives and as the sun moved over the sea burning the sky a rich orange we finally discussed the ocean row.

They were so enthusiastic. I went through the project plan and explained how we could come together as a team. I suggested the charity could help us with contacts and finding sponsorship and we would do our own legwork in Brighton, train and, of course, row. When Jane and Malcolm left, Tommo and I felt excited and resolute. The project was going to plan.

~

September and October

Perhaps the biggest hurdle at the beginning was convincing the trustees to trust us. Jane is a formidable woman, so by the time Tommo and I had organised our first official meeting with them in Halifax, Jane had 'persuaded' the charity to support us.

My personal biggest hurdle was telling Mum, so I decided not to. I dropped the bombshell on Dad over the phone. He sounded a bit shocked, but he promised not to say anything. I wasn't going to be able to keep it a secret for long but I just couldn't pluck up the courage to tell her. In fact, the thought of it brought on more stress and worry than the idea of the row itself.

Although I loved Mum, after years of walking on eggshells I found it very difficult to like her, and that's a horrible thing to say let alone feel. I grew up in a house where Mum was angry nearly all the time. My older brother Steve, younger sister Sam and I soon learnt to read the signs.

Although I do remember sharing some fantastic times together with Mum our home life felt a bit like a pressure cooker. Tension would build up slowly and then explode into screaming matches, mostly between Mum and Dad or Mum and Sam. Where I ducked confrontation, Sam seemed to encourage it, Steve pretended to ignore it. I tried my hardest to toe the line, attempting to keep Mum happy, desperately seeking her approval.

I knew Mum and Dad must have found it incredibly stressful bringing up three young children. By her own volition Mum was a gymslip bride, with a shotgun wedding at sixteen and the three of us before she was twenty-one. Dad had a job as a welder for British Rail; Mum became a registered childminder to supplement their income. With it they had saved hard to buy our modest three-bedroom council house, which sat on a quiet estate in Tamworth, a small town just outside Birmingham. Mum kept it clean and warm and we were always well turned out and very well behaved. Gran would tell me how proud she was of her daughter-in-law. 'Your mum always had the whitest washing on the line.'

I finally moved out at sixteen, Steve and Sam soon after. After we'd left, Mum slowly changed beyond recognition, but I carried the pain of my childhood with me for years. I began to keep parts of my life secret from Mum. We rarely spoke, for most things I told her were met with disapproval. She certainly wasn't going to like the idea of the ocean row, so for now it was better for her not to know. Anyway, without a boat we weren't going anywhere!

~

WE HELD OUR first official meeting at the Sykes homestead, a self-built stone home nestled in a small village just outside Halifax. It was cosy, well loved and lived in, and panoramic windows lined the living room offering a patchwork vista of undulating Yorkshire countryside.

Jane's kitchen was the cluttered hive of a woman who loved to cook and was very good at it. Having discovered the dining room table under scattered piles of paper, boxes and envelopes Jane bought through pudding basins of homemade paté, richly sauced joints of meat and creamy mashed potatoes. Meringues cooled on the hob, and the fridge was filled with whipped cream, its door covered with magnets chastising over indulgence.

Feeling altogether stodged out I stroked their full-bodied Jack Russell, Pip, imagining myself as portly as their pet pooch if I stayed with them for any length of time! Down to business.

Malcolm warmed up the meeting by talking about the trustees' reservations. They had finally agreed to give the go ahead if the project stood alone as a venture, away from the main body of the charity. Basically, if it all went wrong Jane and Malcolm would have to take the fallout. It was a massive responsibility and our commitment would need to be steadfast and absolute if we were to prevent a financial disaster.

Jane came up with the title 'The Epic Challenge for Epilepsy' and to finance its set-up the couple had already taken the very brave decision to invest some of the money raised for the Charles Sykes Memorial Fund. We had £20,000 to get started, £20,000 we would have to pay back. This was more money than I earned in a year, but a boat needed to bought, sponsor packs designed and a website built. Needless to say it was time for us to pull our fingers out.

~

FIRST THINGS FIRST: we needed a boat. Not only did we want enough time to get to know our vessel, but sponsors would want to see the craft we were probably going to drown in. We all came to the decision that even with our combined boat-building skills we didn't fancy the prospect of gluing a flat-pack rowing boat together.

After some Internet research we found a second-hand boat. She was named, somewhat appropriately, *Kaos*. The £15,000 boat was hand-built in a back garden and belonged to Ben Martell ('Ben M') and Malcolm Atkinson ('Malcolm A'), who competed in the 2001 race. We met Malcolm A and the boat at Scotch Corner on a wet and miserable Saturday afternoon. The plywood craft looked exactly like the one we'd seen in Southampton. I stood beside it clutching Pip as Malcolm A talked Tommo and me through the basics. 'This is the front … and … this is the back.' I began to feel a bit sick. Three months in this with Tommo? I can only guess what Tommo must have been thinking.

To get *Kaos* home 'our' Malcolm had borrowed a Land Rover and his son, Ben, had driven us all up from Halifax. (Jane called it 'heavenly knitting' that there were two Malcolms and two Bens: it did seem like an uncanny coincidence.) We hitched our seagoing caravan on to the back and drove her back to Yorkshire. We smiled and waved at the rubbernecking motorists as they marvelled at this strange orange boat trundling along in the slow lane.

November

Malcolm had arranged for *Kaos* to be stored in the mill where he worked, so Tommo and I spent most weekends travelling up to Halifax. Sensibly, Malcolm had decided to buy a second-hand Land Rover from a farmer down the road; until that point we had spent a small fortune hiring cars or enduring an horrendous eight-hour train journey. During our regular four-hour jaunts up the M1 I became used to the Land Rover's idiosyncrasies and fell in love with the old lady.

Tommo made a fantastic driving buddy. Unable to drive himself, he always made sure we had a full Thermos of tea, sweets (usually fried eggs) and a tuned-in radio. He would skilfully avoid the static as we made our way through the broadcast zones. We would also play road games, my particular favourites being 'Mini Coach' for the motorway and 'Snack Bar' on A roads. Both are very simple …

Rules for Mini Coach

1 You each choose a vehicle – preferably not a Vauxhall Cavalier or Ford Mondeo, you want to get to 10 by the end of the journey, not 510! Good examples include mini coaches versus unusual loads or camper versus caravan
2 Whoever has seen the greater number of his or her chosen vehicle type wins!

Rules for Snack Bar

1 There are two different ways to play:
a You take the snack bars on your side of the road, your partner the other side, or …
b You take it in turns with every snack bar you come across
2 Whether you choose a or b, you are looking for the number of cars parked beside the snack bar
3 Whoever has the most number of cars by the end of the journey wins!
(You could invert it – whoever has the most loses. Quite frankly the fun just never ends!)

Tommo and I would always end up arguing about unusual loads. As far as I was concerned a pile of concrete pipes on the back of a lorry didn't count. Giant combine harvesting equipment or rocket-shaped components being delivered to the secret government installation yet to appear on Ordnance Survey maps did.

Also, Tommo talked for Britain, and as my eyelids became heavier as we approached the exit signposted 'The Sculpture Park' (around 11.14 pm) he would launch into another topic of conversation, keeping me going all the way through Huddersfield and on to Halifax (arriving at approximately 12.10 am). On these occasions we stayed with Tommo's mum, Josephine, and her partner, Robin. The Thompson family was incredibly close and Tommo's sister Rachel would often travel over from Manchester to see him. Robin, an ex-colonial in his seventies, born in India and the perfect English gentleman, often sat with us at the kitchen table telling stories that would make one's hair curl. One memorable tale began: 'I couldn't possibly do what you're planning to do, you are both so brave. The only time I found myself in a similar situation was during the war …' He went on to tell us about a reconnaissance mission that had gone wrong, leaving him in a ten-foot dinghy with fifteen other men, 'poor blighters', floating down a river for a week, surrounded by dense forest in which enemy snipers were hiding, ready to pick them off. With no food or clean water many of the men had become delirious and a couple tried to kill themselves. They even considered eating each other … Thanks, Robin! Josephine and Robin were also learning to dance and would often move the kitchen table to practise their tango. They were as strong as their relationship and I remember hoping I would be as happy and healthy in my seventies.

On the Saturday morning, after a hearty breakfast of muffins and poached eggs and with the promise of lemon drizzle cake and chicken with orange marmalade on our return, Tommo and I would head down to the mill to help Malcolm and Ben. They were taking the lion's share of stripping, screwing and nailing the boat back into peak condition and we were keen to know exactly where everything went, from the smallest washer to the solar-powered electrical system. We carefully peeled Malcolm A and Ben M's sponsor stickers off the hull and removed every fixture and fitting.

The mill was so cold I worked in a pair of salt-bleached red salopettes donated by a friend of Jane (our first sponsor!). They were part of a set, which came with a jacket and a hat, held on with an elasticised chin strap. Rigged out in the entire outfit I looked like a giant baby in a generously padded red romper suit – star shaped, stiff and unable to move my arms or legs.

After a weekend or two of hard work the boat stood naked, surrounded by Tupperware boxes filled with every species of nut, bolt and screw. All we needed to do was re-paint her, put her all back together again and then stick our sponsors' stickers on. Trouble was, we didn't have any sponsors, and much as I loved my red salopettes they didn't really count.

~

WITH THESE CONSTANT trips up and down the motorway it was becoming increasingly difficult to keep the project a secret from Mum. Stupidly, in one particularly probing telephone conversation I told Mum a little white lie: Tommo and I were thinking of going travelling, we weren't sure where yet, but we would be away for about three months, we were already saving up for it … I tried to justify it by telling myself I was just paving the way for the big reveal.

I'd been speaking to Dad quite regularly, giving him updates on our progress, but for four months he had been my unwilling accomplice and my conscience was telling me that his involvement in my clandestine activities was unfair. Now that we had the boat we were definitely going, so we agreed I had to tell Mum.

I asked Dad what he thought she would say, especially as I had lied to her.

'She's going to kill you.'

I think Dad had been hoping it was just one of my daft ideas.

Stressed and nauseous with nerves, I waited for the opportunity to arise. I was desperate to put it off and spent many an hour procrastinating with Tommo, asking his advice on the right way to do it. Ideally I'd be forced into it, when not telling her would become a greater sin than lying to her again.

This perfect opportunity arose after a family gathering at my Gran's. My parents were giving me a lift home, Dad had purposely sat in the back and Mum was driving … it would have to be now or never. With one great big breath I blurted out: 'Mum, I lied to you, Tommo and I are not going travelling, we're rowing across the Atlantic next October. We've entered a race and we've already got the boat.'

I don't know what shocked her more: the fact that I'd lied or that we'd managed to organise this behind her back.

'Oh, don't be so stupid, Sally, you're too skinny and Tommo has epilepsy! You'll never make it across!'

Dad waded in with some safety questions.

'Is there a safety yacht?'

'Yes, Dad, a yacht follows the fleet.'

'Has anyone died?'

'No, Dad, this is the third race and no one has died yet.'

'Who enters the race, Sal?'

'Well, a fifty-three-year-old woman rowed across with her son in 1997. She had no experience either, so if she can do it so can I.'

Etc. etc. …

Dad was brilliant. Mum was very quiet, but as far as I was concerned it went better than expected. Maybe the trip appealed to her outdoorsy spirit, because over time Mum became as excited as we were and her growing enthusiasm gave us something to talk about. Amazingly, we were also beginning to get on. Tommo and I began to stop off in Northampton on our way up to Halifax. As I told her about our progress I began to see a changed woman. This was my opportunity to get to know my mother, and she was wonderful, funny, gentle and understanding: all the qualities I had missed out on as a child.

~

December

AS FULL MEMBERS of the Tony Plank School of Novice Rowing, Tommo and I were becoming pretty proficient. Although we had been going regularly, cycling along Brighton seafront to Shoreham Coastal Rowing Club, we'd become slightly less enthusiastic as the days grew shorter and the water colder. The thought of standing in our wellies in the chilly English Channel preparing to launch our sturdy boat into the harbour quite frankly didn't appeal.

Tony seemed rather impressed with our progress so didn't pull too much of a face when we didn't turn up for a couple of weeks when the weather was particularly grim. Anyway, too much exertion and the risk of over-training would have become a real problem: let's not peak too soon.

But like the Christmas turkey, Tommo and I were beginning to fatten up, so I made a firm New Year's resolution to spend more time working out. The facilities at Shoreham were basic to say the least: two manky old rowing machines and the musty smell of well-matured men's trainers did not encourage us to spend more than a minute longer at the club house than was necessary. It seemed we were following Jan's advice to the letter and were well on our way to putting on an extra two stones. I would have been happy to arrive in Barbados emaciated, but my better judgement told me that probably wasn't a good idea. We needed to get fitter, trim down, then build up the seal blubber a month or two before the race.

Tommo got on the case. While researching sporting accessories, he discovered the 'WaterRower', the Rolls-Royce of rowing machines. They were sleek and beautiful, with a three-inch seat cushion and finished in eye-catching teak, and used a paddle to create resistance, which actually sat in a circular tank of water. With every pull the delicate swish tricked the mind into thinking your arse, back and hands didn't hurt like hell! It was the machine for us. I wrote a letter asking if we could borrow one on which to train, and waited patiently for a reply …

When the response finally came we were practically on a sponsorship roll. They were happy to lend us a WaterRower for the duration of the training. Tony had also recommended a local gym as a target for free membership. The Brighton Esporta welcomed us with open arms. It was a swanky all-singing, all-dancing super-gym with pool, sauna, steam room and hot men in tight Lycra. How could I resist?

The WaterRower didn't last long, though. Having taken a day to put the six-piece bit of kit together and having trained on it for only a couple of weeks, the equipment was dismantled, put back in its box and sent back to the suppliers.

Our contact at WaterRower had asked if we could request our gym to install a rower for us to train on. Unfortunately the situation ended in a complete fiasco when the gym said no. After my very best efforts the gym continued to decline WaterRower's offer and finally I thought it best if WaterRower bypassed me and approached the gym themselves. Again the staff at the gym were not happy to oblige, as they had ten perfectly good machines already.

Jane had spoken to our contact at WaterRower a couple of times and was asked to sort out the unsatisfactory situation. Having been caught in the middle Jane called demanding that I sort out the mess. I felt a little unsupported when I tried desperately to explain that there really was nothing we could do. Often a tad parental, Jane tended to browbeat me whenever my decisions didn't match hers, and the tension was beginning to show.

Needless to say, I did sort the mess out. Tommo and I decided to send the WaterRower back, as the gym had all the equipment we needed and the staff were happy to help us every step of the way, but I found the incident difficult to forget. My heart stopped with every email or phone call from Jane because I felt undermined by her. She was a formidable character but the pressure and stress of the project understandably brought out her angst and this in turn echoed my experience with Mum. I was wholly ill-equipped to confront situations with her, however innocuous. Paranoia set in and I began to feel that Jane didn't respect me.

When I looked to Tommo for support and reassurance, the cupboard was bare: Jane had taken Tommo to her bosom as a surrogate son and my position as daughter-in-law was recognisably cool. To me he had positioned himself firmly and squarely on the fence and there he remained for the rest of the project.

FIVE

Ten Tons of Chilli Con Carne

THE FORECAST WAS one of heavy snowfall in the north. It's very rare to get anything more than a light flurry in Brighton, so when Jane and Malcolm invited us all up to their Lake District holiday home for a couple of days between Christmas and New Year I'd hoped our trip would afford me some snowball target practice at Tommo's expense. But in typical British fashion the drizzle left the country lanes of Windermere slushy and grey.

Tommo and I had asked Tony to join us and we travelled up together. Mum and Dad also came, along with Josephine. On our arrival we were introduced to a new member of our merry band, a friend of Jane, Shoena (pronounced Show-na). She had been seconded to help us with the project's PR. Jane and I had previously discussed the publicity plan for the row and had come to the conclusion that we didn't really have enough experience to handle it ourselves. We also needed advice on producing a pack to give to sponsors and the press. It seemed Shoena was the perfect candidate: she ran her own PR company, but more importantly she wanted to get involved with Epic Challenge. She was a slim, attractive, radiantly smiley blonde woman with a soft Scottish accent and I could tell Tommo fancied her the moment she walked in. He instantly changed up a gear into charm overdrive, which usually involved telling jokes at my expense, a habit I found both irritating and demeaning, but he was so good at it I could rarely resist laughing.

The Epic Challenge team settled at the table to talk money. Mum and Dad insisted on going for a walk, even though it was pouring. It was Mum's tactic for not getting too involved – Jane might ask her to do something, and she really couldn't be bothered! Josephine sat by the fire, reading.

The previous months had been a learning curve as we all got to know each other. It had been harder work than I imagined, and I certainly hadn't expected my feelings of alienation and annoyance brought on by Jane's sometimes unsettling behaviour. Tommo was proving to be rather lazy and his attitude left me to hold up our end in Brighton. Shoena was warm, easy to talk to and spoke a great deal of common sense, perhaps an ally amongst the ranks. I instantly got the impression that her calming, steady and authoritative personality would focus the business side of things and help us bridge the gaps between our differing personalities.

At the beginning of the meeting it was Shoena who posed

the inevitable question: 'How are the sponsors going?'

'Erm …' I said. Shit. Should I go for the glass-half-empty or the glass-half-full approach? Let's go half full.

'Well, we have a boat, and we've been given some second-hand wet weather gear. The red salopettes were brilliant when we stripped the boat. We've also got a year's gym membership and Tony has been teaching us to row. It's going great!'

'How much have you spent?' Shoena asked, cutting through my positive spin.

'£20,000.'

'So with only nine months to go, you've spent £20,000 and you don't have any money sponsors? Has anybody shown an interest?'

'Erm … Jane?'

It was embarrassing: we were five months into the project, we'd raised no money whatsoever and we'd already lost a valuable sponsor. We spent the remainder of the meeting deciding on a date to pull out of the project by. 1 February 2003 became our D-Day.

~

THE DAMOCLEAN SWORD of knowing we could fail before we'd even really started must have focused our minds. Although January didn't bring forward any multi-millionaires willing to invest £100,000 (but if we had £1 from everyone who told us to write to Richard Branson I think would have been able to afford to row to Barbados and back again!) smaller sponsors were beginning to climb aboard.

There was a major lesson to be learnt: it's who you know.

Although Shoena had spent the month designing and printing a fabulous glossy sponsorship pack the cold call to big businesses just didn't work. I did feel pissed off when we didn't even get a reply. Just a 'No thank you' would have sufficed. We also learnt that it isn't a done deal until a cheque is in your sweaty, rowing-blistered hands! All too often promises were made, weeks would pass and then the promises would be broken. Gently applied pressure and the enthusiasm of a high school cheerleader was certainly a winning combination. Who could say no to a grinning ocean rower handing out leaflets emblazoned with sick newborn babies?

We combined our sponsorship approaches with fund-raising days and they were going really well. Jane, the consummate events organiser, had arranged a corporate VIP lunch and bucket shake at Wetherby races. As we pitched up on a cold January Saturday, Tommo and I didn't know that we would spend a bone-chilling morning collecting pound coins by the boat. No VIP lunch for us, but bacon sandwiches. We were determined to have a good time and having arrived too early we sat in the car, steaming up the windows with our rendition of 'Barcelona'. We chuckled mercilessly as Jane ran around like a headless chicken ensuring the guests were in the right place at the right time. Shoena, who'd come along to help, sweet-talked the producer of Channel 4's racing programme. It was our first mainstream TV appearance. Never let it be said that we weren't targeting the right audience!

1 February came and went. Jane worked incredibly hard, writing, meeting and calling practically every small business in Halifax. She also persuaded the next mayor to support the Challenge. Councillor Geraldine Carter pledged to raise £50,000 over her

year in office. She proved to be a fantastic ally, with a dynamite personality and the tenacity of a bull terrier. I met her at a ball Jane had organised at the Armouries in Leeds. She was flirtatious, chatty and very much a Yorkshire woman and I pitied the people of Halifax. I knew they would have absolutely no choice – if she asked them to give a pound, they would have felt obliged to give two.

The ball was a huge success and Tommo looked particularly dapper. Because of my own lack of funds I had spent several weeks making my gown. I bought a length of black satin and asked a friend to help me stitch it into a full-length halter-neck asymmetrical wonder dress. I'd unintentionally cut the split in the skirt a little too high, which allowed the tops of my stockings to show. I am convinced to this day that the £10,500 we raised was entirely in support of my thighs.

In our search for sponsors we all agreed that the major donor would have the pleasure of naming the boat. With Geraldine's promise of £50,000 we felt it appropriate that she pick the name. Tommo had me in stitches, he complained about it for days on end.

'I can't stand it!' he would exclaim. 'That boat's going to be called *Yorkshire, Yorkshire, We Love Yorkshire*. If not that, then it'll be *By 'Eck, Ain't Yorkshire Grand*. We don't even live in bloody Yorkshire!'

I thought the county pride was actually quite cool, although I did agree that the majority of the Epic Challenge team were not from Yorkshire, but even if the major sponsor decided to call it *The Fanny Tickle* then that's what it would have to be. Anyway, Geraldine went for *Calderdale: The Yorkshire Challenger*.

March

Tommo and I were training furiously; we were practically on first-name terms with all the staff at the gym. If pressed we could probably have told you what their individual shift times were, how they took their tea and with what biscuit. The Girls at work generously ignored the sneaky letter writing, phone calls and Internet searches and shared my excitement.

As part of the race rules one member of the team needed to gain the Ocean Yacht Master Theory Certificate. Tommo jumped at the chance and signed himself up for a home-study course. I also started the course but was hopeless at making the time to do the homework. The increasingly hectic schedule was exhausting; I'd be into work for 9.00 am, out the door at 5.00 pm and on the bike to the railway station for the short journey to Falmer. I'd cycle round to the gym, train for an hour and a half then head back to the station, cycle home, eat some dinner, answer emails, write letters and eventually go to bed. On Fridays I'd go to the gym, then pick up Tommo and drive to Halifax for the next money-raising activity. After a weekend of bucket shaking, smiling till our faces ached, we'd drive home on Sunday night and the whole cycle would start again on Monday morning. We didn't know it then, but we wouldn't have a weekend 'off' for the next nine months.

My *coup de grâce* for March was a free spot at the Outdoors Show at the NEC, the biggest exhibition for outdoor sports in the country. After several clandestine phone calls at work I'd managed to blag a spot for our boat for three days in the 'Canoes and Kayaks' hall. I wangled a day off work and as Jane trundled down the motorway with the boat, Pip for company, I spent the train trip to Birmingham throwing up in the toilet. Stress and exhaustion were making me feel wretched most of the time and I was beginning to dread the thought of three long days of rowing-related questioning and marathon grinning. Tommo and I were now becoming experts at the 'rowing inquisition' and we soon discovered an emerging pattern. Kids would always ask about the toilet arrangements, and I would delight in making it sound as gruesome as possible ...

'We have to poo in a bucket and throw it overboard, sharks will probably smell it and attack the boat and try to eat us! We'll have so many boils on our bum that they'll probably become infected and go green and pussy. Our hands will be covered in bleeding calluses and we'll probably argue all the time, I'll then try to murder Tommo by hitting him over the head in his sleep with a giant flying fish. Then I'll throw him overboard and tell everyone at home that he fell in! If they ever find the body the police will never guess that it was me who did it! So, do you fancy going?'

Women always asked how we'd cope with the isolation and the fear of knowing that the ocean was several miles deep. I just told them we were likely to lose two stones. Most wanted to come after that. The guys generally queried the electrics, ballast, plywood hull and watermaker, asked about the nuts, washers, rudder and the rowing seat/oars/gates/runners. I diverted them to Tommo but often discovered he'd escaped to get the umpteenth cup of coffee.

It seemed most visitors to our boat were familiar with the

tale of Debra Veal and her husband, the couple who attempted to row across the Atlantic in 2001. They told me with glee that Andrew Veal had abandoned boat two weeks into the trip, leaving Debra to finish alone. With several resupplies from the race organiser's yacht and the world's media ready to welcome her in, Debra had hit the headlines. I was only hoping that Tommo wouldn't drop out several days in, leaving me with little choice but to 'do a Debra'! Finding him wandering off for a coffee, I have to admit I didn't feel that confident.

Whilst at the show we met some lovely people, all keen to talk to us about our adventure. We also spoke to the amazing Peter Bray, who kayaked across the northern Atlantic. His tiny custom-made canoe was on display. If we thought our boat was small ... He gave us his last tube of 'super' cream for sore, cracked skin – he thought we'd need it for our hands and backsides. We were also given several pairs of gloves by a small family-run clothing company called Trident, and Gul (the offshore clothing specialists) also promised to sponsor us with some top-of-the-range wet weather gear. I'm always touched by people's generosity, they all wanted us to succeed and did what they could to help us get to the start, even if it was just a kind word or £1 in our charity buckets.

Tommo and I stayed with my Gran. Tommo described her as a creaking gate: riddled with arthritis, my Gran had a catalogue of complaints that would fill a nursing dictionary. She smoked like a chimney and loved Richard Whiteley from *Countdown*, although how the virtual relationship blossomed was a mystery as she generally managed to miss the programme having fallen asleep just after lunch. I felt very lucky to have her around and we were incredibly close, especially during the period of my ailing relationship with Mum. So for me it was very difficult when I was given strict instructions not to tell her about the row. Both Mum and Dad felt she'd fret herself into an early grave, so Tommo and I kept our promise not to say anything and used our best diversionary tactics, leaving her none the wiser to our covert day tripping. Having a Land Rover parked right outside her front window with 'Atlantic Rowing Team' emblazoned on its doors was hardly stealthy, but I told Gran we'd borrowed it and rapidly changed the subject. It seemed that of all the new skills I was learning my ability to lie was rapidly becoming the most honed.

As Tommo ploughed through the astro-navigation course we booked ourselves on to the compulsory race courses. We spent a weekend in Southampton catapulting unsuspecting yachty types into, under and over life rafts. We also learnt how to use a VHF radio, I went a bit doolally on cheap vending machine coffee and became hysterical at one point when I got a bit mixed up. I was both *Sexy Lady*, the boat in trouble, and the coastguard, which resulted in some wayward Maydaying. Another delight for the other course attendees was my attempt to master the phonetic alphabet. Needless to say, when Mike became Mango, various fruits and related delicacies started appearing as alternatives to the conventional terms. Apricot, Banana, Cherry … Doughnut!

The first aid at sea course was pretty useless, really. Not only was it led by a paramedic who'd never been at sea but he just didn't seem to understand that calling an ambulance probably wasn't going to help us! Quite frankly, if you have a heart attack in an ocean rowing boat, waiting a week to be rescued just isn't going to work out. You're more likely to be tossed overboard to reduce the smell of your dead carcass. Anyway, we dutifully put ourselves into the recovery position and waited for said ambulance to come and resuscitate us. I think we all came to the conclusion that we ocean rowers needed to be a hardy bunch. Broken leg? You've got another one, so get on with it!

Southampton became a welcome distraction from the stress and strain of the project. On the Sunday we did what normal couples do: we spent the afternoon shopping! I bought a pair of the most amazing shoes – grey and pink stripy flats with cloven toes, which I proceeded to wear every day until the soles fell off. Tommo indulged in four buns from the Cinnabon shop. Simple pleasures.

Before we left we stopped off for a quick lesson in how to repair our watermaker. After just half an hour we were able to break one down and put it back together again, blindfolded and with our arms tied behind our backs. It's amazing how knowing your flange from your nipple can boost one's confidence.

April

Six months to go. Still no let-up and still not enough money.

Some wavy wallpaper and a few ping-pong balls on a tray were all it took to explain 3,000 miles and the gimbled stove to 50 under-10 year olds. We also parked our boat in the playground and encouraged the kids to lock themselves in the cabin whilst we threw buckets of water over the bows. In fact, we so impressed the children at Vale School in Worthing that Tommo and I were accosted for autographs after our morning assembly. We loved days like these: in fact, we also seemed to love each other more on days like these. Perhaps it was the excitement of our adventure coupled with the simple enjoyment of drinking lukewarm Thermos tea and looking at the pictures the kids had drawn. They usually had us flailing in the storm-tossed ocean, surrounded by sharks. Actually, I lie, they usually had Tommo flailing in the water with me screaming on the deck! It was also interesting to see the kids draw the increasing number of sponsor logos on our hull. The power of marketing.

One sponsor had lived up to its promise. Gul sent through a catalogue for us to look through with instructions to choose whatever we wished. We just couldn't believe it: mail-order *Supermarket Sweep*! Although we were sorely tempted to pick outfits from the surfing section because they were just so damn cool, we were sensible and chose some offshore wet weather gear. We also picked some high-performance rash vests, two dry suits and a couple of holdalls in which to take it all to Gomera.

When the gear turned up at Tommo's he called me at work so excited he could barely string a sentence together. I rushed over to his place that evening and we had a fashion show in his front room. Everything was so tight: water sports are just not for the body conscious. I gave Tommo thirty seconds to put the dry suit on. It was the most complicated bit of clothing I've ever come across. Ugly, too. With a diagonal zip, rubber feet and gloves and a rubber neck that stops water getting in, you really would have to be in a life-threatening situation before you even contemplated putting it on. And bugger you if you actually want to get into it in an emergency. Poor Tommo was all over the place. First of all he couldn't work the zip out – he didn't realise you needed to climb in through the middle of the suit, arms and legs first, then pull the top half up and over. Eventually we both fell over laughing: well I was laughing, Tommo was suffocating; he got his head stuck in the neck bit, all you could see was his curly hair poking out of the top and his face frighteningly morphed in the black rubber. We hoped we wouldn't have to use the dry suits.

~

Launch I – The Epic Challenge for Epilepsy

DUE TO THE project being co-headquartered in Halifax and Brighton we went a bit 'launch' crazy. Never has one boat been so blessed. I decided we needed to launch *Calderdale* in the sea properly, which was probably a complete waste of time (and as you can tell I had plenty of time to waste), but I wanted to use a Brighton-based event to thank all those who had supported us so far who were not from Yorkshire. So the plan on the Saturday was to take the boat down to the seafront, shake buckets and invite the local television news. On the Sunday we'd launch the boat in Shoreham Harbour, have a little row and go for a pint. That was the plan – and I needed help to pull it off. Unfortunately it was at this point that I started to become incredibly frustrated by Tommo's lack of action. Although he didn't work and spent most of his time at home, he wasn't helping in any way. I was doing absolutely everything and although I appreciated his company on long drives and bucket shakes I would have liked it if he had approached some sponsors or encouraged his friends to help out. This was all too obvious to my own friends and family, who could see that he wasn't pulling his weight, but it only began to worry me seriously when Shoena told me she felt Tommo just wasn't 100 per cent behind the project. Until now I had decided it was easier to get on with it myself than to try and explain things to him. I just wished he'd take a little bit of initiative.

Anyway, the weekend went without any major hitches, although the news team didn't turn up and I couldn't get the Land Rover to start. This was also the very first time we'd taken the boat out on the water, and when the wind caught her she drifted uncontrollably towards the tall ship *Endeavour*, moored in the harbour. We had to be saved by Tony, who came out in a RIB (rigid inflatable boat) and towed us safely back to land. The Mayor of Brighton did the honours with a bottle of Asda's finest cava.

May and June

Five months to go, only one trip out in the boat ... At this point I'm not going to bore you with our full social schedule, needless to say the summer months were the busiest time for the team. The highlights:

- The ORS dinner – meeting previous ocean rowers and muscling in on all the official photos
- Shaking our buckets outside our gym on the hottest day of

the year, standing in a suntrap for eight hours: good
experience for our trip in the tropics

- The Girls at work helping me organise a sponsored walk
along Brighton seafront ... all seven arduous miles of it.
My twenty walkers managed it in an hour and a half! It
absolutely threw it down, leaving the walkers feeling very
sympathetic to our own potentially soggy mid-ocean
plight. We managed to rack up three casualties: one
broken thumb (I know, I wondered how that happened
too), blood poisoning from an infected blister and a
twisted knee. I didn't include these in my risk assessment!
The team did manage to raise £5,000 – quite an incredible
sum

Launch II – *Calderdale: The Yorkshire Challenger*

Geraldine announced her charity (i.e. us) and we took the boat
to Halifax for her official naming. The launch took place during
the Yorkshire Mayors' Day, when all the mayors paraded through
Halifax in full regalia. It's these traditions I hope we never lose.
It looked incredible: there was more bling on display than at a
gangsta rapper convention.

Along with the launch, the weekend from hell included:

- A school visit
- Stewarding at the Yorkshire Bike Ride
- Bucket shaking at the Halifax gala, which involved
driving the boat round the town in a procession, with
small children standing on the side of the road
throwing pennies as hard as they could

- A black-tie dinner at the Royal Rishworth Hotel, where I drunk way too much and warbled 'Someone to Watch Over Me' in the wrong key
- To top it off we also ordered our dehydrated chilli con carne from a dehydrated chilli con carne company (I lie: they do also do dehydrated chicken curry)

The bike ride did have its highlights (getting up at 5.00 am wasn't one of them, but once we'd slurped a cup of coffee and collected our fluorescent tabards we were on a roll). As cyclists approached our corner of Yorkshire countryside Tommo and I launched into our special moves. We were to direct them through a taxing right-hand turn with calls of 'You're almost there, keep going! Not long now, downhill all the way!' In fact, they still had sixty miles to go. We'd adopt our positions: I went for the 70's high-collared sequin-studded white-catsuit-clad knee-bended arm-swinging-over-the-top Elvis-style double-armed point, complimented by Tommo's straight-standing arm-extended village-policeman-come-country-signpost deadpan directionism. Did we laugh! My mother and Josephine were also up at 5.00 am to go stand in the road at Filey for twelve hours, but at least they had a cafe close by where they could get a fresh cup of tea and go to the loo. Tommo and I had to pee behind a bush.

We also went to sea: actually, Chichester harbour on a choppy day. Tony helped us organise it, he also persuaded a friend to accompany us in a RIB. Due to my atrocious rudder skills we only narrowly missed a rather large red buoy, several dinghies and a couple of sea kayaks. Tommo looked resplendent in his new Gul wet weather jacket and salopettes. I looked grumpy in my tight rash vest. I'd forgotten the rowing footplates and left the Land Rover's petrol cap at a station in Brighton. It felt like one of those days.

July

More events ... will this never end?

- There were more schools visits, including one at a tiny village school in Farley, just outside Salisbury. They'd organised a table-top sale to raise funds for us. Tommo managed to pick up our mascot for the boat: he named him Farley the Elephant. He was gorgeous – hand knitted with a wonky trunk, and an orange and grey stripy jumper. A bargain at 7p.
- My Dad organised our first bucket shake in Northampton. We were also featured in the local rag and on the BBC radio station. Whilst doing our bit with the buckets and trying to avoid going over to the Cornish pasty shop opposite I met a young woman called Claire Mills. We talked for ages, as she'd also planned to row an ocean. She took my contact details, but I never expected to hear from her again
- I'm sure we did more events in July, but it all just melts into one great big bucket shake after another ...

I decided to reduce my hours at work, so I went part time, working Tuesday, Wednesday and Thursday. Unfortunately, any good intentions of concentrating on project admin on Fridays and Mondays pretty much went out of the window. This was possibly because it was actually a lot easier to make calls, scour the Internet and write letters at work. But it did encourage me to spend more time at the gym – in fact I ended up going twice on Mondays. Horrendous!

Perhaps at this point you'll understand why I was so glad just to get in that bloody boat and disappear into the middle of nowhere.

August and September

I'm a bit of a first aid fanatic, so much so that in the summer of 2002 I took a train to Cornwall for a two-day course. It cost a packet, but it was entirely my idea of a weekend well spent. A city break in Amsterdam? Nope. It's a weekend fishing broken Polo mints out of 'unconscious' car drivers for me. (You often break your teeth on the steering wheel when you have an accident.) After two days I learnt that the best and probably only bit of first aid kit you need to carry with you is a roll of masking tape. Sod triangular bandages: a T-shirt wrapped with tape will help to stem even the most bloody of wounds. My trainer was keen to let us know that casualty doctors want their patients alive. They don't have to be clean with a beautifully folded bandage! For weeks afterwards I scanned the streets for potential life-saving situations. I was on red alert ready to practise my skills, and exactly a year later that opportunity came about.

The day had come for me to try out our rowing schedule of two hours on, two hours off. I arrived at the gym at 9.00 am: two sessions in and my brain was turning to blancmange, as were my bum cheeks. I decided to enjoy one of the sunniest days of the summer and made a beeline for the outdoor pool. Children were splashing about, their parents sunning themselves on loungers around the pool, and a child's body lay floating face-down in the water. Everything went so quickly: after screaming for the lifeguard to help, two women dragged the little girl out of the water. I didn't do any of the checks St John Ambulance had taught me. Her face was blue, her body floppy and lifeless: no more checks were going to tell me this child wasn't breathing. I tipped her head back and gave her two gentle breaths. Frantic parents were gathering around us, my heart was beating so loudly I could barely hear as another lifeguard offered to take over. As I passed her over, three-year-old Minty began to breathe, then cry, then bit my finger! She was alive, and I disappeared off to the changing rooms to call my parents and tell them with pride that I'd saved someone's life.

~

TOMMO FINISHED THE astro-navigation course! It only took him eight months. I was so proud of him, especially when he actually completed the final exam in 'exam conditions'. I would have cheated, but Tommo packed all his books away and did it properly. He's much cleverer than I am, that was always so attractive. But with only a couple of months to go, I knew deep down that our relationship was no longer working. Pulled along by the riptide of the adventure we were drifting apart. It seemed this adventure was threatening to separate us.

I came to the realisation that it wasn't because of Tommo that I wanted to row the ocean and, if I was honest with myself, I began to doubt his ability to make it across. Perhaps at this point I should have faced this reality and told him my feelings but at the time it really wasn't an option.

When tensions grew between Jane and me he was never there to back me up, even if I was wrong. Instead I grew tired of being the butt of his jokes, so much so that I found his company more of a strain than a pleasure. In essence I didn't feel good about myself when I was with him; even Robin was quick to point out that I was Tommo's foil, a position I would have gladly traded. I suppose that's why I enjoyed spending time in Halifax: his Mum got it instead of me! Anyway, with £500 of dehydrated chilli con carne zipping to us in the post this really was no time for second thoughts.

With a great deal of sadness and excitement I left Colleys. I needed to spend more time fitting out the boat so she could be shipped to Gomera. I had saved a little bit of money to tide me over until October. Once we'd left, the plan was to rent my flat out until our return. We didn't go to the gym again: if we weren't fit enough by now we would never be. Anyway, my backside needed the time off.

Over the last few months the boat was slowly prepared: she got a new paint job, the hatches were resealed and the third coat of anti-foul applied. We managed to persuade a small boat building company to design a rudder system for us. The very lovely Burt at Hillyard Boat Builders invested hours into our high-tech footplate system. Unfortunately he didn't manage to fit it before we had to drive the boat to Halifax for the final weekend of events. Malcolm almost had a heart attack when he saw the four-inch hole in the hull, but it was nothing a bit a Sikaflex and a rubber boot couldn't fix.

Launch III – The Final Blessing

To say that Tommo and I had very little water-based experience is certainly an understatement, but we did spend one night in the boat in the middle of a water-skiing lake.

Maybe you're wondering why we didn't spend a weekend pottering in the English Channel or the Irish Sea. Well, we were heavily advised not to. Ironically, our aforementioned inexperience could have been deadly. The Channel is incredibly busy: a small and relatively immobile ocean rowing boat would probably come off the worse for wear in a collision with a tanker. Also, the likelihood of being troubled by the strong currents and tides between the islands definitely put me off. I can see the headlines now …

L-Plate Ocean Rowers Lost at Sea

An epileptic man and his girlfriend have gone missing during preparation for Atlantic row. The harbour master commented: 'They told me they'd never been to sea before. In fact as they left they began arguing about who would make the first cup of tea.'

We did spend a weekend on a yacht skippered by Ben Sykes. We left Plymouth on the Saturday morning and Tommo and I vomited all the way to Fowey. At one point we were sharing the same bucket. The next morning I felt much better. Unfortunately Tommo remained below decks or sat looking green until we tied up in Plymouth. A little advice to the seagoing uninitiated: pressure point bracelets do not work! And whoever came up with that 'look at the horizon' claptrap needs to be shot.

So, it was our third and final launch in Halifax. After rowing leisurely around the circumference of the White Rose Lake we found a buoy in the middle, tied ourselves on and stayed there for the night. As I parked my bottom over the side for a quick wee Tommo rocked the boat for ocean-like authenticity. After a Cup-a-Soup, some chocolate and a romantic moment staring at the stars we retired to the cabin, not to the sound of waves gently lapping the hull but to the clink of glasses and chatter from the pub 200 yards away.

The following morning, our beds damp with condensation, we crawled out on deck, put the kettle on and took to the oars. With warm tea in our bellies we decided it was probably best to use the loos on shore. The last thing the Sunday drivers would want to see was a young couple responding to the call of nature.

We were really pleased by the number of supporters who joined us for the blessing, in fact the pontoon became so overcrowded it began to sink. After an emergency evacuation the ceremony began. As the priest sat with us on the boat and Jane and Geraldine stifled tears, Tommo deliberately shot me a glance that left us both stifling giggles. I had that gut-clenching feeling that comes from desperately trying not to laugh, and we sat there like two naughty schoolchildren. With some relief we all said 'Amen' in unison.

~

WE SPENT THE following weekend packing the boat. My parents came up to help. The food had taken over Josephine's dining room, and they marvelled at the sheer quantities of chilli con carne and porridge oats. Our plan was to consume upwards of 7,000 calories a day. This would consist of a bowl of porridge, three dehydrated meals, two dehydrated puddings, two bars of chocolate, three sachets of powered energy drink, a piece of tiffin cake[2] (over a hundred portions had been homemade and individually wrapped by a good friend of Jane and Malcolm), a selection of sweets, a Cup-a-Soup and any other snacks we could force down our throats. I just couldn't imagine eating all that food, and seasickness would definitely reduce our intake, but as Tommo began to tease me that I was 'eleven stone two and living on Pringles' I actually began to appreciate the extra two stone of fat that would fuel any calorific shortfall.

With the oars secured on deck, the fluffy sheepskin seat covers acting as packing around the delicate electrical equipment and every hatch crammed with our 630,000 calories, Tommo, Malcolm and I pushed our heavy and now cumbersome fat-bottomed boat out of Josephine's back yard.

We towed *Calderdale* down the A1 to Newark, playing Snack Bar as we went. When we arrived at our shipping agent,

---

[2] A lovely rich chocolatey fruit cake

Calderdale was manoeuvred into a container ready for the long journey to La Gomera. The boat was on her way. All that was left for us to do was meet her there.

Tommo and I had spent some time discussing the odds that one of us might not make it to the start line. The chances of being hit by a bus were pretty slim, but the opportunities for getting injured were becoming a distinct possibility. Breaking a leg or spraining an ankle could seriously jeopardise the project so it was time to think about a reserve.

Our first choice was obvious – Tony. We both thought he'd jump at the chance of getting in the boat. When we finally plucked up the courage to ask him he was as keen as we'd thought he'd be. So, if I became incapacitated for whatever reason, Tony and Tommo would merrily take to the oars.

Now for Tommo's replacement. Well, I was sure none of my friends would be happy to spend three months in a boat with me, so I started looking closer to home. Sam? Even if my sister didn't have her son, Lincoln, to consider, she'd probably throw me overboard before we reached the harbour entrance. Dad? Nope … that's just wrong in too many ways! Brother … again wrong. Mum?

You know what: no one is as bloody minded as my mother, and she likes a bit of camping! She hadn't disowned me now that I'd spilt the beans so I seriously started to believe this could be the most amazing opportunity to build some bridges. In fact, Mum was beginning to get really excited about the project. One Sunday afternoon, I had blurted it out: 'Mum, if Tommo couldn't go, would you come with me?' To my utter amazement she had said yes.

October

Tommo recommended a friend who would move into my bedsit, paying the mortgage whilst we were away. By now I'd been out of work for almost two months and I was definitely feeling the strain financially.

Moving out of my flat was more emotional than I expected. This tiny little room was more than just my home – it symbolised my independence. I packed away my books and winter clothes and struggled with my furniture down the narrow five flights of stairs. My sister and parents had unwillingly volunteered to store my belongings and they were not over-impressed with just how much I'd managed to squeeze into my little apartment. As I looked back at the sparse room I felt entirely overwhelmed by sadness. Tommo returned to his mum's for the final few weeks of preparation and I settled into my old room at my parents'.

SIX

Three Weeks and Six Days in Gomera

MANY OF THE ocean rowers we'd met had told us that getting to the start was more difficult than the row itself. Well, here we were, having successfully convinced hundreds of people to hand over their cash. 'Why are we rowing 3,000 miles?' I asked. Tommo didn't answer. We both stared at the grey, swirling sea from the plane window. Something in the pit of my stomach was telling me we were being incredibly stupid! Tommo wasn't giving anything away, he just grinned inanely, obviously extremely excited about our impending adventure. Did he know something I didn't? Perhaps I was underestimating our newly acquired abilities? Let's look at the evidence:

1 We'd only been out on the water in our little boat
   three times
2 The one weekend we had on a yacht was so nauseating
   we spent most of the time counting carrots
3 Tommo has epilepsy, a condition that kills people
   every day
4 Finally, if by some miracle we made it across alive, as
   the most argumentative couple in the world it was
   highly likely we'd never speak to each other again

Jane and Malcolm had risked their reputation to support us and because of this the charity coffers were looking very healthy indeed. However grey and threatening that sea looked, soon it would be our time to deliver. Everyone was relying on us.

I looked down at my pre-packed in-flight salad and pondered how far I'd come. At university I'd worked for an in-flight food company, adding the tomatoes as the trays rolled past, dressed in a blue hair net, disposable plastic apron and wellies, being shouted out by my supervisor for not placing the tomato in the right place. I never imagined I'd be here.

~

WE CAUGHT OUR first glimpse of La Gomera as we sunned ourselves on the ferry's deck, drinking ice-cold Fanta Limôn. We definitely didn't miss the British winter. La Gomera looked like the island from *The Land That Time Forgot*. Almost perfectly circular, its pinnacle is covered with lush rainforest, and deep scars run down from its peak, leaving much of the land too steep to be inhabitable. The majority of its inhabitants reside in small harbour towns. We were staying in a small fishing village called Playa de Santiago.

Arriving in San Sebastian on the south of the island, where we would eventually row from, we hopped on to a small 'cat', which took us round to Playa. This short ferry ride allowed us to see the true beauty of the island's coastline. The steep terracotta cliffs had been stripped by the ocean and carved out by the rain as it ran down from the forest at the centre of the island. Fish were leaping beside the boat and the water looked refreshing, clear and icy blue.

We arrived at the smaller harbour of Playa and stepped off the ferry with tons of luggage. Not knowing the address of the hotel, we thought it would be best to grab a taxi. The cab drew up and in our hopeless Spanish we asked for the Apartmentos Tapauga. Of course, I didn't have a cue what the driver said in reply, but Tommo translated, reassuring me he knew exactly what he meant, so we jumped in. Ten seconds and three hundred yards later we pulled up outside our apartments. You could actually see the three-foot-high name (in lights) from the harbour. Brits abroad!

As a team we had decided to give ourselves three weeks in Gomera – we thought we'd be able to make the most of the time, tinker with the boat and then launch her in good time to gain some much-needed sea experience and confidence. But of course even the best laid plans can go wrong. Tommo caught a stomach bug, so I went to San Sebastian alone to see if *Calderdale* had arrived. A quick look round the harbour told me she hadn't, so off I went to find 'Our Man in Gomera', Doug. I paced the pontoons looking for any yachts with a British ensign, but a woman from Yorkshire(!) told me there had been bereavement in the family so Doug and his wife had returned to England. No boat, no contact, no boyfriend to have a cup of coffee with ... Anyway, I ended up with a cheese sandwich when I had asked for a café Americano.

With nothing else to do but sit back and relax, Tommo and I re-established ourselves again in that first week. Because Tommo was a professional loafer he encouraged me to slow down. We spent hours in the roof-top pool, splashing about like teenagers; we ran races and practised holding our breath under water, a useful skill considering the circumstances.

The boat arrived at the beginning of the second week. The marina soon became busy with boats, crews and equipment. Everybody's boat sat out on the hard standing, and it was certainly reassuring that other teams were also struggling to get everything done in time. Non-stop tinkering began at the crack of dawn and tools did not down until the sun set.

Jane and Malcolm flew over in the second week and Malcolm immediately set to work helping us get the boat ready for launch. Jane marched on with the website, which was proving to be a complete pain in the arse, as was bothering to pack the boat on the hard standing: the race organisers had decided they all needed to be weighed, which meant they needed to be empty. As the first rains in six months lashed the car park concrete, we took everything off *Calderdale* and soggy we all became. Malcolm had scoured the length and breadth of Yorkshire looking for a weigh bridge so we could weigh her before we packed, but race rules were race rules and as we begrudgingly re-packed at least we knew all the teams were in the same boat, so to speak.

With the help of the yacht crews, one by one the boats disappeared from the car park, arriving at the slipway ready to glide gracefully into the water. Once rowed round the pretty marina they would spend the last week sitting along the pontoon closest to the passing tourists. It was soon our turn to join the rest of the shoal in the twinkling waters of the harbour. So I ask you to picture the scene … I'm sitting in *Calderdale* as she heads down the slipway, the ballast is still to be packed and the rudder yet to be attached. After a little pushing and pulling from members of the support crew, standing in the water up to their waists, I begin to row off round the marina as Tommo and Malcolm run down to the pontoon ready to catch my lines and tie me off. I dip the oars in and glide off towards the sea wall. There's a tight corner … I'm almost round … no, just a bit more … wind's got the front end … I'm not going to get it round … I'm heading straight toward the sea wall … CRASH!

I grabbed a round fender instead of a sausage one and shoved it off the bow, it didn't fit between the boat and the wall, so proving my skills as a competent skipper I tossed it overboard and grabbed the boat hook instead. With all the strength I could muster I pushed myself off and drifted rather alarmingly towards one of the Challenge Business support yachts. I became the first ocean rowboat in the race to be rescued.

I chose to sleep on the boat the night before we set off. We would launch on a Sunday morning and the Saturday had been very fraught. The final preparations had been manic, especially when Tommo disappeared to watch the rugby with half the contents of the boat still out on the pontoon. My parents were avoiding us by staying in an apartment on Tenerife: they didn't want to get under our feet. Many family members were hanging around wondering what to do to help. In fact, Kenneth had recommended months before that we encourage our families to stay at home. As Mum was our reserve rower we needed her close by, but I can only imagine the anxiety of our parents, who must have been looking out into the Atlantic desperately trying to picture their children making it across alive. Mum did come down to the boat one afternoon to present us with a packet of cress seeds. The paper sachet had been turned over twice at the top and secured with a wooden clothes peg. With glee I jumped on the boat, rootled through a net attached to the side wall of the cabin and re-emerged with a similar packet of cress seeds, turned twice at the top and secured with a clothes peg! Mum couldn't believe it. I am my mother's daughter.

I spent the night writing all our 'Diamond Donors' (individuals who had sponsored us) on to the ceiling of the cabin. There were hundreds of names. I remember thinking how amazing it was that so many people had been touched by the project.

Race Day, 19 October 2003

All rowing boats had to be at the start line by 10.30 am. A flag aboard one of the Challenge yachts would be raised at 10.55 am, indicating five minutes to go. A foghorn would be blown and the flag lowered at 11.00 am. The boats would leave, and that would be it, the start of the Woodvale Atlantic Rowing Race 2003.

Tommo joined me on the pontoon at 8.00 am. He was in high spirits, excited and chatty. I, on the other hand, felt sick to the stomach. I found it difficult to look anyone in the eye without my gut wrenching and my eyes filling with tears. In the final minutes before launch hundreds of people packed the pontoon. My own family, Josephine, Rachel, Tony, Jane and Malcolm gathered around *Calderdale* for photographs. My Dad hugged me like I was going to die and his tears ripped me in two as he whispered 'Bring it back for the family, Sal, bring it back for the Kettles!'

I didn't feel frightened, it was more a feeling of dread, and I'm not sure which one's worse. As I sobbed silently behind my sunglasses, Tommo chuckled and whooped as we rowed, and I felt glad he was sitting behind me taking the bow position. I didn't want him to see how upset I was, especially as it was obviously proving to be one of the best days of his life.

I imagined the view from the harbour wall. With every boat sporting multicoloured sponsor stickers it must have looked like a pileup at Silverstone, boats zigzagging everywhere as they jostled for a good position on the line. The flag dropped, the foghorn blew, and at a G force-inducing two knots Tommo and I set out to sea, arguing about the footplates. I think Ben could hear the expletives from the yacht he had chartered to follow us out.

Within the hour all fifteen teams were out of sight and aside from the occasional yacht we were alone on *Calderdale* with only 3,000 miles of ocean between us and the next time we would step on land. As the swells grew and the sea gradually darkened, the sun began to set and the lights twinkled in the harbour, we prepared for the next twelve hours of complete darkness alone in our little plywood boat.

Six Days Later ...

We were interviewed by BBC Radio Northampton the day after
we returned to England.

~

*Northampton's Sally Kettle and her partner Marcus Thompson were
forced to quit their attempt to row 3,000 miles across the Atlantic
Ocean due to illness. Just six days into the race team* Calderdale *had to
pull out because of the effects of seasickness on Marcus. But Sally plans
to embark on another 3,000-mile Atlantic challenge with her mum in
January, making them the first mother-and-daughter and all-female
crew to enter the race.*

    *Despite their disappointment, Sally and Marcus were in high spirits
when they dropped in to see us to talk seasickness, bruises, arguments
and peeing in a bucket.*

Can you just talk us through why you decided to turn back?

Marcus   *'I was very, very sick. I never overcame my
             seasickness, which meant I was very dehydrated as
             everything I ate or drank came back up. For the
             six days we were at sea I ate four pieces of
             crystallised ginger and six penny chews and
             that's what kept me going! I didn't eat anything
             else. On top of that, when I was having a rest
             at one point I had a seizure in my sleep and then I
             didn't have the energy to overcome the seizure, to rest*

up. So I was getting worse and worse and worse and not drinking and it got to the point where if there had been an emergency it could have been tricky going. So we decided to stop before it became an emergency and requested a tow back.'

Sally   *'It was a huge decision to make. We'd been passing it around for a few days before we decided just because Tommo was feeling so wretched. We saw the support yacht and we asked them for some advice on what was best for Tommo and what sort of things he could take. They said just stick it out, as most cases of seasickness last seventy-two hours. We both knew we were going to be seasick – everybody is. But it was coupled with the seizure, which we weren't expecting at the beginning. I was expecting we'd be seasick, we'd both recover, get going and then maybe through exhaustion Tommo might have a seizure later on and we'd deal with it when it came. It just wasn't good for Tommo to go on and I couldn't row for the two of us so it was best that we came back while we had the boat in good condition. As we were only thirty miles off the coast they could still give us a tow back, but any greater distance and they would have scuppered the boat, which was another thing that came into our decision.'*

Q   It's a stupid question, but how did you feel when you had to turn back?

Sally   *'Bloody awful, we were devastated.'*

Marcus   *'I felt I'd let Sally down through my health, I felt I'd*
          let myself down, I felt I'd let the charity down – The
          Fund for Epilepsy – and I felt I'd let other people
          with the condition down by endeavouring to do
          something so huge that people would say "You
          shouldn't be doing that," and I thought people are
          going to think that you can't do these things if you've
          got this condition, which is, of course, nonsense. And I
          still feel the same. I still think I've let lots of people
          down. I know there's been some achievement – in my
          head I know – but emotionally I don't feel that.'

Q   How long did you wait for help?

Marcus   *'There was no rescue – that's an exaggeration.*
          Basically they had to take us off our wooden boat on
          to their steel yacht and you don't want the two to
          crash as the wooden boat would certainly come off
          worse.'

Sally   *'We phoned them when it was quite late on the*
          Thursday night. They were fifty miles away with
          some other crews so it took them twelve hours to get
          to us. So it wasn't this huge dramatic rescue with
          helicopters and things.'

Marcus '*It was quite straightforward: a transfer of people from one boat to another boat. They put a dinghy between the two boats. We then attached lines to our boat, which is when the boat was damaged from the sheer force of the swell. We then climbed into the dinghy and then into their boat.*'

Q What experiences are you going to take home from your six days at sea?

Sally '*The boat is amazing. I spent most of the time on deck and I never felt unsafe. I never thought "We're going to die" or "This huge wave is going to come over us and tip us over." It was just like a bobbing cork, and that for us was a huge relief. We both got blisters after the first day and my arse was sore; God it was sore! It was also very hard to get around the boat. They say the first two weeks are the worst and they were. We were constantly arguing ...*'

Marcus '*Well, you were constantly shouting at me! There's a difference!*'

Sally '*It was very stressful. Tommo has some amazing bruises!*'

Marcus '*I slipped over on deck at one point and I landed on the tracks of the seat and I got a six- to eight-inch bruise on the back of my thigh. I got something else similar on the inside of my thigh – and I don't know how I got it! I think I was asleep and Sally just hit me with a screwdriver or something. You get lots of bumps and bruises.'*

Sally   *'Plus, everything is inconvenient. Going to the toilet is inconvenient. Just getting stuff out of things is really hard work. But it's been a great learning curve towards our plans to go in January.'*

Marcus   *'There are things you learn about the boat – how it moves in the water and how you feel completely comfortable in it. Then there are things you learn about life on the boat: peeing in a bucket is not easy.'*

Sally   *'Oh yeah, and we tried doing it in the cabin too as we were locked in.'*

Marcus   *'It was raining and we were locked in and we tried to wee in the cabin.'*

Sally   *'In a drinks bottle, urghhh!'*

Marcus   *'I was alright. Sally was less successful, and that's all that needs to be said on the matter! You looked like a naughty puppy! It's also about things that you learn about yourself.'*

Sally   *'I was horribly impatient and easily frustrated. I didn't realise I'd be so bad, actually.'*

Marcus   *'It was a question of not getting angry about things*
          you can't control. You can only do what you can do,
          so don't get upset about what you can't do. And if you
          get upset about what you can't do, don't shout at me!'

Q   So, judging from your six days at sea, how do
          you think you would have coped with the full
          ninety days?

Sally   *'We'd have definitely made it.'*

Marcus   *'If I hadn't had the seizure and the seasickness*
          combined, we'd be out there now. We'd be getting into
          a routine and there's no reason to suggest we wouldn't
          have made it.'

Sally   *'Seasickness is seasickness. You eventually get over it*
          and get on with it. It's just Tommo didn't get over it.
          But then it might be genetic because his mother is not
          a good sailor, is she?'

Marcus   *'No, she gets seasick in the shower.'*

Q   So you're planning to enter the Ocean Rowing
          Society Atlantic Rowing Regatta in January?

Sally   *'When we got back I was keen to get back out. I was*
          ready to grab anyone who was willing to come,
          actually! The boat had to be repaired and we

rang the Ocean Rowing Society and provisionally
they've said yes, so we've got to get myself and
my mum back to full fitness. Mum's got to learn how
to navigate, how to read charts and bits and bobs and
now we're going to sit down and make a plan. There's
never been a mother-and-daughter team and there's
only ever been one other all-female crew, so we could be
setting some records.'

Q Is it pretty much the same as the race you've
just embarked on?

Marcus *'It leaves from the same place, it arrives at the same*
place, but it's unlike the race we were in as all the
boats had to be identical. With the regatta everyone
has different boats; you have crews of four, single
crews, but mostly pairs, and it's not a race.'

Sally *'You try and get across as quickly as you can and you*
can set a record in your class — it's not a race against
each other. So we're now in training and I'm looking
forward to it.'

~

Six Days at Sea

When we first rowed out to sea the exhilaration staved off
the seasickness. We were so excited nothing could go down or
come up. It was only when the sun began to set and darkness

enveloped the boat did our stomachs begin to protest. Although we were taking anti-seasickness tablets the tiredness and the dark overrode their effects and the first night was just horrendous. We had found it very difficult to prepare for the all-night rowing and we began to regret not spending more time training for it. We were just going to launch into our schedule of two hours on, two hours off during the day and four hours on, four hours off at night, effectively suffering the consequences when they came; anyway, we weren't racing so we could choose to stop and rest up if necessary. There was so much we just couldn't prepare for, but other rowers had said the first two weeks are the worst, so as the first days passed we really began to understand what they meant. In lots of ways I was far better prepared than Tommo, maybe the nights spent visualising the pain and discomfort had given me the upper hand.

What we also completely underestimated was the effect of seeing land for such a long time. I think we both thought Gomera would disappear over the horizon within a day or two but by day four the looming mass of rock continued to taunt us. Perhaps it seems odd that we so desperately wanted to be in the open ocean, but if we were at least we could fool ourselves into thinking we were well on our way.

Life on board was incredibly frustrating, stressful, tiring, emotional and painful. We stumbled about the rocking boat knocking ourselves on anything and everything attached to the deck. Arms, legs, feet and foreheads were covered in scrapes and bruises. Profanities were flying. The waves grew as we made our way into the Acceleration Zone, a natural phenomenon created between the small islands. As the wind and water gets squeezed between each landmass it's forced to speed up, producing ferocious winds and very choppy, confused waves. *Calderdale* coped fantastically: we didn't.

Tommo spent more time in the cabin sleeping; he'd been sick a couple of times but something else was definitely wrong. He slept for hours and barely ventured out to take to the oars. He refused water and pushed me away when I attempted to coax some food into him. I began to feel that he'd given up. I was on deck most of the day and joined him in the cabin at night as we slowly drifted out to sea. The two Challenge support yachts came to visit us and we took the opportunity to ask them for any advice to combat Tommo's sickness, but the only action they could recommend was to sit it out and hope it would pass.

As I sat out on deck, already bored of the view and of rowing, stories of failed attempts came back to haunt me. Chay Blyth had made it very clear that any crew who decided to turn back lacked the balls to complete the row and quite frankly should never have entered, and in doing so they would be marked for ridicule.

I began to resent Tommo and his condition, I resented him sleeping, I resented his complaints every time he came to the oars. I resented having to be the skipper, the one in charge. I resented Tommo for not working harder during the last year and a half. The cursing in my head grew louder and louder until eventually I couldn't keep it in any longer. The wind had changed direction and we had to launch our jellyfish in a bag, the para-anchor. The ropes had become twisted into an unfathomable mess and I couldn't undo them, my fingers blistered and stiff from rowing. I called Tommo out to help, but as the frustration grew there was nothing he could do to stop me from finally lashing out at him.

'I fucking hate you for putting me in this position!' I screamed through tears.

Tommo went mute with shock. He eventually managed to talk me down and I successfully launched the para-anchor, allowing us to stay relatively still in the water. I got into the cabin beside him. We lay silently, listening to the water. The boat creaked and groaned with the rise and fall of each wave. It was time to abandon the trip. I sobbed and sobbed, not able to look Tommo in the eye, not able to verbalise my own thoughts of failure. We both knew enough was enough and it was time to call the support yacht. I have to admit when he told me he had had a seizure in his sleep I didn't believe him and although I didn't say it he knew that was how I felt. He was incredibly hurt by my lack of support. I was infuriated when he made excuses, blaming the condition for his lack of motivation, playing the victim.

It sounds so heartless as I write it now, but at the time I had a raging anger that drowned out any empathy for his situation. But Tommo was unwell: his body was covered in bruises, the skin on the backs of his legs was beginning to break down, and large red, raw sores were spreading from his groin to the backs of his knees. We did share a laugh when I saw the sunburn on his thighs, which looked like a pair of bright red stockings. That was the only laugh we did share as we lay there waiting.

So here we were. We had only lasted a few pitiful days at sea but there was still a chance we could get back to Gomera, and although we had clocked ninety miles on our GPS we were only thirty miles as the crow flies from port. There was a very real chance the boat would be towed back by the support yacht and not scuppered. We talked about this eventuality and I decided I would row it alone if Lin Parker, skipper of the Challenge yacht, decided to blow up *Calderdale*. Abandoning a boat at sea, leaving it to drift, can create a hazard for other ships. If we both got off the boat she would have to be sunk. There was no way we could leave her behind, especially after the time we'd spent and the money we'd raised. *Calderdale* represented all our dreams.

After several hours wallowing in self-pity I picked up the satellite phone and with a very heavy heart I called Lin. After explaining the situation she told us to stay on our para-anchor and they would make their way back to us. They were fifty miles south of our position but it would take twelve hours tacking up wind to get to us. We had to wait till dawn until they would be able to attempt a tow.

I then called Simon Chalk to ask him if he'd take Tommo's place. We'd met him at the very first meeting in Southampton. He had rowed across the Atlantic in 2001 and after two attempts successfully rowed the Indian Ocean, solo. His company, Woodvale, was sponsoring the race and so he had come to Gomera to see us off. Whilst there he'd mentioned that he'd jump into any boat if it was ready to go and all he had to do was row. I was clutching at straws and although I rather fancied his amazing blue eyes I was thinking more selfishly. I just wanted to get across. As you can imagine he was rather shocked to get the call and of course he wisely said no! Keen to help, he recommended a friend, and said he'd get her to call me. We sat and waited for the phone to ring. Simon's friend Janette giggled nervously on the end of the line. I briefly explained the situation and she told me she would have to talk to her family and with their blessing be packed and on the plane as soon as she could.

I came off the phone feeling like I hadn't really thought this through: surely I'd prefer to go by myself than with a total stranger, however gorgeous his eyes were. I really hadn't been very fair to Janette either: here I was offering an adventure on a plate, but we didn't even know if we'd get on. I had to think long and hard about my reasons for wanting to row this ocean. Was it an adventure with Tommo? For the charity? No, it was a promise I had made to myself.

It was time to call Mum. I didn't really want to ask her to come. I felt horribly guilty, because if she said yes what would Dad do? More importantly, did she really want to come with me? Her daughter sobbing down the phone, her dreams smashed with only her mother to save the situation … if she did say no, she knew it would crush me. I rang Dad's mobile.

SEVEN

The Old Woman of the Sea

'HI MUM, IT'S all going wrong, we're coming back ... You really, really don't have to say yes ... but will you come with me?'

'Yes, Sal, of course I will!'

'Mum, are you sure? Please be sure.'

'Sal, I'll do it!'

'Ok, well, we'll be back at port tomorrow afternoon, will you meet us there?'

'Do I need anything?'

'No ... Oh, perhaps more teabags!'

Dad told me later that Mum then went to the kitchen and started packing cans of baked beans. She has coeliac disease, where the gut is unable to digest gluten, therefore she can't have bread, flour, pasta – in fact anything containing wheat. She was worried she would have to come out on the support yacht and they wouldn't have anything for her to eat. So, as we bobbed helplessly out in the ocean, Mum had shocked my entire family with her plans to row an ocean with her daughter, armed with cans of baked beans! At this point she hadn't even stepped on the boat.

I couldn't believe it. Mum was actually going to come with me. It seemed the advice she had been given by an elderly lady, whose garden she tends, had hit home. 'Sarah, you get to a point in life where you wish you could do things, but your body doesn't let you. If there's an opportunity then take it before your body tells you you can't.'

I called Janette and told her the news. Her response was a mixture of relief and disappointment, but she understood my predicament. I also told her that I'd asked my mother: whether this would prove to be the right decision, we both agreed time would certainly tell.

~

WHEN THE YACHT arrived at dawn the next morning, Tommo and I shoved our passports down our pants, struggled into some shorts and T-shirts and stepped out on deck in our lifejackets – the most clothes we'd worn in days. The ocean had been swept up into white-topped peaks and the para-anchor was pulling the boat head-on into them. Foamy water was cascading over the bow of the boat, washing down the deck and soaking us to the bone. We were incredibly anxious about the pick-up. I was worried Lin would decide they couldn't tow the boat back and we would be faced with the prospect of me rowing it alone. The voice of one of the crew began to crackle intermittently over the VHF.

One lesson we learnt all too quickly was the limited range of the radio: radio waves don't pass through water. We had to get the aerial as high as possible, which meant standing astride the footwell, clinging precariously to the roof of the cabin, one hand on the boat, one hand holding the VHF, neck craned, with the volume at its highest. With the wind whipping round my ears and the boat tipping wildly below me, I guided the yacht to our position.

We were heaving our anchor in as Lin skilfully drew the support yacht up beside us. Her crew shouted instructions, telling us to attach water bottles and fenders, in fact anything that would offer us some protection from the steel hull of the yacht, along the side of our boat. The plan involved a transfer from our boat to theirs. We would need to bring ourselves alongside them and climb aboard – there'd be no hunky coastguards dropping in from the heavens from a helicopter.

The crew threw us a thick rope, which I tied to the para-anchor bridle, attached to the towing eye at the bow of the boat. I had worried for months about my poor rope skills. Perhaps it was the seriousness of the situation, but my fingers flew into action and I tied off the rope with a firm bowline without even thinking. The crew threw a further two lines for us to tie to the side of *Calderdale*. Tommo attached one to a large silver cleat on the side of the cabin … with a sickening crack the cleat ripped away from the wood, leaving a gaping hole. The rope, with the cleat still attached, floated away in the water. We both dived for the boat hook in an attempt to fish the elusive cleat back out. More ropes were being flung from the support yacht, followed by inaudible cries. If we didn't tie this boat off now Lin would have to abandon the first attempt, wasting valuable time and pushing her and her crew to their limits. I frantically began tying the second line to the struts, which supported the rowing runners. They'd been built into the superstructure of the deck. If the force of the waves pulled the rope away with the runners the deck would go with it. Tommo triumphantly retrieved the lost line and after we'd cut away the cleat we tied it as securely as we could to the struts. We were now attached by umbilicals to the mother ship and the Challenge crew began to pull us towards them.

The waves were not helping as we pitched and slammed against the yacht, the makeshift fenders were proving to be useless, the water bottles collapsing with every impact. Lin decided to create a buffer by throwing an inflatable dinghy down between us. Tommo went first, stepping tentatively on to the unstable floor before being hoisted up under the armpits and unceremoniously dragged and dumped on to the deck of the yacht.

Me next. A couple of hands grabbed my backside, another accidentally pulled my knickers up to my bra line and into an uncomfortable wedgie. Whacking my knees and hips against the side of the yacht I scrambled up and over the side of the rails, collapsing into an undignified heap on the deck. *Calderdale* drifted from the towing line behind the yacht. Lin steered us back toward La Gomera.

We all sat in silence, the crew not knowing what to say, Tommo and I not knowing what to tell them. I would have been happy helping out, anything to keep my mind busy, to take away the feelings of shame and disappointment. Lin insisted we take it easy and enjoy the sunshine, so we sat watching *Calderdale* bobbing away behind us, the island growing bigger on the horizon. For all the sadness associated with our time on the yacht I actually really enjoyed being there. In fact it was the first time I'd been on one without feeling sick!

~

WE NEEDED TO row *Calderdale* back to the pontoons; the restricted space wouldn't allow Lin to tow her in. Tommo understandably decided not to board the boat again but waited on deck as one of the girls from the crew joined me at the oars. We leapt aboard quite easily, rowed her in and tied her off, no fanfares, no crowds, just Malcolm and Mum on the pontoon ready with fenders and hugs.

I thought I'd break down when I saw Mum but I threw my arms around her thanking her for agreeing to come with me. She looked a little shell-shocked. I think she was secretly pleased when she saw the hole in the cabin: the repairs would buy her some time to get herself together.

Tommo joined us on the pontoon, melancholic but desperately trying to put a brave face on the situation. Malcolm was fantastic, reassuring us that we hadn't let anybody down, that we'd made the right decision and he would support us even if we decided not to try again. I suspect his and Jane's disappointment was as great as ours, although Malcolm tried his very best not to show it.

As we wobbled up the stairs towards an apartment Malcolm had hired, our land legs having not yet kicked in, my mind was racing. I was keen to get on the case and ready the boat for our re-launch. Strangely, I felt excited, in fact practically elated, about the prospect of going again. I suddenly knew that I had faced my worst fear and survived. It wasn't a fear of death, of drowning, or capsizing – it was the fear of failure that had haunted me. And now we had failed with a big fat F. We had fucked it up, but we had survived six days at sea together in a twenty-four-foot wooden boat! But Tommo certainly wasn't seeing the positive side: I could tell he felt like shit and wished he'd given it a bit more time.

Re-launching straight away wasn't going to happen. Jane and Malcolm had spoken to Mum and asked her not to go without some proper training and Challenge Business also said no, again because Mum had no experience. It all made sense really, and having spoken to a local boat builder it would also take some time to repair the hole in the cabin. We would have to return to England, leaving *Calderdale* behind. Mum and my family jumped on their original flight home. Tommo and I stayed with Malcolm in San Sebastian. We put the boat to bed and took a road trip round the island.

With *Calderdale* left in capable hands, we boarded the ferry for Tenerife, made our way to the airport and flew home to London. Tommo came to stay with me at my parents' and after a brief flurry of media attention he returned to Halifax to stay with his mum, although I don't think even her lemon drizzle cake could cheer him.

During those first few days neither of us followed the remaining crews as they continued their adventures. I cared for our friends' safety, but selfishly I wanted to move on from that race and start a second attempt. Pining over what could have been wasn't something I was prepared to do. 'Move on,' Mum would say: 'Move on!'

The tenant in my flat hadn't paid any rent whilst we were away. Disappointed and worried, it seemed cake wouldn't cheer me either. In fact, I felt like I'd been hit across the face with a large wet fish, especially as I considered him a friend. But there you go: just a week or two before Christmas I had to initiate the battle to evict him.

The Eye of the Tiger

Soon after we'd made the decision to take part in the Challenge Business race we'd received word of an alternative event, a regatta organised by the Ocean Rowing Society (ORS). It would leave Gomera in January 2004, taking the same route across the Atlantic with teams eventually arriving in Barbados. We began to weigh up the pros and cons of both events. As newcomers to the sport Tommo, Malcolm, Jane and I were a bit overwhelmed by it all. We spent some time discussing the options and although we felt the regatta reflected our ethos of 'just getting across and having a good time' (i.e. not racing), Challenge Business had already organised two successful events, and nobody had died whilst taking part in them! So we decided to stick with Chay Blyth and his team. There really wasn't much in it; it was just the 'death factor' that tipped the balance in their favour.

I was so grateful that we made this decision, as it meant we were left with a chance to try again. For the first time in ocean rowing history there would be two events leaving La Gomera within a couple of months of each other. Mum and I would return in January as entrants in the regatta. All we needed to do was register and pay another entrance fee. We'd be taken under the wing of the exuberant and rather eccentric Kenneth Crutchlow. With a voice that bellowed like a foghorn and sporting a rather bushy grey moustache, Ken, who was well into his sixties, was undoubtedly the godfather of the sport.

You might be interested in a little bit of ocean rowing history. Kenneth's account would take several days so I'll abridge it for you. It's not that Kenneth's tales are boring, on the contrary, he's achieved so much in his eclectic life that he always has a story. Anyway, Ken set up the ORS on a promise to his friend Peter Bird, who died during an attempt to cross the Pacific in 1996. Although Ken had run the length of Death Valley and swum across to San Francisco from Alcatraz in a pair of alarmingly small knitted swimming trunks, he'd never in fact attempted to cross an ocean in a rowing boat. Perhaps it seems odd that he would devote himself entirely to the sport, but he had promised Peter that he would set up a society that would support the needs of anyone who wished to row across an ocean, and that's exactly what he did. It culminated in a very swanky website, a source of advice, statistics and comment for nearly ten years. In fact it was one of the first places I looked the day after Tommo first threw down the gauntlet.

So here we were with our place booked in the regatta, and there was only a month and a half for Tony and me to prepare Mum for her 3,000 mile row. Although she regularly walked the dogs it's safe to say that she was in no way match fit. She also needed to gain some weight, and with Christmas just around the corner her preparations for physical greatness were about to begin. To get the ball rolling I paid a visit to the river rowing club in Northampton. Amused and somewhat amazed by our predicament, the club committee took pity on us and offered us both free membership until the start of our race.

It wasn't until the first weekend in December that Mum ventured out on the River Nene for the first time. She waddled down to the water togged out in a thick woolly jumper, bobble hat, gloves and wellies. Like all newcomers to the sport the club had provided her with a bright yellow plastic bucket of a boat called a Virus – its fat bottom is ideal whilst you're learning as it gives you the reassurance that you won't tip up and fall in as you flail about trying to master the oars. The Viruses are also a lot shorter than the average sculling boat, perfect for kids and perfect for Mum: at five-foot-three she fitted rather snugly into her little bucket.

Tony had made the trip up from Brighton and kindly offered to coach from the safety of the riverbank. You could hear him shouting instructions all the way to the M1 as Mum slowly began to master the technique, although she accidentally hit a couple of swans before careering off into the bank, entangling herself in bulrushes. Still, there are no banks or bulrushes at sea, so there was no need to worry unnecessarily, and after an hour on the water she dragged the boat on to the pontoon and I could see confidence glowing from her reddened, wind-chapped cheeks.

The following day I came downstairs to find a pair of short plastic oars tied to the dining room chairs with my Dad's work ties. Mum had been practising the sculling technique at the dining room table, her arms whirling about in what looked like a pretty realistic attempt to ocean row. She was keen to demonstrate her commitment and I actually thought it was a brilliant idea. With the constant pitch of the boat Tommo and I had thrown our technique out of the window. Mum's mock-up perfectly reflected the futile asymmetric dipping of the oars as you tried to catch the waves.

~

WITH THE ROWING technique mastered, it was time for Mum to acquaint herself with the gym. Not a natural athlete, she certainly didn't look that excited. In fact I've never seen her look so grumpy. There was no mistaking the vibes she was throwing out – she did not like going to the gym. She lasted all of five minutes before the novelty of sitting on your backside to get fit wore off. After only a couple of days we both knew it would be a struggle for her to commit to this kind of training regime. We decided brisk daily walks with Pip and Scruff would have to suffice.

With the 'walking and occasional rowing' regime well underway we also needed to get Mum up to speed on astro-navigation, first aid and sea experience. The first aid course was easily done: a day with St John Ambulance and she knew how to resuscitate, place the patient in the recovery position, tie a neat bandage and call an ambulance.

We booked ourselves on to a two-day intensive astro course. The regatta rules didn't require the skills, but Jane and Malcolm were keen for us to qualify: 'Belt and braces, Sally, belt and braces!' Mum hadn't attempted complicated maths for thirty years, yet she methodically and patiently worked through the course, passing it with flying colours. I felt the pride of a parent. I think she even surprised herself.

For the much-needed sea experience we called Challenge Business for suggestions. 'I can't wait to be sick in a bucket' Mum told friends triumphantly when we secured a weekend on one of their sixty-foot ex-racing yachts. She felt that no trip to sea would be complete without a bout of vomiting.

The weekend 'Competent Crew' course would take her out of London and into the Channel, making berth at Southampton. In preparation for the British weather she even took the bright-red wet weather jacket, salopettes and hat. Annoyingly for us both, she wasn't sick. It seemed I would be the only one spending time at sea with my head over the gunnels. Her constitution kept her stomach contents in place, and although the schedule of four hours on/four hours off was tiring, with tea on tap my mother remained unfazed.

Mum had enthusiastically collected a mass of useful items for the boat, from storage tubs to a foam mattress to cut up for seat cushions. In fact, the dining room table had practically disappeared. With every trip to the supermarket we were also dropping extra packets of gluten-free ginger cakes into our trolley. God only knows how we were going to get all of it into our already overstuffed boat!

The Christmas holidays gave us ample opportunity to work especially hard on our diet. Turkey, gluten-free mince pies, trifle, chocolates, Christmas pudding – we never refused an extra helping. Dad joined in, even though he'd promised to lose two stones before we got back from our trip. Mum made a point of reminding him with every mouthful. We teased him, but his comeback was always the same: 'I'm empathising with you, Sarah.' Quite frankly that excuse didn't wash with me!

With Mum's help I found the weight gain easier to handle, together we began to celebrate our additional rolls of tummy fat, pitching our inches with pride. Although I still didn't like what I saw when I looked in the mirror, the feelings of intense revulsion were beginning to fade. Additionally, that December I had the privilege of really getting to know my parents as friends. What a surprising twist that an ocean row set to split our family apart by several thousand miles had actually bought us all closer together.

Everything that needed to be done had been. We all accepted that Mum wouldn't be Steve Redgrave or Ellen MacArthur in just a month and a bit, but she was as ready as she'd ever be. Mum had shown that she was prepared to row and make her own cups of tea, and more importantly after everything that had happened she was prepared to go with me. It was more than I could have hoped for.

~

AWAY FROM BRIGHTON, I had time to think seriously about my relationship with Tommo and after much to-ing and fro-ing I finally came to the decision to end it. Sadly, I hadn't missed his company and I certainly hadn't missed our constant squabbling. I had loved him for four years and now only feelings of friendship remained. Although we spoke regularly on the phone, I found myself struggling to remain genuinely excited to hear from him. I asked Mum what I should do. We eventually came to the conclusion that it would be best for me to tell Tommo after our row. It sounds heartless now, but we both thought the disappointment and upset of the first attempt, coupled with my announcement, might be enough to trigger a bout of depression. So I pretended, saying 'I love you' at the end of conversations, creating diversions if the topic of commitment came up. I always knew this row would make or break us, and after all we'd both been through during the last year, I think we had seen the very worst in each other. I was relieved that I'd finally made the decision and I think my family was too.

~

MUM AND I flew out of Luton early on 2 January. We were lucky enough to have a small entourage who'd made the effort to come and see us off. My parents' friends, affectionately known as the Stumpies, Mum's brother Peter and his wife, Carol, had faced a bitterly cold snowy morning to come share a cup of tea with us the in a concourse cafe. Wrapped up in several layers, I found it hard to imagine how hot it would be in Gomera, and I began to worry that I hadn't packed enough jumpers.

We left it to the very last minute before we made our way through security. Mum had given us all orders not to cry – she's not one to wear her heart on her sleeve and the last thing we needed was sobbing relatives looking at us like it was the last time they would see us alive!

The two-hour flight went by quickly and we soon found ourselves engaged in a conversation with a woman in the seat next to us. The chitchat started when we asked her for her orange juice carton. They were small circular plastic tubs, and we needed four. Amazingly Mum and I had spooked each other with the same idea – the pots would be perfect for growing cress! I suggested we place one of my cotton wool face pads in the bottom, soak it in fresh water, and sprinkle the seeds on top. Mum suggested we put two together, held with an elastic band, the 'lid' perforated with pin holes to allow for condensation. Hey presto, fresh greens.

Malcolm had taken an earlier flight from Leeds so we rendezvoused with him at the airport. Jane had been left behind in Halifax so she could prime the press, update the website and find her line.

Dropping our kit off at the apartments, Mum and I slipped into shorts and T-shirts before flip-flopping down to the harbour to find *Calderdale*. She sat at the top of a scaffold storage frame within the harbour compound. Blue tarp had been stretched over her, so we couldn't be sure of the repair to the cabin's roof. The wonderful José and 'Our Man' Doug had taken care of her whilst we were away, so she hadn't been sitting open to the weather.

I scuttled down to José's office to ask him when we could bring her down. He met me with a broad grin, obviously pleased we'd been able to come back for a second attempt. He explained it would take a day or two to organise the crane to lift her: 'Mañana, mañana!' he said, smiling.

I trusted José, so although the Spanish have a reputation for putting jobs off I knew he would have lifted her himself if he'd time that day. Tanned and toned, his jeans were slightly too tight, pulled up too high and his T-shirt tucked in a little too securely, but he possessed that Mediterranean sexiness that leaves many a woman weak at the knees. That included me!

Again, we had to potter round San Sebastian waiting for the boat. We hadn't been to any regatta get-togethers, but it didn't take long to spot the crews. We'd clock them as they disembarked from the ferry, carrying overstuffed holdalls over one arm, an EPIRB[3] under the other, floppy sunhats shading portly but athletic physiques. It also helped that they had all been given the tip-off about the Blue Marlin, the official ocean rowers' bar.

Mum and I soon discovered that we were the only women taking part – female ocean rowers were still a novelty, it seemed. I took the opportunity to enjoy the company of the male rowers, although not in the biblical sense, I must add.

The atmosphere was very different from that of the Challenge race. The crews were more approachable, every team giving time to help others. The ever-boisterous Kenneth Crutchlow had also invited ex-rowers along to offer much-needed advice and reassurance. Jan Meek was spreading her vivacious enthusiasm,

---

[3] Emergency Position Indicator Radio Beacon. Race rules require you take this kit, as it is your final get-out clause. Once activated the signal is received by Falmouth Coastguard. This is the case wherever you are in the world. The coastguard then engages the nearest vessel in your vicinity to come and get you. Serious stuff!

whilst Diana and Stein Hoff, a couple who had both rowed the Atlantic solo, were providing lunchtime waffles on their catamaran. Isn't this the life? It's sunny every day and the only thing you have to worry about it is finding your way to the tropical Caribbean island paradise of Barbados!

Kenneth was keen to encourage camaraderie amongst the teams, encouraging us to all go to dinner together. The restaurateurs of San Sebastian were either dreading our arrival – thirty rowers with associated taggers on – or they were welcoming the opportunity to earn more money in one night than they would during an entire month. Either way, Ken would insist we all stood up and introduced ourselves to the group before proposing the next toast of the evening. We soon found out that the party wasn't over until the third toast[4] had been announced, by which time most of us were under the table. Except Mum, who doesn't drink (a by-product of a rather nasty week-long hangover induced by way too much dry cider two summers previously) and was the paragon of virtue.

Calderdale finally came down from her boat-sized bunk bed. We unleashed her from the tarp, threw any equipment on her decks into wheelbarrows before the port official lashed her up to the crane and slowly dropped her into the water. Having learnt my lesson the first time, both Mum and I jumped aboard, easing her round into the harbour; the wind was light enough to avoid another embarrassing break for freedom. Malcolm tied her off on a pontoon at the far side of the marina and together we set to work, enjoying a little privacy from the constant interruptions of curious passers-by. I felt a bit like the old woman of the sea: I'd

---

[4]The third toast being 'To those at sea'.

survived six exhausting days out in the unforgiving ocean, which I suspected was more time than any of the other crews had actually spent in their own boats. Several people asked for my advice and I obliged as best I could, but the only real feedback I could give was that seasickness was a real bastard. Mum thought this was hysterical: well, she would, having not actually been seasick yet.

The boat packing wasn't as traumatic this time. Most of it had already been done and so we just re-jigged a bit, adding stuff and taking stuff away – all very technical. Mum pottered about under my watchful skipper's eye.

Calderdale was slowly taking shape again. The main cabin was cleared and clean, the sleeping bags tossed to the back ready for our first night; cotton buds and emergency Sudacreme cream stored in the cargo nets we'd attached to the sides of the wooden interior. The front was packed to the gunnels with extra food and tools. Two crash helmets had been thrown in on top. Mum had decided we needed them in case we capsized. She'd heard news of a couple of lads who attempted the Indian Ocean the previous summer: they'd tipped up and one of them had smashed his head against the ceiling, rendering him unconscious. So she went out and found some canoeing helmets, and my Dad 'sponsored' one and the Stumpies' 'sponsored' the other. The Stumpies had written 'Tell 'um shit' across the brim of theirs and Dad 'The sun will come out tomorrow.' 'Tell 'um shit' was a reference to what my Gran had told my Dad when he complained that the Stumpies teased him relentlessly; the latter took the piss out of my somewhat theatrical nature. Either way both phrases were there to brighten our spirits at a time when thoughts of dying at sea would probably be at the forefront of our minds.

Talking about heads leads me rather aptly on to the psychos. I'm not sure who decided the crews needed to be psychologically tested before the row, but two doctors from Cardiff University lurked around the teams, asking them to undertake a series of written tests. Mum and I were worried. Both of us felt it was all a bit 'quacky', and we'd already faced our fair share of sceptics. Even *The Times* had doubted the likelihood of our success ... 'Mother-daughter relationships are extremely complex ... If there are historical problems, they will come to the fore on a trip like this.'[5] Argh.

We spent about an hour separately talking about our relationship, our reasons for taking part and our expectations, but the psychologists refused to give anything away, except a bundle of papers that needed to be filled out during the expedition. We were given explicit instructions to complete the forms during or after a particularly traumatic situation. There were questions like:

1 Did you want to turn round and go home?
   Rarely   Sometimes   Often
2 Did you have thoughts of suicide?
   Rarely   Sometimes   Often
3 Did you want to chuck your partner overboard?
   Rarely   Sometimes   Often

How often would we be ticking 'Often'?

[5] *The Times*, 1 January 2004.

115

~

WITH ONLY A few days left to the start Tommo had made arrangements to come to Gomera to help us with our final preparations. I felt a bit apprehensive about him coming over. I was worried a return to the place where he faced what he saw as his greatest failure would be far too stressful for us both. But as he stepped off the ferry from Los Cristianos I was actually really pleased to see him. We gave each other a massive squeeze before heading to the apartments we'd spent so much time in only two months before.

In his buoyant and charming way he introduced himself to the other crews as 'the boyfriend who failed', laughing at his own misfortune before offering up advice on how to tie a good strong bowline round the runners and not round any cleats attached to the cabin roof. He offered reassurance to those who feared failure: here was a man who'd been unsuccessful and survived, apparently coping well with the disappointment. But I knew deep down he wasn't coping very well at all, although I was happy to share his enthusiasm for being the 'failed ocean rower' whilst he had the opportunity to flaunt it.

Tommo wasn't the only visitor to come and see us off. Mayor Geraldine Carter, the Yorkshire dynamo, came over with her husband, Brian. I could tell she was a little overwhelmed by it all because she was uncharacteristically quiet. Having given her blessing for the second attempt, seeing the reality of it probably made the dangers seem all too real. And her efforts had funded it!

My Dad joined us, along with Jane and a lovely bloke called Mark from the BBC's *South East Today*. Our own camera crew in tow. Check out the media queens! My brother Stephen had told Mum he wouldn't be able to take the time off work to come over, so you can imagine her surprise when he arrived on the pontoon. My nephew Lincoln and sister Sam were staying on Tenerife, and would come over on the Sunday morning – regatta start day.

Our entourage tried to be as helpful as possible without getting in the way. The men made themselves useful by attempting to fix a speaker system to the gunnels. Tommo and I had previously brought along a small pair of plastic speakers for our minidisc player, the plan being to stick them in a plastic bag and sit them out on deck. (These were pre-iPod days, when a minidisc player was the height of musical technological sophistication!)

As the final day of preparations ended I fished out a pair of my biggest, baggiest pink knickers and tied them to the mast beside our Fund for Epilepsy mascot – a fluffy curly-fleeced white lamb. *Calderdale* was now officially a girls' boat, the only girls' boat in the fleet, and we were proud of her. We stood there watching the pants flapping in the gentle breeze and knew she was ready to go for the second time.

We all went out to dinner the evening before the start and I couldn't speak. For some reason this was even worse than the first time we left, so much so that I couldn't look anyone in the eyes for fear of throwing up on them or bursting into tears. It feels like you're about to step out on to the stage at Wembley having only warbled a couple of 80's numbers at the local pub karaoke. It's the stuff of nightmares: a diarrhoea-inducing mixture of guilt, fear, apprehension and queasiness. Everything is telling you not to do it, but you know that too many people are relying on you, so you can't not go.

Unlike me, Mum was on top form. Jane had organised some pre-dinner snacks at our apartment and Mum had taken the opportunity to jump in the bath and shave her legs for the last time. It was obvious that she had no idea how bloody awful this was going to be!

I didn't sleep on the boat; instead I spent the night tucked up next to Tommo on the floor of the apartment, using the cushions from the sofa. Mum and Dad were sharing the pushed-together single beds. Not able to sleep, I watched the hours ticking away on the watch the Girls had bought me as a leaving gift. It was one of those super-chunky sailing watches capable of telling you the time several miles under water. The blue figures glowed ominously:

$$01:31 \quad \ldots$$
$$02:04 \quad \ldots$$
$$04:56 \quad \ldots$$

Part Two

The Epic Challenge for Epilepsy Family Tree

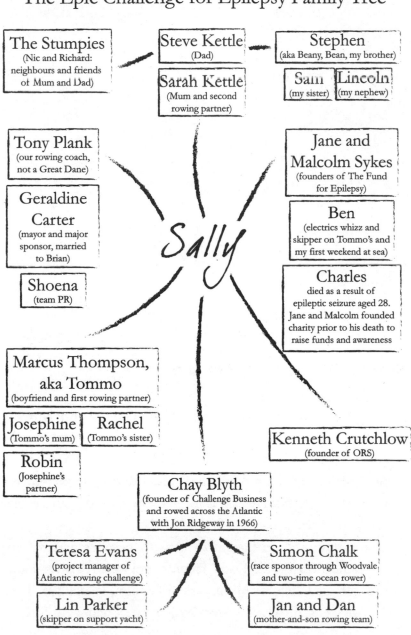

The Stumpies
(Nic and Richard: neighbours and friends of Mum and Dad)

Steve Kettle
(Dad)

Sarah Kettle
(Mum and second rowing partner)

Stephen
(aka Beany, Bean, my brother)

Sam
(my sister)

Lincoln
(my nephew)

Tony Plank
(our rowing coach, not a Great Dane)

Geraldine Carter
(mayor and major sponsor, married to Brian)

Shoena
(team PR)

Sally

Jane and Malcolm Sykes
(founders of The Fund for Epilepsy)

Ben
(electrics whizz and skipper on Tommo's and my first weekend at sea)

Charles
died as a result of epileptic seizure aged 28. Jane and Malcolm founded charity prior to his death to raise funds and awareness

Marcus Thompson, aka Tommo
(boyfriend and first rowing partner)

Josephine
(Tommo's mum)

Rachel
(Tommo's sister)

Robin
(Josephine's partner)

Kenneth Crutchlow
(founder of ORS)

Chay Blyth
(founder of Challenge Business and rowed across the Atlantic with Jon Ridgeway in 1966)

Teresa Evans
(project manager of Atlantic rowing challenge)

Lin Parker
(skipper on support yacht)

Simon Chalk
(race sponsor through Woodvale and two-time ocean rower)

Jan and Dan
(mother-and-son rowing team)

EIGHT

Finding Mum

Regatta Start Day, 20 January 2004

I DIDN'T NEED the alarm. At dawn I walked down to the telephone by the harbour. The only other person mooching round the boats was 'our man from the BBC', Mark. I gave him a weak smile. I picked up the receiver and called Radio Northampton: drivers on the A45 were about to hear the first of our regular progress reports.

The pontoon soon began to fill with families and rowers. Mum came down with Dad; Tommo appeared with a Fanta Limôn for me, a tea for Mum. Jane, Malcolm, Geraldine, Tony and Dad were all wearing matching Epic Challenge T-shirts

– our team out in force! Mum had given Dad strict instructions not to cry, so they'd both resorted to wearing sunglasses. In the twenty-odd years they'd been married this would be the first time they'd be away from each other for any length of time. I can only imagine what my Dad must have been thinking and feeling. Lincoln couldn't look at his Gran, and kept his arms firmly by his side when we both tried to give him a hug. He has a habit of offering his forehead when you try to kiss him, but as tears trickled down his cheeks he tipped his head even further, leaving you kissing his soft curly black hair. Sam maintained her steely demeanour – like my Mum, she didn't wear her heart on her sleeve. Instead she told us to get on with it, she had a suntan to top up and all she was getting was a vest mark.

I, of course, couldn't contain myself, especially as I watched the other crews hugging their own distraught families. We probably wouldn't see any of the friends we'd made until we returned to England. Honestly, it's so traumatic I really can't do it justice! Why didn't we listen to Kenneth and leave our loved ones at home?

Tommo grabbed hold of me. 'Look after each other and stay safe. Promise me you'll stay safe.'

'Of course I'll look after Mum.'

'You won't shout at her like you shouted at me?'

'I'll try not to!'

We stepped aboard *Calderdale* and pushed her gently away from the pontoon. Keep smiling, I reminded myself. Boats were slowly making their way out of the marina into the harbour; yachts and motorboats headed out past the harbour wall, their crews ready with foghorns and cameras. Ben had chartered a yacht offering my Dad, Malcolm and Tony a lift out to the start line. Tommo and Geraldine found a spot on the wall amongst the thousands who had turned up to see us off. We bobbed about in the harbour, boats jostling for position on the start line, yachts swaying in the breeze.

And They're Off ...

28° 05 371N
017° 06 521W

11.00 am. The boom of the starting cannon reverberated across the island and the flag was hoisted up the mast of our support yacht *Kilcullen*. The Ocean Rowing Society Regatta 2004 was underway.

We were out of the shelter of the harbour and into the open ocean at a heart-stopping 1.5 knots. Although Mum and I only had the two weeks in Gomera to practise rowing together, I have to admit we did look the part. The timing of our oars as they broke the water was perfect and once we found our rhythm my spirits began to lift. I knew right there and then that we would make it across.

I'd love to tell you the first day of our adventure was filled with wildlife sightings and wild, wind-whipped waves, but it wasn't. The sea was reassuringly flat and the only wildlife we saw was my Dad shouting 'Girls, wave for the camera!'

The boys on Ben's yacht just wouldn't bugger off. They'd been following us for over an hour, and we were desperate for a wee! There's only so long you can sit there waving at a few blobs on a yacht before you're more than happy for them to leave you alone.

As the other rowing boats disappeared we took a course due south, taking a direct route to 'where the butter melts' – a rather lovely piece of advice given to sailors who are heading for the Caribbean. 'Go south until the butter melts, then turn right.' I had planned to row west until we hit land, but Kenneth had insisted the slower rowers (i.e. us) took a route due south to pick up the stronger trade winds.

Once we were alone on the ocean I whipped off my T-shirt and shorts and slopped on a load of factor fifty (there have to be some benefits of rowing with your mum – an all-over tan must be one of them!). Mum, fearing Ben and the boys would make a surprise reappearance, stayed put in her T-shirt, hat and black bikini bottoms.

'It didn't take you long, did it?' she said. 'Just like your father!'

At lunchtime we tucked into rice cakes and jam, Mum had her cup of tea and we set to our two hours on/two hours off, only to change it to one hour on/one hour off four hours into the row. We both decided two hours was way too bum-numbing for the rower and too horribly boring for the person stuck in the cabin. Also, it didn't take long before the rice cakes and raspberry jam made a comeback, shortly followed by the Fanta Limôn and last night's dinner.

Staying in Touch

Communications with the outside world were surprisingly abundant, even on our little wooden boat. The VHF radio enabled us to contact ships in our vicinity, although, as Tommo and I had already experienced, ships would be practically running you down before you could achieve some sort of unbroken signal.

We had also packed a laptop. Stored in a giant yellow pelicase (a bomb-proof, leak-proof, floating suitcase) it was the most cost-effective, if somewhat cumbersome, way to produce email-able updates. '*Calderdale* Calling' was emailed back to Jane, who in turn sent it on to a growing list of avid supporters. This was a major task for us both. It would take a week to hand-write the diary in an increasingly battered exercise book before I set to work one-finger typing it on to the laptop, which I had to balance precariously on my legs with my feet up on either side of the cabin door, a small puddle of sweat gathering around my belly button and trickling down the backs of my knees – eek! Not only was it time consuming but it would also play havoc with our power consumption. I would type during the middle of the day so that the sun could produce just enough power to blast out a page or two. The screen saver reminded me of my priorities on the boat – after a couple of minutes' inactivity WHY AREN'T YOU ROWING? would scroll in pink across a bright purple background.

For all the inconvenience, I loved writing '*Calderdale* Calling' – it kept my mind occupied for hours on end. I sat at the oars, driving my mother crazy as I'd giggle away over my ideas for the diary. The ocean is an awesomely beautiful place but after a day or two it loses its appeal, so having something else to think about saved me from jumping overboard.

We also had a satellite phone and talked to Dad every Sunday evening. We'd often receive impromptu calls from Jane and Malcolm, my Gran and other relatives. Unfortunately news from home did become more of an annoyance as the trip progressed and we both developed a love–hate relationship with the phone. For me, it would become a lifeline in times of stress and worry, as I'd often call Tommo when it got really tough: he would lift my spirits and I would return to the oars with a smile on my face. Mum decided not to answer the phone after our first month at sea. I think she envied Jan and Dan, who weren't able to afford a phone for their crossing, and because they weren't able to talk to anybody they didn't have to 'perform' for relatives at home. Mum felt the pressure to be in a good mood all the time, to tell everyone that we were enjoying it. We'd worry that bad news from the boat would translate into disaster at home. 'It's crap weather today and the waves are huge. We're pissed off ...' might become 'They're in a storm, they might capsize and die!' I'd do all the talking, flippantly underselling tough situations so as not to panic everyone.

~

I DON'T THINK the team realised how stressful the row would become for us all. Perhaps that sounds stupidly naive? Well, we all knew the rowing would be tough, painful and boring. We also knew Mum and I would need to look after each other if were to get across as friends. Also, the changing moods of the ocean could, potentially, place us in many life-threatening situations. But, with the single mindedness needed for an expedition like this, I don't think any ocean rower truly realises the pressure placed upon his or her family and friends left at home.

~

Skipper's Log

21.01.04   On anchor all night. Mum sick. But good progress made yesterday.

23.01.04   Fantastic night. Flat. Lots of stars. Stayed off anchor to drift. Heavier winds & seas from 2.00 am. First ship sighted.

25.01.04   Flat calm all day. Fantastic time, saw whales, a moth, some birds. Whales singing into night. Saw another rower. Couldn't hail him. Crew v. happy.

From: Sally
To: Jane
Date: 26 January 2004
Re: *Calderdale* Calling

We're a week in and only now can I look at a screen and not feel too sick. So here's my first attempt at a diary.

Tommo told me this morning that Mum and I have done 105 miles. Fantastic! Because we've not been feeling 100 per cent we've decided to row all day and sleep at night to be sure we don't get too fatigued. Mum was very sick the first few days but amazingly I've only thrown up once. We haven't really fancied the food yet, but we've been forcing down Smash and boiled rice.

The weather has been different every day, practically every hour. The first couple of days were very windy, brilliant for getting away from La Gomera. Today it's practically dead calm, no wind and hardly any swell.

Mum's been complaining that we haven't seen any wildlife. Not even a stickleback! She ate her words when a moth and two whales visited us. A huge bird flew past as well. We weren't sure what it was.

We really love it so far. There have been a couple of grotty days, but now we are eating and getting into a routine.

Speak again soon,

Sally & Sarah xx

PS Since this we've seen even more whales and a sea turtle! At night the ocean glitters with phosphorescent algae, which drips off the oars. The stars at night are also amazing: they fill the whole sky. There are millions of them.

It's been dead calm for the last couple of days so we haven't been able to make a huge amount of progress; a bit frustrating but we're hoping the weather will change in a day or two.

I couldn't believe it had taken us a week to travel just 105 miles. I've driven that distance in an hour and a half. But at the time it felt so monumental. Within a couple of days we'd left Gomera behind us, its rocky mass having finally sunk below our horizon. The only teams within twenty or so miles were the solo rowers; the other pairs were well ahead. In fact one crew, a four-man team in a boat called *Queensgate*, had already rowed six hundred miles!

Unfortunately Mum and I soon realised that if we wanted to achieve a half-decent daily mileage we really needed to row at night, but as women who like their beds we rarely took to the oars after midnight. The fact is, we hated rowing at night and we both worried that if we confessed to everyone at home that we weren't out at 3.00 am they might start telling us to get on with it. Quite frankly, that's the last thing we wanted to do, so we decided not to mention it in the hope that nobody would notice. Anyway, we sometimes drifted further at night than we'd rowed during the day!

In that first week Malcolm must have called us every day. He'd traipse across the Yorkshire moors until he found a field where he could secure a good signal on the second satellite phone. No doubt his Pip would be mooching along behind him. Although we loved to hear a familiar voice, he always called to ask the same bloody questions: 'Are you eating?' 'Have you checked your hatches?' 'How's the watermaker?' Being a kind and thoughtful person, he was understandably concerned about our welfare, but after the fifth call of the week Mum and I were beginning to feel a tad annoyed by this constant mollycoddling.

Unfortunately it didn't take long before it became a constant source of complaint on the boat. The phone would ring and we'd sit at the oars meanly mocking his predictable questioning.

'Are you eating, Sarah?'

'No, Malcolm, I'm wasting away!' Mum would croak before pretending to wither up and die.

We were laughing about it, but eventually it began to annoy us and I was also beginning to take it personally. At home you can giggle about it with friends over a glass or three of wine; but on the boat unwanted conversations and comments rattle round your head constantly. I started to dread the phone ringing in case Malcolm was on the line ready to badger us. I felt like Pavlov's dog, the ringtone triggering an ever-repeating mantra: 'You're not good enough. You're not good enough. You're not good enough.'

Although Malcolm was trying to help, his offers of support were in fact slowly undermining my confidence. I wanted to confront him, explain that we were quite capable of handling ourselves, but when the calls came the words didn't come. Instead I sat on it for another week in the hope that he would realise that we did indeed posses a natural ability to stay alive and therefore would stop mothering us. It didn't happen!

Skipper's Log

27.01.04   Good sleep. Overcast start to day. No wind. Flat calm. V. good day's rowing. Rowed together. Saw turtle. Interview Radio Northants. Tanker & amazing sunset. Still calm seas. In good spirits & eating well.

30.01.04 *Rowed throughout night till 5.00 am. Slept till 8.00 am. Both exhausted. Long, hot day. Both feeling a bit low. Did see huge whale - dorsal fin only though. Readying for another long night.*

From: Sally
To: Jane
Date: 30 January 2004
Re: *Calderdale* Calling

We're moving painfully slowly. We're making progress, but on the charts it looks like nothing at all, and as we woke up to another dead calm day I'm sure we won't be breaking any distance records.

Mum and I have been building up to a twenty-four-hour routine. Last night was our first all-nighter and it was awful. We're both absolutely exhausted. How do you prepare to row non-stop all day and then all night? Billy (one of the other rowers) mentioned that his father had advised him 'When eating elephants, small bits at a time.' I can't help but think this is one bloody great big elephant.

For all my whinging Mum and I are still in good spirits. We're been receiving texts from friends and we're receiving masses of emails, all of them are hugely appreciated.

Mum's still concerned about the apparent lack of wildlife. We've seen a few petrels and we have a resident stripy fish but not much else. What's been quite saddening is the amount of plastic floating around. The ocean is so utterly beautiful, tranquil and strange and then you see a plastic cut-out of a Christmas tree floating past! In fact seeing all this has affected Mum and me. We had no intention of throwing any rubbish overboard, only food products, but now we're adamant that nothing unnatural goes over the side (having said that, I did lose a washing-up sponge in the drink yesterday!). We've also decided not to fish. I've grown rather attached to Stripy and I wouldn't want him or any of his family flapping around on our deck with a great big hook in its mouth.

All that's left to say is that we're having a fabulous time, even though it's frustrating at the moment. I'm enjoying Mum's company – a lot!

S & S xx

PS Please pray for better weather, we need a good north-easterly to help us on our way, otherwise I calculate at our current speed it could take us 150 days! We don't have enough chilli con carne for that.

~

MUM FINALLY 'PERSUADED' me to call Malcolm. 'Do something or put up and shut up – your choice. Either way, I'm fed up of hearing about it,' she said, curtly. It was obvious she wasn't prepared to pick up the phone, although she was happy to whinge with me.

I called Malcolm and as diplomatically as possible told him to stop fussing over us. The watermaker was fine, and anyway, if it wasn't we'd have dehydrated and shrivelled up days ago. The hatches were a bit leaky, but we'd lined them with bin bags. And yes, we were bloody eating ... We had two stone to shed; we certainly didn't want to come back with it! He didn't call for a while (what a relief) … then the emails started.

Skipper's Log

01.02.04   Uncomfortable night, lots of rocking & rolling. Sea-me[6] busy! Winds strong. Pants flapping well! Good rowing, big seas & strong winds but little distance made – v. strange.

02.02.04   Made good ground again in night although both v. uncomfortable. Hounded by other ships. Sea-me went crazy! Big winds & waves. Sally v. sickly today. Encountered ship at 7.30 pm. Monitoring its progress. Securité[7] given three times. Five-min. watch started.

From: Sally
To: Jane
Date: 4 February 2004
Re: *Calderdale* Calling

Heaven is a can of pineapple chunks.

The last couple of nights have been pretty sleepless. There's a ship roaming in our waters and the sea-me (aka the stress-me) is blinkitty-blinking like there's no tomorrow. We discovered the

---

[6] A radar reflector that allows other vessels to see you as larger than you really are.
[7] Attention all ships!

ship responsible was a fishing trawler but I'm sure when Mum and I first saw it it was an enormous can of pineapple chunks floating along with fishermen waving on top of it. I freaked out when it decided to do a figure of eight around the boat, as usual I was in just a T-shirt and I was shouting at Mum for some underwear. Mum thought it was best to hide out in the cabin so I could pretend that my 'boyfriend' was in there. The flaw in that particular plan was that I had no idea how to say 'My boyfriend's sleeping the cabin' in whichever language they happened to speak. I reassured Mum that fishermen were not in the habit of kidnapping ocean rowers, so she came out and watched the pineapple chunks watching us.

We can't believe we've made it past two weeks. It's the law that we get across now. Kenneth C. keeps saying, 'The first two weeks are the worst, get through those and you'll definitely get across.' Well that's that then, a foregone conclusion. We'll make it into Port St Charles.

Our only problem at the moment is our taste buds, they haven't just changed, they've gone on strike. Pretty much all the food on board tastes awful. We're both still very queasy and Mum is sick almost every other day. We've been amusing ourselves with the energy bars we can't face eating – we fashion them into poo shapes and leave them around the deck for each other to find. We laugh hysterically when we discover them stuck to the side decks or beside the runners. With that and the extra body hair I think Mum and I are going to arrive in Barbados as men.

News of Stripy – he's either been 'ad or he just hasn't been able to keep up with us. We haven't seen

him for about three days now. We miss him, but he
has been replaced by two moths and a butterfly, who
seemed to have stowed away with us. There's a big
fat moth who likes Mum and a little white moth who
flutters about the boat worrying us; he gets so close
to the water a wave will probably swallow him up.
The butterfly is a beautiful red admiral and reminds
us of home.

   We're making progress every day, more on some
than others. We're hoping to squeeze out another
fifty miler in the next few days but that very much
depends on the weather. We've changed our course
slightly, also. The wind isn't helping us to go
south so we're now heading for N20 W30 rather than
N20 W25. Hope that's ok for all you back-seat drivers
out there!

Still trucking,

Sally & Sarah

I always thought I'd be amenable to the odd bit of advice about
our route, but after several emails about our choice of course
– mainly from Malcolm – I was practically tearing my hair out.
Checking and rechecking our route, I was again beginning to
doubt my own judgement: perhaps we were going in the wrong
direction?

   We'd planned to row south, head towards N20 W25, then
turn right. I'd adjusted our course according to the weather
conditions, so we were now heading towards N20 W30. We
were following the 'south-till-the-butter-melts' advice, and our

progress was steady if a little slow.

Perhaps if we'd had the opportunity to track the routes of the other rowers then maybe we'd have taken a different route, but we were unable to log on long enough to gather that sort of information. Also, we didn't have a clue what weather was waiting for us around the corner, so we did what we thought was right in the conditions as they presented themselves. As I checked and double checked our charts, read through the emails to be sure I wasn't being entirely oversensitive, I couldn't help but wonder why Malcolm was getting on our case about this as well.

We knew it must have been incredibly frustrating for those at home who were following the regatta on the Internet: every day the coloured dots, which represented the other crews, were drifting across the chart. Perhaps it looked as if the other boats were zooming along to Barbados, unlike our own little pink dot, which seemingly bobbed about whilst we drank tea.

137

We later found out that Dad had settled into a daily routine of staying up till 1.00 am waiting for our positions to be updated on the ORS website. He'd despair at our lack of progress, thinking that we were also struggling with the disappointment. So he spent sleepless nights worrying that we were worrying about him worrying about us! Luckily for us, Dad couldn't afford the £1-per-minute it cost to call the satellite phone from a land line. Instead he would ring on Sundays with a progress report. Anyway, I don't think I could have coped with any more well-meaning criticism. 'Sally, remember what my yoga teacher said – don't compare, don't compete' were Mum's words of wisdom whenever Malcolm's messages began to wind me up.

Of all the problems we'd anticipated before the row, being stressed out by our own team was not one of them! We were back in the same position as before. I needed to confront Malcolm again, and this time I would have to be a lot firmer.

I set to work on a very testy email.

```
From: Sally
To: Malcolm
Date: 5 February 2004
Re: (no subject)


Dear Malcolm


This is my opportunity to prove to myself and
others that I am a capable and confident woman.
Your constant calls and emails telling us what we
```

should and should not be doing are not helping. We
are doing our best and I'm sure if we were men you
would not be so keen to butt in.

Sally

Ouch! He sent back an apology via Jane and we didn't hear
from him for a while. I felt relieved, although disappointed in
myself for not having the guts to sort out the problem straight
away and therefore not embarrass poor Malcolm, who, after all,
was just trying to help. The importance of face-to-face contact
was re-enforced: without it so much can be misconstrued and
misunderstood.

When Malcolm, Mum and I were working on the boat in
Gomera there were no tensions between us at all – any niggles
were solved with a giggle and a beer. Unfortunately there would
be no such release on the boat. Phone calls and emails between
me and Mum/Jane and Malcolm were often ambiguous in their
tone and meaning, which eventually led to a complete breakdown
in communication. These misunderstandings were to jeopardise
our enjoyment of the adventure, although my diaries would
never let on how serious the situation would become.

~

Skipper's Log

05.02.04   *Didn't lose ground overnight. Regular checks as*
            sea-me flashing. Strong winds this morning. Too
            sick. Close call with fishing boat.

01.02.04   Big moon still up. Still sick. Mum rowed. Strange black sea.

08.02.04   Was sick!

09.02.04   Where's the bloody wildlife? Had to clean cabin. Mattresses mouldy/then deck/Mum's legs!

From: Sally
To: Jane
Date: 9 February 2004
Re: *Calderdale* Calling: The Glamour Edition

Mum and I have been looking at our bodies and we've come to the decision that our careers as supermodels are now well and truly over. Our skin looks like the hairy hide of a rhinoceros; I'm covered in red spots, which Mum first thought were measles. I was inclined to agree with her, especially as I get a bigger sympathy vote. Eventually she put it down to the fact that I hadn't washed for over two weeks! Mum's luminescent legs are covered in bruises.

We've discovered over the last week or so that our challenge is not in fact about rowing – it's about dealing with sickness. We've both been incredibly sick. At one point when I was vomiting over the side, stupidly into the wind and therefore spattering my T-shirt and myself, Mum said, 'Don't cry.' My reply was, 'I can't help it, Mum, rice pudding doesn't taste as nice as Smash on its way back up.' We managed to force a laugh. Mum reckons that if a woman can suffer with morning sickness for nine months we can too. Anyway we've got plenty of rice cakes, rice pudding and rice rice to last us three months. I have to say I'm feeling less optimistic.

We have discovered that the Atlantic is not an untouched wilderness. We have seen another boat pretty much every day so far. In fact, we had a bit of a run in with one last Wednesday. Mum was on watch and called me outside as a monster fishing trawler came over the horizon towards us. Mum was in a T-shirt at least four sizes too big, which came down to her knees, and I sported a rather fetching Don King hairdo. The spotlight on the boat suddenly came on in a 'You are in enemy waters … I repeat … You are in enemy waters' stylie, engulfing our little boat in light. Honestly, I don't know what the fishermen were expecting, but they were rather excited. They must have thought this was their lucky night, saving too devastatingly gorgeous damsels in distress.

The shouted conversation went a bit like this …
'You ok?'
'Yes thanks, we're fine.'
'You need agua, food?'
'No thanks, we have agua and food.'
'No? You have no agua, no food?'
'Yes thanks, we have agua, we have food.'
'Yes! You want agua, you want food?'
'No!! We are ok. No food or agua needed. Thank you.'
'Agua, agua?!'
'!!!!!'

As so it went on, and the steel hull of the trawler was bobbing ever nearer. We started shouting with flaying arms 'Too close, please. Too close!' They started up their engines and moved slowly away, promising to tell everyone in Tenerife that they'd seen two mad English women rowing about with no idea whether they had enough food or water.

To all you Stripy fans out there: HE'S BACK! With friends. He must have returned to the clan telling them that there's an all-you-can-eat chez *Calderdale* with enough regurgitated Smash for all the family.

Mum's becoming incredibly protective over a bag of jelly sea monsters her friend Nic bought her. The problem is she ate way too many in the first couple of weeks and is now very despondent that she doesn't have enough to last her till we get there!
    Anyway, must go, have whales to watch, jellies to steal and a boat to row.

Sally & Sarah

By now life on board was starting to get to us. On the face of it we were enjoying ourselves, but our emotions seemed to follow the ebb and flow of the water that surrounded us. One minute we were up, singing away to Dido at the top of our voices, and the next we were delving deep into the murky depths of a dark depression. Although Mum hadn't cried in front of me, I suspect she'd spent some time in the cabin silently sobbing. I know whenever she'd disappear on her break I'd take to the oars and wallow in my own self-pity.

    We were both very careful not to share our misery. I'd be sure to dry my tears before Mum came out on deck. I didn't want her to think she'd have to comfort me, especially as it was my idea to go on this bloody trip.

It was the futility of the whole exercise that really pushed my buttons. That slow, punishing plod over the never-ending swell of the Atlantic – there was just so much ocean ahead of us it felt overwhelming. I was still worrying that everyone at home was worrying that we were worrying! It played on my mind that our family, Jane, Malcolm and our supporters were thinking we weren't working hard enough. There was an invisible pressure to perform.

By now, Mum's lack of training was also beginning to take its toll on her physical wellbeing. Her hips and back ached constantly, which meant she couldn't get comfortable in the cabin, and she was struggling with persistent nausea. She ate very little, sticking to potato soup and a bowl of boiled rice.

Of all the challenges we were facing I think Mum found being constantly dirty the most difficult, which surprised me. With only a packet of wipes and a one-litre plastic water bottle – which we'd adapted by piercing the lid for that rainforest shower experience – our hygiene routine was very basic. It was incredibly inconvenient to have a thorough wash but we eventually mastered the process after several weeks at sea.

If we timed it well we'd be able to achieve an all-over body wash just before the warm sun had set. Standing naked in the footwell we'd squirt fresh water over our goose-pimpled bodies, soap up, wrench a comb through our scraggy knotted hair, and then shave our legs before rinsing down and patting ourselves off with a salty beach towel. If we started the regime too early we'd still have a stint at the oars, getting sploshed by salty water. Leave it too late and we'd miss the chance to dry off using the sun's dying rays.

It didn't help that we only had seven T-shirts to last us the entire journey; even at a modest ninety days we could only change into a crisp new one once every two weeks. As they grew ever saltier and stiffer, orange with sweat and sun cream, this was slowly turning into hell on water for Mum.

Skipper's Log

10.02.04   Saw pod of six whales. Mum saw even bigger one but too quick to identify. Problems with lighter caused much stress. Pressure still low.

11.02.04   Shit day. Mum sick.

12.02.04   Radio Leeds interview. Good strong winds. We're on next map – YIPPEE! Fun day. Over 100 miles done! Still having problems charging laptop. Malcolm & Ben on case.

From: Sally
To: Jane
Date: 18 February 2004
Re: *Calderdale* Calling: The 'What Mother's Up To' Edition

Breaking News: It's the Pants or Me!'

Atlantic mum threatens to leave boat
if smelly pants don't go

These were Mum's exact words: 'Those pants look like dead man's pants. A man who has been dead for more than two days!' I thought that was a bit strong. My 100%-cotton 'Authentic' M&S boxer shorts (large) are so gorgeously soft that, admittedly, I haven't washed them since we set out! Unfortunately if you wash anything out here it becomes salt encrusted and never dries properly, so what's a girl to do? I have to keep my dignity when sleeping in the cabin with Mum, and anyway, the £10 M&S gift voucher could only stretch to two pairs and they have to last at least another week!

Mum also told BBC Radio Leeds that I was 'a bit stinky' and I thought fresh air was 'a natural cleanser'. Again, a bit harsh. It seems Mum's nose is becoming very sensitive. I can't smell anything. Anyway, I'm conducting a social experiment. How often can a girl be allowed to fester? If you were out here you'd think three washes in one month was pretty good going too! One other thing … does anyone know if gaffer is good for waxing?

So, as you can tell, Mum is becoming a bit of a handful. She's recently discovered that there's more to do on the boat than row and make cups of tea. She became rather despondent when I asked her to deploy the para-anchor. 'That's not on my remit,' she said. 'Row and make tea only, you said. Row and make tea.' I told her to get on with it. Honestly, you can't get the crew these days!

One thing that's sure to pick her spirits up is seeing some wildlife. We're harbouring some rather lovely Concorde fish at the moment. Their skin shines like silver pennies in a wishing well. They're about a metre long with a yellow tail and fins and blue-green bodies. They leap from the water and land with an almighty splosh. Mum saw one leaping, kamikaze style, right next to the boat. She shouted, 'Oh, that was a rather meaty one. Quick Sal, grab the fishing line!' I gave her a stern look and told her how disgusted I was that she'd thought of such a thing. I retired to the cabin and daydreamed about a succulent freshly grilled tuna steak served with buttersnap peas, steamed broccoli and new potatoes.

We're becoming rather obsessed with food.

Mmmmm ... pineapple chunks.

Mmmmm ... curry.

Mmmmm ... sticky ginger cakies.

Accompanying crew update

Travelling Ted, donated to us by a school in Northampton, has been earning his keep. He's on sea-me duty, looking out for all the beeping ships, of which there have been a few. In fact we were very close to one only a few nights ago. We tried hailing them on the VHF ... nothing. When it went past there was no one on deck and it looked like it was travelling on autopilot. Very worrying.

Farley the Elephant has been keeping us company in the cabin. He's very content and loves the ocean.

Weather report

The wind, being only a fair-weather friend, is currently in the doghouse. It's going in completely the wrong direction and we're not moving very far. Also, there's a storm coming, so we're battening down the hatches, making extra water and planning for a couple of roastercolar days (as Lincoln my nephew would say).

All in all, we want nice food, Mum's going over if she doesn't change her attitude and I'm hoping to hold out on a wash for another couple of days.

Sally & Sarah x

Mum was becoming increasingly agitated with the phone, laptop and emails, and she was becoming annoyed with me because I spent so much time faffing with them. Mum rarely answers the phone at home and is a complete technophobe when it comes to computers. It aggravates her that society has become so dependant on these electrical pieces of plastic. Mobile phones have only heightened her loathing of constant communication. Unfortunately, in this respect we were on opposite sides of the fence.

Before we left we agreed to leave the satellite phone on between 12.00 noon and 1.00 pm GMT; this gave my Dad, Malcolm and other well-wishers a pocket of time where they knew we'd be 'in' if they called us. But as the days passed by Mum started refusing to answer the phone, especially if she happened to be on her break during that golden hour. I would scuttle down the deck, tumble into the cabin and answer the ringing phone whilst trying to avoid Mum's mouldering feet.

For a start, she didn't want to talk to Malcolm, particularly after the 'Are you eating/going in the right direction/is the watermaker working' fiasco. She refused to speak to radio stations and journalists because she didn't want to tell them everything was fine and that we were having a good time, particularly when she didn't feel fine: she felt dirty, tired, frustrated and lonely.

Also, she was finding it harder to talk to Dad, partly because she missed him so much, but mainly because he kept going on about our stats. He'd ask us how far we thought we'd rowed that day/how far we thought we'd row tomorrow, then he'd give us a run down of all the other teams' progress. I loved getting this information – not only did it give me an overall picture of our progress but it also made Dad happy; he had a job to do, which served to relieve the impotence of being the one left at home.

Communications with Malcolm were reignited when we started having problems with the laptop – it was beginning to overheat and the fan was whirling like a helicopter about to take off, and the Internet dial-up connection became infuriatingly intermittent. I was incredibly nervous when I first spoke to him on the phone. I'm not a confrontational person and having sent my testy email I was worried he would be cross with me. But I needn't have worried; he was his kind and thoughtful self, happy to help and ready to advise.

It was such a relief to be talking to Malcolm again, but the situation would prove to be a huge learning curve for me. During the build-up to the race there were many times when I had bitten my lip, hiding my agitation and annoyance about the way certain things had been done – of course, that's life, you don't get everything your own way. I'm sure all members of the team had similar experiences; but finding my voice and expressing it was going to be as difficult as the row itself. Although my differences with Malcolm had been resolved for the moment, I never thought relationships between Jane and Malcolm and my mother and me would continue to be challenged throughout the remainder of the journey. There were more misunderstandings to come!

As for the laptop, I think Mum would have been happy to jettison it overboard. As far as she was concerned it would be one down, only the sat phone to go. She irritated me with her complete lack of concern, winding me up with statements like, 'Oh well, let's throw it overboard, it'll make the boat lighter' and 'You can write your diaries in the book and type them up when you get home.'

'That's not the point, though, is it?' I'd retort. 'Why would people want to read the diaries after we get back?'

You could hear my profanities for miles around as I desperately tried to repair the bloody thing. I had to fix it before I lost my mind – the diaries were my salvation, giving me something to think about during my hours on the oars. If the laptop blew up I would too! Anyway, people were texting to tell us how much they loved reading them. Now my ego wouldn't let me give them up!

Skipper's Log

19.02.04   V. rough seas. Stayed in cabin all day.

22.02.04   Two ships in night. Both responded to Securité on VHF. Had conversation with guy on bulk carrier to Brazil. Woke to find v. large ship off stern. No *radar ... no sea-me. Also VHF not charging & battery on multi-meter dead. V. pissed off. No Kilcullen. Flying fish spotted - eaten by Concorde fish. Mum had coeliac sickness from apple & custard.*

23.02.04   *Kilcullen arrived late last night, 9.30 pm. Had Mark Mortimer's[8] boat in tow. Didn't stay long. Sighted sea chicken! Tanker with no beep. Effluent stream v. disgusting. Rubbish everywhere.*

24.02.04   *Good peaceful night. Mum on br'ly watch. No shipping. Lots of leaping Concorde fish in the night. Funny day. Annoyed with negative comments from home.*

25.02.04   *Problems with watermaker - v. stressful but resolved. Both bit weepy today. Getting hotter by the day.*

From: Sally
To: Jane
Date: 25 February 2004
Re: *Calderdale* Calling: The Quarter of the Way There Issue

'It's a Man! It's a Man!'

We've been lucky enough to be visited by three ships in one night. Not only did two of them not have their radar on and therefore could not see us, but also

---

[8] Mark, in his boat *Acorn Atlantic Warrior*, retired from the regatta having had problems making headway in the Acceleration Zone just off Gomera.

one was coming directly at us! It's the oestrogens; it attracts men from miles around.

Both Mum and I can't believe how other rowers have been able to get across without seeing one other ship. Why is it that one has visited us almost every night? They're like moths to a light bulb.

I got on the VHF and half-heartedly did a Securité position check. On every other occasion we've not received a reply but to our amazement a man responded. In fact I didn't shout to Mum 'It's a man! It's a man!' I screamed 'We've got an answer! We've got an answer!' Needless to say he'd only said 'Can you repeat your position? Over' but the sheer joy of being heard by a ship with its nav lights pointing directly at you is insurmountable.

I decided to have a quick chat with our man on the airwaves, his silky French accent and perfect English wooing us with every 'Over'. He seemed very perplexed by the idea that we were sitting out on our para-anchor. He said there was over 4,000 metres of sea below us, I was tempted to reply that we had a very long chain but decided to try and describe our anchor set-up in as simple a way as possible.

I was very pleased when he asked me if I was the officer on watch … ooooh, he had such a way with words! I told him it was just me and Mum and we were rowing, and as his bulk carrier disappeared over the swell the VHF cut out leaving us with only the destination of his ship, but alas not his name. He was heading for the country of love - Brazil.

But with the ships comes pollution. We rowed straight into a distinct line of effluent and rubbish.

You could see it stretching for miles, a flat calm strip with brown frothy bubbles on its surface. Our oars created more bubbles with every pull. We suddenly felt very protective of our fishy family below the hull and we turned our watermaker off. Our moods dropped and we despaired at the damage these ships were doing.

The storm

Last week we had our first storm. How exciting is that! We battened down the hatches and prepared for the worst. Mum was particularly excited because it meant that we could crack open the remaining can of fruit salad. We'd opened one in the first week and ate it like animals, sticking our hands in and scooping out the contents with relish. This time Mum carefully divided the contents into two bowls and we ate each succulent piece of fruit one at a time. Of course, as always, I dribbled the juice all over myself. Honestly, if I haven't left half my food on my T-shirt, I haven't eaten!

Mum was laughing hysterically on the Friday when the waves were at their largest and the wind was whipping around the boat. Every time we stuck our heads out of the cabin a props boy would throw a bucket of water over our heads. She said it reminded her of a Morecambe and Wise sketch. Going to the loo was also a nightmare and the constant splish-sploshing of the water around the sides of the cabin made matters worse.

We came through it unscathed, if a bit smelly and fed up of being in the cupboard. The following day we were struck by a flat calm. We sacrificed a peg to the water gods, asked for some wind and waves in the right direction and rowed very slowly west, trying to make up for the ground we'd lost during the storm.

During our time in the cupboard I sat with nothing on in the staggering heat and Mum poked my fat tummy rolls. 'Look at them,' she giggled. 'Don't you ever take the mick out of my stomach again!'

'I'm supposed to be emaciated, Mum, emaciated. I don't know what's happened!'

'It's down to one grain of rice for you, my girl.'

I bent over further in an attempt to make seven belly rolls, but had to be content with only six.

We're having a fantastic time (now that we're not being sick!).

Rowing at night

There are absolutely no merits to rowing at night apart from the fact that you get to Barbados quicker. It is TORTURE! When has a night-shift worker ever had to suffer the torment of staring at his or her own bedroom door for hours on end? I look at the hatch levers, ever hopeful that they will turn and the shift ended. Mum seemed rather pleased that my attitude was even worse than hers. I wasn't awake at 3.00 am when she'd actually done a figure of eight. She even admitted that on a previous night she had gone in completely in the wrong direction!! Neither of us can focus on the compass properly and the nocturnal habits of our Concorde fish can no longer sustain our interest for more than a half hour. But the stars and sparkling water are fantastic and I spend quite a lot of time checking constellations. Either way, no amount of Etta James can lighten my mood after a night at the oars. IT'S HORRIBLE!

Our friend the para-anchor

A girl should never leave home without one. The para-anchor is by far the best bit of equipment on the boat, apart from your sleeping bag. Not only does it look really cute in the water, like an enormous red and yellow octopus, but also it has this amazing ability to stop you dead.

In the stormy conditions we had a week ago it came into its own and we only lost about five miles. Other boats had drifted nearly thirty miles in the same time. WE LOVE OUR PARA-ANCHOR.

N20 W25

How close can a girl get? Thought to be the directionally challenged of the sexes it seems us ladies have managed to get ourselves successfully to our first important waypoint and almost touch it.

Sunday evening

Three days later, the trade winds have kicked in and we're HEADING WEST!

Tales from the aquarium

Stripy's had BABIES! There are loads of them. Mum and I are in raptures as they swim out every morning and check out our oars. The littlest are about an inch long and there are about thirty of them.

Two lovely flat brown fish have also joined us. They have two fins, one at the top and one at the bottom, and they wave at us. We've decided to call them Lincoln and Andre after my nephew and his best friend.

Sam (named after my sister) is a beautiful spotty fish who also hangs out below us. She's brown with mustard coloured spots. She's so deliciously fat and fishy you just want to squeeze her!

A badge is winging its way to Ben in Aberdeen who told us that our Concorde fish are in fact yellowfin tuna and they have been entertaining us no end. We awarded one magnificent triple leap down a wave with a 10.0, 10.0, 10.0, 10.0, 9.5. Fantastic! Ben also told us they eat flying fish. By coincidence, just before we received his email we'd seen five tuna hunting in the calm water. It was carnage. Tiny little flying fish were, er, flying all over the place, springing up from the water whilst the tuna swam around with open mouths. Oh, the circle of life. We feel so proud that our vomit has cultivated such a wondrous array of happy fish!

Sea chicken[9] feathers Tommo, sea chicken feathers!!! He's close. Love you our fantastic Oracle.

X Congratulations to the Fours X

... who came in just an hour ago.

S & S x

---

[9] A sea chicken (*pelagus pullus*) is a much talked about but rarely seen sea bird which lays its eggs on the crests of waves. Relative of the *batterius pullus*. Tommo and I had taken it upon ourselves to find evidence of the bird and bring it back to England.

'Pain is only temporary, failure lasts a lifetime' was the cringingly gung-ho sticker affixed to the cabin of *Queensgate*, the fours' boat crewed by three blokes from Devon and a chap from Yorkshire. Anyway, after just thirty-six days, fifty-nine minutes and thirty seconds they arrived in Barbados having missed the speed record by just sixteen hours. Mum and I were so proud that they'd made it across so quickly, but how depressing that we were still only a quarter of the way there.

Soon after this boats were coming in one every few days, compounding our sense of helplessness. Still, we tried to reconcile our torment with the thought that these quicker crews hadn't really had the time to appreciate the beauty of the ocean or the truly irritating habits of their crewmates – or perhaps that's what spurred them on?

Skipper's Log

26.02.04   Bird on boat 7.00 am. Petrel with little webbed feet.

27.02.04   Mum's had miserable day. We've gone miles but both feel pretty low. Culmination of lots of stress & feeling sick.

01.03.04   Shit night. Sat on compass till 3.00 am. Mum fell asleep! I curled around it. This morning grey, wet, gloomy. On rudder again today. Waves wild & huge. No one phoned!

02.03.04   Must have made HUGE mileage today. Still v.

windy/choppy. Couple of scary waves. Shoal of happy-Happy fish & red-billed tropical bird. Both in better spirits. Hope tonight not too hairy/rocky.

From: Sally
To: Jane
Date: 3 March 2004
Re: *Calderdale* Calling: The Jane Fonda Issue

Mum and I have convinced ourselves that gravity is much stronger out here at sea than at home. Everything's dropping. Even Mum's stretch marks are starting to smile! Mum's becoming a little concerned and has begun to design a training programme to shape our wasting muscles. We're contracting a serious case of the jelly legs and the slightly dodgy condition 'rowers' bottom'.

First, she came up with the idea of a run around the block, but after several nasty collisions with the rudder footplate and the fact that we were having to hurdle over the oars and each other, she thought running on the spot would be better. We've started running in the footwell in front of the cupboard.

We started enthusiastically but the regime didn't last long. 'We're not getting anywhere,' said Mum.

I agreed.

Mum and I have been thinking about the kind of goodies we'd want to be dropped if we were unfortunate enough to run out of things halfway. Not that that would happen, of course. There's enough chilli con carne on board to feed a small country.

- Several c of pc (obviously!)
- More loo roll
- I'd like another book. I'm reading mine through a second time already
- A copy of *The Times*
- More Rice Crispies
- Rob Hamill[10]

A modest selection, but essential none the less.

Mum found sheer joy in the unwrapping of a clean, damp-free sleeping bag. I think it made her year! She looks like a giant orange grub in it.

I'm having to train Mum in the art of festering. She's getting there slowly. She's managed to wear a T-shirt for three weeks with much whinging, but the Sacred Road to Fester is a long and arduous one. I've never met a woman so obsessed with cleanliness. Maybe that's why I'm so put off by it, years of cleaning whilst living at home.

It isn't about the rowing ...

One thing about this adventure: you find out a lot about yourself that you really don't like. I've discovered that I'm capable of going from calm to extremely frustrated in less than a nanosecond. I swear too much. I'm often petty and angry and I don't give myself an inch. I can begin to see why the challenge is exactly that.

'Rowing' is just a title: it describes what you're doing in a very basic way but it doesn't tell you anything about the intricacies, like the way Mum and I laugh about our antics. We've managed to find ways of living on the boat where we're not left cursing

---

[10] Gorgeous New Zealander who'd rowed across in 1997 setting the fastest time for a pair – forty-two days. But at this point it wasn't his rowing technique we were after!

each other or ourselves. We can now get around without getting covered in bruises. The rowing has become relatively insignificant in comparison to these daily achievements.

But for all the laughter, Mum and I have been feeling pretty low recently. The weather has been wild (rough seas and strong winds), which only makes every movement on the boat more frustrating and dangerous. Just lying down is hard work! I whacked my head twice on the cupboard door, which left me practically inconsolable. I had a cracking headache, a squinty eye and a limp but otherwise there was no permanent damage done.

What's been concerning us most is that friends and family are worrying about how long it's taking. We've always known that it will take as long as it takes, that's the nature of this kind of project. Just by staying out here long enough you can't help but get across! We wanted to reassure everyone that apart from the constant rolling of the boat and the numbness of our still-boil-free bottoms we're actually having a brilliant time. How often can a mother and daughter say that they've had the opportunity to get to know each other really well? I love it when Mum tells me about the films she likes or the time she spent living with my Auntie Mandy. I can only hope that she can put up with my singing for another month or so.

Tales from the aquarium

We've been going so fast recently that we're worried that our smaller fish haven't been able to keep up.

I saw a baby Stripy desperately swimming beside the boat, but that was three days ago. Yesterday we had a whole shoal of happy-flappy brown fish. There were hundreds of them following the boat. Lincoln and Andre must have let their mates know that we're here.

We've seen flying fish. There must have been at least thirty of them flying above the waves. It was incredible. They're able to use the wind to help them go for several metres. They haven't started landing on the boat yet, that's still to come.

A pod of whales came to visit in the night. We could hear them blowing, but unfortunately we didn't see them. Some species aren't that keen to come up to the boat. We're hoping to see some more before we get to Barbados – they do like flatter seas, though.

We've seen a red-beaked tropical bird and plenty of petrels. It's really difficult identifying the birds because they fly past so quickly. I was almost convinced we'd seen a masked boobie, but our wildlife book told us they can only be found off the northern coast of Canada.

A beautiful petrel landed on our boat in the middle of the night. He had webbed feet and because of this couldn't walk properly on the deck. We found him struggling in the footwell. Mum picked him up and off he flew. I wanted to keep him but Mum said no.

Sally & Sarah

The relationship between Mum and I had progressed during my time at home over Christmas, but by now we had reached another level. It shows in my skipper's log that Mum had a miserable day on 27 February. In fact, it was the first time she'd shown her emotions in front of me. It was incredibly disarming and I too got into a bit of a state. We barely spoke that day; we just wallowed, rowed and went to bed exhausted.

Perhaps there's a point in every adult's life when he or she needs to see a parent as a person. I know now that I needed to see Mum as Sarah; that she's as human as we all are. We all know our parents are fallible but when Mum struggled it finally felt like the relationship was an equal one.

From this new level playing field I really began to understand what made my mother tick and also how her coded sense of humour worked. It's difficult to describe, but imagine seeing a poster on the side of the road, which takes you on a journey in your head from the image to a memory or a feeling, then back to a TV programme you saw a week ago where the presenter had said or done something funny or strange. Mum would see something on the boat, or out at sea, take a journey in her mind and four steps later come out with something seemingly unrelated to the original thought. We'd be laughing hysterically, because I had found a way of tuning into her complex thought processes.

I have to admit it: Mum is far funnier than me! (I'm just wittier.)

Skipper's Log

04.03.04   Halfway in days! Woke up late. On oars today. Made good progress in night. First flying fish casualty! Saw lots today. Amazing progress. Contact with Random House.[11]

05.03.04   Second flying fish casualty. Three flying fish today. One huge one. Cooker packed up, fixed it. Email from Malcolm. Chilli con carne for third time! Otherwise just another day.

06.03.04   Thick heavy fog this morning – quite spooky. No flying fish yet. Saw five pilot whales – four adults, one calf – hunting tuna under & around boat. Absolutely incredible. Singing & surfacing almost close enough to touch. 11:30 am–12.00 pm. Tried to video, ran out of bloody tape AGAIN! Photos good though. Also saw a cupboard.

08.03.04   BIRTHDAY!! Hope the sun shines so we can have shower. Got cards to open & turkey curry to eat. Mum found more fruit salad & another turkey curry! Opened cards & got calls from Gran/Bean/ Dad. Made amazing progress too.

From: Sally
To: Jane
Date: 10 March 2004
Re: *Calderdale* Calling: The 'Did You Know it was My Birthday' Issue

---

[11] It was at this point that I thought I'd write a book, so I decided to strike whilst the iron was hot and call Random House. In fact they had published the only book we had on board. I looked them up on the Internet, found their number and rang them. As you can probably tell, this pre-emptive strike didn't actually work.

IT'S OFFICIAL ... First There Was One, Soon There Will Be Many!

Team *Calderdale* move swiftly into the ranks of the ocean rowing great and good ... they have now joined in the annual flying fish cull!

A bog-eyed fry landed on deck last Wednesday evening, followed by three more the following morning.

Holding the stiff fish, Sally said, 'Can we eat him, Mum?'

Sarah's reply: 'No, we'll save up a few and make a proper chowder!'

An expert said, 'These fish look remarkably cute, their eyes are big and therefore disproportional to their bodies which gives them an appeal not unlike a baby's.'

Sally said, 'They give me the heebie-jeebies!'

Mum and I have been finding some common ground: shopping. A conversation on recycling started one evening last week. We chatted about the finer details of recycling points – there's not enough of them – and how the one at Sainsbury's always seems to be full, and this led on to plastic bags. Mum will always take a handful of her own to the shops and the girl at the checkout will look on scornfully as she pulls out an extra-large Argos bag for her purchases. I interjected here to tell her how annoying it is when people take a bag just for a packet of sandwiches. I also told her, at length, about the merits of

Baxter's Royal Game soup (a lovely soup), which I regularly buy from the same supermarket (it was on 3for2 offer and after that I was hooked!). This led on to a brief diversionary chat on the programmes *Tough at the Top* and *Back to the Floor* and 'What's his name?'

'Sir John something Jones.'

'Sir John Harvey-Jones.'

'That's it!'

Anyway, back to shopping. We discovered that we both love to pack our own bags. No spotty teenager was going to bung our tins of tomatoes in with our pot of natural set yoghurt and a cabbage! We brought it down to several categories: one bag each for freezer food, fridge food, veg, cans, boxes and non-food items. Of course, there's the obligatory packet of biscuits at the top of the bag closest to you for a swift nibble on the way home. I sometimes go for a packet of wafer-thin ham, but it depends on the mood I'm in: sweet or savoury. Mum's penchant is a packet of Snack-a-Jacks. I think I impressed her with my thorough explanation of the careful sorting of my purchases into equally weighted bags when I have to cycle to the shops. You can't be unbalanced on your bike.

Anyway, Mum and I touched a chord. We are similar in more ways than we thought. As my hair turns ginger in the sunlight, Mum's starting to believe they didn't swap me in the hospital.

My birthday!
On Sunday we had a surprise visit from *Kilcullen*. A mast appeared in the morning mist and I was back

on the VHF 'Securité-ing' our position to the as-yet-unknown yacht. Phil, crew member and ex-rower, replied, and after several position checks and a rush round to get decently dressed Phil asked, 'If you can hear me loud and clear say "Yes, Yes, Yes!"'

'Yes, Yes, Yes!'

'Right, this is for tomorrow … Happy birthday to you, happy birthday to you …'

He sang the whole lot beautifully. Mum and I were laughing our heads off. He didn't even break off in the middle through embarrassment. A VHF-a-gram!

As they pulled up to say hello in their Bermuda shorts and dodgy 80's T-shirts, cameras out, Mum and I wondered if we were in the same weather system as we sat freezing in our wet-weather gear. Phil asked why Mum was always the one rowing when they came to visit. ''Cos I'm the skipper!' I shouted back.

The truth was that she knew they were coming and she wanted me to enjoy their attention on my birthday. She also hates using the VHF, and who can blame her? Us girls can't keep our conversation down to one sentence at a time.

I treated myself to a day of pampering … I had a shower and a new T-shirt (much to Mum's relief), opened my birthday cards, Mum found another can of fruit cocktail, which we shared, and I ate a pasty with a little snap-light sticking out of it. Mum was going to share her last blueberry sponge finger with me; she was even going to let me have the paper casing to scrape with my teeth and then suck to within an inch of its life. But I'd treats enough and we decided to keep it till the halfway point.

It was a rather lovely day. I didn't miss the parties at home. Mum spent more than her allotted time on the oars and I received calls from my Dad, Gran and Uncle Paul. I also had time to read through my birthday emails. What a way to spend my twenty-sixth.

Tales from the aquarium

Wow, have we got stuff to tell you! Everyone is eating everyone else! To start with, the weather has been pretty strange recently: on Saturday we were hit by a suffocating sea fog, it was drawing in during the night and by morning we couldn't see further than 200 yards. It was spooky in that pirate-ships-out-of-the-mist kind of way. The waves were the only sounds we could hear. At 11.30 am a very large black pilot whale appeared out of nowhere and was heading straight for the boat. I shouted at Mum to come out and take a look; I was worried he wouldn't stay long as they are very shy and tend to just disappear. We could hear him singing under the boat, amplified through the hull. Another whale appeared through a wave behind us, then another, and within minutes we were surrounded by four whales and a calf! They were so close to the boat we could almost touch them, and we tried, leaning tentatively over each side of the boat and getting splattered as they surfaced and blew water from their blowholes. Whale snot! They were after our Concorde fish, hiding beneath us. The whales were attempting to rouse them out by blowing huge bubbles from beneath the hull. As we looked over the side we could see their pure-white underbellies.

How lucky were we to have a pod of pilot whales hunting and singing beneath our tiny boat? They didn't touch us once, we weren't frightened, just overawed by their gentle magnificence. They left after half an hour, one with a tuna dangling from its mouth. We're not sure how many more they'd caught but the day's hunting had been successful and they were gone within minutes. Only one Concorde appeared alongside the boat after that.

We're constantly surrounded by shearwaters at the moment. They zoom over the top of us, wonderfully fat and feathery in comparison to the much smaller petrels. They hunt the flying fish. We spot them gliding effortlessly over the water for metres at a time. I saw a shearwater dive for a fish in mid flight, he missed him, the fish flew again and this time the bird grabbed the fish in its bill. Got him.

Stripies are back! They're hiding at the front of the boat, obviously flying along off our bow wave. Mum's also spotted a little brown fish that follows us at the back. She's named it Winnie the Fish.

The rarest of ocean discoveries was made on Saturday: the little-known brown-speckled kitchen cupboard. We saw this thing floating along on the waves in the foggy distance and lo and behold it was a proper kitchen cupboard. I mean, there are things that should be given to the sea gods, but an MFI kitchen unit is maybe being a little bit too generous.

Halfway

YES! WE' RE ALMOST HALFWAY! Time wise, we' ve been halfway for a long time, but by next week and the next issue we should be the good side of the Atlantic Ocean, and we can begin the countdown to Barbados. Those who are following our progress will know that this will be the quicker half as we don' t have to travel so far south, it' s east … sorry, west … all the way! How did I pass that navigation course?

So, we' re almost there! Get your bags packed and your flights booked and come and see us in. How often do you have the excuse to holiday in Barbados?

Lots of love, your intrepid ocean explorers

Sally & Sarah xx

PS Does anybody know how 'I Don' t Wanna Fight No More' by Tina Turner goes? Mum' s desperate to find out and I' m desperate to get some sleep!

Wildlife Update

Whilst out in our little boat we've discovered a lot about the wildlife around us. Here is predator and prey diagram of all the animals we've seen so far

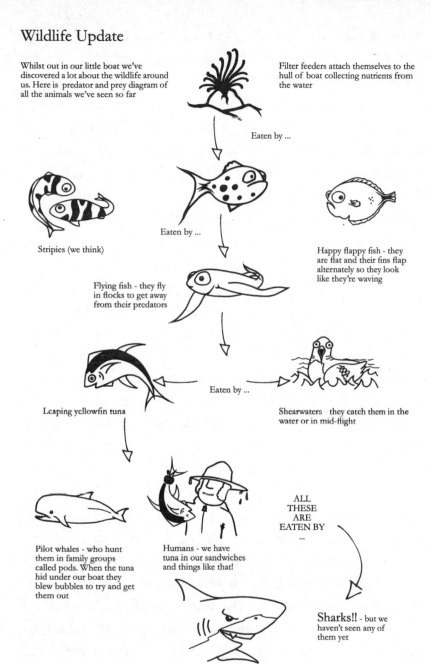

Filter feeders attach themselves to the hull of boat collecting nutrients from the water

Eaten by ...

Stripies (we think)

Eaten by ...

Happy flappy fish - they are flat and their fins flap alternately so they look like they're waving

Flying fish - they fly in flocks to get away from their predators

Eaten by ...

Leaping yellowfin tuna

Shearwaters they catch them in the water or in mid-flight

Pilot whales - who hunt them in family groups called pods. When the tuna hid under our boat they blew bubbles to try and get them out

Humans - we have tuna in our sandwiches and things like that!

ALL
THESE
ARE
EATEN BY
...

Sharks!! - but we haven't seen any of them yet

When a yacht occasionally came to visit, its arrival on our horizon was inevitably accompanied with a mixture of elation followed by a profound feeling of disappointment. Having spotted a blip on their radar, curious crews would often change course, come over and investigate. Spotting their sails on the featureless landscape of the sea would make my stomach turn with the growing excitement of seeing somebody 'out here' in the middle of nowhere.

But after the briefest of 'Hellos' and 'Where're you heading?' they'd drift off again, amazed at the sight of this little wooden rowing boat hundreds of miles from land. Unfortunately this would be followed, all too quickly, by the realisation of our own isolation, leaving us to regret having seen the yacht at all.

We soon discovered that getting what you want doesn't necessarily give you what you need. After *Kilcullen*'s birthday visit I just disappeared into the cabin and cried – a self-pitying cry brought on by jealousy. Their crew: eating great food, sleeping on a better bed, enjoying each other's company, with only days ahead of them before reaching land. Us: bored, missing our own friends, still months from land.

I'm not sure Mum felt the same way. The only emotion she did display openly was panic! She was worried our 'secret weapon' would be discovered. Having become frustrated with our lack of progress, compounded by the fact that crews were arriving in Barbados thick and fast, she decided it was time to take action. Diving into the front cabin she found a couple of large beach towels and, giggling away like a naughty schoolgirl, she carefully hoisted them into position off the guy ropes that held the mast in place. A couple of pegs and a bit of string later, our makeshift spinnaker filled unconvincingly at the front on the boat, breaking the first cardinal rule of ocean rowing – NO SAILS. Mum said menacingly, 'If you tell anybody about this I will kill you!' Looking at the GPS it made absolutely no difference to our speed – we were still plodding along at 1.5 knots. Quite frankly, we didn't care about the rules. We just didn't want to get caught!

Skipper's Log

11.03.04   Mum wanting loo in night was annoying. Got sore bums, otherwise boring.

12.03.04   Saved flying fish in night, couldn't reach one more, died on deck. Had great interview on Radio Leeds. Yorkie Lomas (ours) there. Carlton TV interview with Stuart Boreham.[12] Funny day – went slowly. Sharks? Two of them. Got soaked continually. Waves huge. The Times called.

13.03.04   Horrible night, very bangy. Mum bailed water from footwell at 2.30 am. Flying fish almost in gusset of grey pants. Boring day again.

15.03.04   Now three hrs behind GMT!! Nice day. Got email from The Times. Flappy fish around. Deeply concerned about Villa Nova sponsorship. Only one room! How ridiculous!

---

[12] Stuart rowed solo across the Atlantic, leaving just after the Challenge Race in 2003. Although he has cerebral palsy he successfully made it across, becoming the first physically disabled person to row an ocean.

16.03.04 HALFWAY!! Tommo said 'as crow flies' we were at halfway on Sunday. Celebrated with turkey dinner. Concorde fish did magnificent display - 30 leaping together.

From: Sally
To: Jane
Date: 17 March 2004
Re: *Calderdale* Calling: The Halfway Issue!

WE' RE HALFWAY!!!

Smoke us a Flying Fish,
We' ll be in Barbados for Breakfast!

At 18.20 on Tuesday 16 March we reached N15' 14' 964 W38' 00' 000, the Middle of the Atlantic. We'd reached the middle point 'as the crow flies' on Sunday evening but Mum and I had decided to have our midway celebrations at W38. I had a can of spaghetti bolognese and Mum had a can of baked beans. We only have twenty-three degrees to go before reaching Barbados and as I look at the maps we're a very small boat finding a very small island in a very large ocean. We only hope the second part of our journey is as uneventful – in the best possible way – as the first. It should be a lot quicker. The winds are steady and more reliable and we're making a degree every day and a half. If we keep on a steady course we should make it into Port St Charles thirty days from now, give or take.

Our weather report from Central Briney

The ocean needs a psychiatrist! It's really confused out here. In the morning it rains and the sky is covered with a blanket of grey cloud; but by afternoon it's scorching blue skies and the temperature on the boat is almost unbearable; by nightfall the sunsets are grey and pink like 80's wallpaper. The sea is also in a state, sometimes it looks like a photograph of the Swiss Alps in a travel brochure, steely grey mountains with frothy white tops. Both Mum and I love the way the sunshine changes the colour of the water as the clouds pass over it - cold steel to an amazing deep turquoise.

The waves are all over the place as well, rogues are constantly sideswiping us when we're not looking. We took a direct hit a couple of days ago, which almost took my teeth out and sent Mum flying into the electrical panels. We both thought she'd come out in two shiners but thankfully she just had a couple of small bruises to add to her growing collection. I'm not sure what she's been up to but her legs and arms are covered in them.

All in all the weather in the middle is much the same as that off the coast of Great Yarmouth.[13] The sun is hot but in the wind it's absolutely freezing. So, if you want to get that mid-Atlantic feeling for half the price, head to the coast.

---

[13] Insert any British seaside holiday destination

Dad, call the coastguard

Mum in 'I don't want a cup of tea' shocker!

Anyone who knows my Mum knows that she'd have tea intravenously. This woman can easily get through twenty-five cups a day. Well, it's frightening but true, she's now on only one cup of tea a day. She's even beginning to regret not bringing the detox kit from Boots my sister Sam bought her two Christmases ago on the proviso that Mum 'detoxed' in a week when Sam was not around.

But it seems that there hasn't been a Jekyll-and-Hyde-style transformation and Mum is coping perfectly well. Admittedly she now enjoys poetry, a spot of classical music, she's looking forward to her menopause and hoping to experiment with fruit and herb infusions when she gets back, but other than that she's completely normal.

Whatever happens, Dad, don't blame me!

By the way, we're both suffering from a rather nasty case of trench foot, something for the men in our lives to look forward to. Mum said her feet look like a zombie's: they've got rotting flesh peeling away from around the toes. 'You need a pumice on that,' I told her, but unfortunately in my gloating glory I soon discovered that my recently painted orange-toenailed tootsies had also begun to decay. Nice.

Chilli con carne

I must officially apologise to chilli con carne. I've done nothing but badmouth this food for nearly a year now. I love it and I'm eating it every day, in fact I can't wait till dinnertime. Feel free to ridicule me on my return for not having seen the virtues of this spicy tomato-based heaven in dehydrated powder form.

Tales from the aquarium

We've seen some amazing things whilst we've been out here and Mum and I have been wondering how many others have been lucky enough to have pilot whales hunting under their boat, flocks of flying fish being argued over by shearwaters, and yellowfin tuna. We have been extremely fortunate, but today we were whinging. It has been over a week since we've seen anything different from our usual aquarium. A killer whale would be nice!

Our Concorde fish could sense how despondent we were feeling and came up trumps. I've mentioned before how they leap from the water and belly flop with an almighty splosh. Well, it seems they've been practising. About fifty of them started to leap in unison towards the front of the boat, not flappy belly flops but proper, beautiful dives, up to five in a row. Mum got overexcited and I dropped the oars to take a look. The sight was surreal. They were leaping towards us at such a speed it was almost frightening. One moment a flash of mirrored blue and sparkling water in all directions and the next … nothing.

Who gets to see this? It's incredible out here.

Lots of love,

Sally & Sarah

PS We're going mad out here … Please save us!

NINE

Downhill All the Way

I CAN'T REMEMBER why Mum and I started worrying about accommodation in Barbados. I think Mum might have asked me questions about the arrangements and I hadn't been able to answer them. I thought it had all been sorted out before we left, but Mum was keen for me to double check.

During preparations for the row with Tommo, a friend of Jane and Malcolm's had recommended we contact the Villa Nova for sponsorship. Built for Anthony Eden in the 1830s, the original country house had been converted into a boutique hotel, which now has a reputation for entertaining the powerful and the famous – in the summer of 2003 the press had a field day when Tony Blair and his family had stayed there. How terrible it was that tax payers' money was being spent on luxurious holidays abroad! We never thought it would come off, but after some tenacious negotiation Jane had successfully secured sponsorship whereby Tommo and I could stay at the hotel upon our arrival in Barbados. I'd asked Jane if Villa Nova would agree to extend the courtesy on completion of the second attempt. Jane reassured us that all arrangements had been made. It was at this point when I regretted not having double-checked with Jane what the arrangements actually were.

Mum asked me to call Jane just to clarify everything for us. She joked, 'I bet they've only got one room for the two of us. Three thousand miles and I won't be able to sleep with your Dad!' (Translation: 'Three thousand miles and I'll have to spend another bloody night with you!') She was right. Unfortunately Jane hadn't told Villa Nova that we had partners and would therefore need two separate rooms; also she questioned why we would change the booking at this late stage. Oh dear, our first night in Barbados wouldn't be spent with our loved ones and from our conversation Jane seemed to misunderstand our concerns.

I relayed the conversation to Mum and she went ballistic. 'Call your Dad, tell him there's no way I'm staying in a posh hotel without him. Either the sponsorship changes or he has to book us somewhere else to stay. I don't care where I sleep as long as it's with him.' Mum was crimson with anger. I called Dad and as I sat in the cabin she shouted through instructions from the forward rowing position.

'Tell him to book another hotel! Tell him to tell Jane we've changed our minds!'

Poor Dad was a bit bewildered; I was crying as I tried to

explain the situation, Mum was so upset she was also in tears out on deck. Why hadn't I checked before we left? What a complete cock-up.

Fundamentally it was a situation easily solved: a quick call to Villa Nova or an Internet search for a new hotel would be all it would take to rectify the problem. From the comfort of your own home it's not a major disaster, but again on the boat these things intensify. The damp, salt-ridden mattress was the only bed we had to look forward to. Chilli con carne or potato soup were the only meals that tasted good enough to eat. In our minds this simple mistake was a fundamental fuck up.

Dad told me not to worry, he'd sort it out and get back to us the following Sunday. Mum made me promise not to call anybody for the next week, not even Tommo. As far as she was concerned this would be sorted out in private. She didn't want her family to know how upset we were.

Skipper's Log

20.03.04
Uneventful. Growing concerned about pace S. Will have to try adjust during day. Feeling v. concerned, although held course. Cross-wind & waves. Had first big argument with Mum. Computer emails not working. Trying to sort but basically buggered!

21.03.04
Went loads S in night. Plan to spend day compensating. Cabin getting v. v. warm during night. Flying fish carnage. Eight this morning. Worked hard - one hr on/one hr off shift on NNW

*track to reduce track S. Worked brilliantly, we
didn't lose at all! Made decent progress N too.*

24.03.04   *Flying fish hitting cabin all night - sounded like
they did damage. Dropping wind made for pretty
calm conditions - hardly a breeze. Didn't make
great distance, only just on next map. Computer
buggered, as is phone.*

From: Sally
To: Jane
Date: 24 March 2004
Re: *Calderdale* Calling: The Into Boredom and Beyond
Issue

Whilst being out here Mum and I have had ample
opportunity to ponder. My thoughts have generally
concentrated on the fact that I have no job and
nowhere to stay when we return to Blighty. It's
actually an exciting prospect, but not one that
doesn't concern me a little. Mum has helped me come
up with a top five of money-making and therefore
rent-paying suggestions:

1 Win prize money by entering donut-eating
   competitions
We've discovered the canny ability of not licking
our lips or sucking our fingers when eating. The
salty environment just makes it impossible to get a
good nail biting session in. So with these amazing
new talents I can sweep up at all the donut-eating
competitions.

2 Become a market gardener/fluffy knicker
   manufacturer

Never buy sea salt from the supermarket again! We can harvest it out here in the mid-Atlantic, guaranteeing its quality and purity. Honestly, selling sea salt … what a con! This is why we thought we could also make fluffy knickers, we can sew them as our fortune crystallises around us.

3 Get a job in PR for the ORS

Want to row an ocean? Not only can I make it sound like the most fun you've ever had in your life but I could also persuade you to take a parent with you for that bonding experience.

4 Become a critic of the BBC World Service

We listened to a rather evocative magazine programme on 'The Re-introduction of Wild Boar into the English Countryside'. I awarded the presentation as follows: Originality – 8/10. Content - 7/10. Relevance – 4/10. In conclusion, ours is a much-needed service.

5 Go and work in a factory

Now, this one's Mums favourite. I'm not so keen. I'm slightly concerned I would not be making the most of my obvious talents, illustrated above.

We're so bored we've begun recounting our dreams. You know you must be bored if other people's dreams become interesting. I woke yesterday and told Mum that I'd dreamt Matt Boreham's wife, Ali, had turned up in Port St Charles dressed as a giant lobster. Kenneth Crutchlow thought this was a terrific idea and that all the families should come in fancy dress. I imagined my sister as an octopus, her friend Helen as a mermaid and my Dad as a Dover sole – a desperate attempt to convince Mum that he had stuck to his diet whilst we've been away.

Mum's dreams are always about my brother, Stephen, as a child. In one dream he'd named the family dog – a Great Dane – Plank. We've never had a Great Dane but I'm sure our friend and coach Tony Plank will be chuffed to hear that in the event we'd have to call it after him.

The cressery

Yep, we've started to grow the cress! Mum and I think so alike sometimes it's spooky. I never thought growing cress could be so complicated. I thought you just bunged it into an empty eggshell with a smiley face drawn on it. Oh no! There's got to be holes along the container side to allow the air to circulate, a decent medium for healthy root growth – we used a cotton pad – and sun from dawn till dusk, but not direct sunlight, as this scorches. See, it's hard work! But hasn't it paid off. Our first crop has just matured, and our meal choices have quadrupled: cress con carne, cress and custard, cress à la rice cake, cress soup ... oh, and cress tea (recipes will be available).

Atlantic Nudity Day

I've declared 23 March Atlantic Nudity Day. It's so hot out here – 33° in the shade – that even a hat and

a coat of factor sixty is still too much clothing!
So off it all came on Tuesday. Mum was having none
of it.

Tales from the aquarium
Aside from the normal Concorde belly flops there's
not a great deal to tell you. We have been asking
for a killer whale but Neptune hasn't been listening
lately. He's sent us another dead calm, but that's
not quite what we ordered, we're sending it back.
Making the most of it, we've sorted out our kitchen
cupboards. If the wind doesn't pick up soon we're
out here for some time to come. Uh.

Still trudging on, but happy …

Sally & Sarah xx

PS Congratulations to Billy and Nat, Sam, Pavel and
the *Against All Odds* boys.

We tried to keep our spirits up. I wrote the diary as if nothing
had happened, telling everyone at home that we were still
happily bobbing along. Within a day or two I had broken
my promise not to call home. Choosing a particularly blowy
afternoon, whilst Mum was sat outside with her wet weather
jacket tucked up around her ears, the wind drowning out my
clandestine activities, I called Tommo. I just wanted to vent my
frustrations. Tommo listened patiently, although he infuriated
me by sitting on the fence again, saying Jane had behaved with
the best intentions, which I believed to be entirely true, but in

my state of mind I just didn't want to hear it! I asked him if he wouldn't mind calling Dad just to make sure he was ok and not too anxious about us.

Maybe other crews were having arguments with their support teams? But so many crews were at the end of their journeys there were barely any of us left out at sea, it was getting increasingly lonely. Even a Ukrainian gentleman in his sixties, a solo rower called Pavel, had now made it across.

When Sunday finally arrived the phone rang just after noon.

'How did you get on?' I asked Dad.

'Well, I told Jane and Malcolm that you didn't want to stay at Villa Nova, but I'm having trouble finding hotels near Port St Charles,' he said anxiously.

'Dad, we didn't say we didn't want to go to Villa Nova, we just need Jane to ask them to extend their sponsorship to two rooms. If they say no, then that's cool, but please ask her to try again. It'll save you some time and effort.'

'Ok, I'll do that. Is Mum alright?'

'No, she's pissed off and she won't talk to you. But don't take it personally, she's not talking to anybody!'

Again I relayed the conversation to Mum. She just sat there with a face like thunder.

'Have you turned that phone off?' she snapped as we swapped places.

'Yes, I have,' I snapped back. 'Oh, and by the way, I did make a call in the week. I spoke to Tommo. I had to talk to someone. Anyway, he said he'd speak to Jane and help Dad find a hotel.'

She wasn't going to tell me what to do – I'm skipper!

~

Skipper's Log

21.03.04   Nothing happened last night. No noise apart from Happy sponsor sticker. Tuna glittered beside us. V. warm night. Grabbing some N back so happy with that. Wind increasing slightly. Where's the bloody wildlife? Computer & phone working!

27.03.04   Boat kept course well. Could stronger winds be back? Hoping to continue making good ground to beat 100 days ORS predict.

29.03.04   Carnage on deck this morning. Blood on gunnels, fish everywhere. Didn't hear thing in night. Also Mum not up to tinkle! Great watermaking day. Wind v. strange, quite S hence track N. Eating more chocolate.

31.03.04   Why the hell do we bother? Rowed hard all day AGAIN, still made exactly same distance as ever. Saw whale - glimpse. Fucked off.

01.04.04   Famous last words! Didn't go anywhere but N in night. No wind. Both pissed off. Wind S-ly. Both tired, aching, frustrated. Rowed together all day with little break. Still made v. little distance N. Para-anchor out for night, both feel sick from vitamin drink.

From: Sally
To: Jane
Date: 1 April 2004
Re: *Calderdale* Calling

ATLANTIC MUM PLANS SOLO PACIFIC ROW –
SPONSORS WANTED

Daughter Needs 3 for Women's 4s' Record

It seems the Atlantic pair has caught the ocean rowing bug. Sarah Kettle said 'I love the tranquility of the ocean, it's given me time to reflect and take stock. I'm hoping to go again but as a solo rower. I think I've come to a new point in my life, one far from the hustle bustle of everyday gardening.'

Sally Kettle also commented, 'I've taken my time on this row, getting to know my Mum and finding out about myself. Next time I want to get the record, the fastest-ever women's crossing. I just need to find three girls who want to come with me. Night shift workers are welcome, and hopefully one will be in the army because their food is really good!'

Oh dear, it's the first day of another month and we're still out here! In the last couple of weeks we've been feeling quite low. A combination of exhausting heat, no wind (and therefore reduced progress) and the growing monotony of the task has ground us down

Tommo and me, my hair looking miraculously vomit free after our first trip on a yacht

Mum – the explorer

Back at port we unpacked the boat and put her to bed. The blue plastic covers the hole in the cabin roof. As you can see, we packed everything. (You can't see the kitchen sink, it must be in the cabin!)

Mum's first time at the oars, only 2 weeks before our 3,500-mile journey!

Our supporters. Their names written on our cabin roof

Mad dogs and Sally's mum
row out in the midday sun

I refine my pose for the camera!

Proud Dad – 105 days later we step on land for the first time and look how glamorous
and healthy we look! (Unlike the male rowers, who step off their boats looking like the
Beasts of Bodmin Moor!)

Small boat, big sea – and this was a calmer day!

Claire's Christmas pants

Jo leaves the boat. Rowgirls are therefore disqualified from the Woodvale Atlantic Rowing Race 2005

Sue and me with yet another broken oar

First three to row an ocean! Claire, Sue and me

a little; so much so that a few days ago we had our first argument. It was over the smallest of things but it culminated in my wearing a watch and the two of us spending more time out on deck together.

Although the heat makes it practically impossible to enjoy standing in the footwell in front of the cupboard door, our spirits are dramatically lifted when we spend time talking to each other, even if it is about the best way to clean the oven or the merits of a turkey baster!

I asked Mum what cheers her up, she said she loves the Concorde fish belly flopping gracefully around the boat. She says they look so silly as they launch their shiny bodies through the air, their tails flapping for extra momentum. I asked her what else made her smile. She said, 'Seeing my grandson and him saying "Hello, Gran."' She instantly burst into tears. I recommended she choose a different 'smile-making' thought; that one definitely wasn't working!

There's been a strange role reversal on the boat. I spend half an hour at night reading Mum a story from our *Chicken Soup for the Ocean Lover's Soul* book Jan and Dan (the mother-and-son team) bought us. They've been a fantastic support over the last year, giving advice and cheering us with their tales. I think our journey has a lot in common with theirs: they were determined to enjoy their experience together for as long as it took to get across. Their biggest piece of advice has always been ENJOY YOURSELVES and we've been trying to take it.

Guinness Book of Records

We've both been wondering if we'll end up in the big book – 'First Mother and Daughter to Row an Ocean', that sort of thing. It would be absolutely fantastic if we did. Since watching *Record Breakers* as a kid I've always wanted to break a record – I remember a moustachioed German man came on to the show with his daughter, and they had an apple peel the length of a football pitch (or something like that). I thought that was cool and that I could do it.

Thinking about it, I may have to settle with the 'row an ocean' record instead. We'll just have to call Norris McWhirter and ask him to meet us in Port St Charles with an adjudicator and a stopwatch.

Notes from the arboretum

Mum felled the final mighty stems of our first batch yesterday to add to her mashed potato so I've sown some more seeds this morning. These succulent tufts have satisfied not only our hunger but also our need to nurture. If the cress is happy then so are we!

```
Recipe to Cut Out and Keep

CRASH

Serves 1                Ingredients

1 Dollop of piping-hot Smash Instant Mashed Potato
1 Thimbleful of Freshly Chopped Cress


Method

Add one to the other. Enjoy!
```

Tales from the aquarium

Two new fish have joined our happy aqua-clan, albeit briefly. The first was a strange but very large grey fish, which we mistook for a dolphin or a shark, about two metres long if not more. It was light grey in colour and swam near the surface of the waves. Because of its colour it was difficult to distinguish any features; we couldn't make out the fin or the tail shapes. I've decided it's got to be a shark, certainly until somebody can tell us any different.

The second arrived today with several friends - GIANT STRIPIES!! They were about a metre long, skinny and, of course, stripy black and white. They look similar to pike - a narrow long head, small fins and well 'ard. They saunter menacingly around the boat. Let's hope they don't get too friendly with our mini stripies - they're still wiggling away at the bow, keeping up as best they can.

Tommo's worried about our wishing for a killer whale, he's basically concerned because they have a rather nasty habit of 'killing'. Well, I'm sure they won't find much sport in killing a wooden boat. Much as I would like to credit them with a great deal of intelligence it's unlikely they'll know their lunch is pottering about on the deck. Anyway, Mum and I are convinced our Concorde fish are biding their time and just waiting for the right moment.

Concorde 1	'See the skinny little one? She's out on deck but for the plan to work we need them both out at the same time.'
Concorde 2	'Yeah! That fatter one with brown hair looks like a good lunch to me!'
Concorde 1	'Yeah! If we belly flop enough they may come to the edge of the boat and take a closer look … then … bump … Oh dear, over the edge … and we'll have 'em!!'
Concorde 2	'Hahahahahaha …'
Concorde 1	'Heheheheehehe …'

Mum got hit by a flying fish the other night and she screamed like a girl. We've been making a tally of the cull and we'll let you know in the last week how many we've managed to lure to their deaths on our decks!

The weather
We need your help! We're fed up out here and we want to get home. The waves are coming from the south and the wind from the south-south-east, any way you

look at it they're both pushing us in the wrong direction. We've been struggling for days just to stay in the same spot and it's doing nothing for our frown lines, except deepening them.

We need a peg sacrifice on a very large scale and we need your help to do it. Grab a wooden peg, and not the mankiest one either - pick one you're going to miss. Then find a suitable body of water: a river, stream, lake or pond will do (a washing machine will do at a push). At 7.00 pm on Tuesday we'll sacrifice our pegs together and this is what you need to say as you toss it into the water: 'Please grant Sally, Sarah, Matt,[15] Richard, Henry and Moose a steady force five with strong east-north-east winds to speed them to Barbados to their much-missed family and friends. Thank you.'

If we all do it together maybe the clerk at the ocean weather desk in the sky will do something about it!

Thanks,

Sally 'Have we done our quota?' and Sarah 'What're the scores on the doors Miss Saggy Drawers?' Kettle xx

I didn't envy Dad, as he was in a practically impossible position: not only did he have to re-organise the hotel but he also had to try and estimate what date we'd be arriving so he could book flights that would get him, my brother, sister and nephew to Barbados in time. This was a difficulty all the families were facing. Changes in the weather could delay rowers by weeks, so

---

[15] Matt, Richard, Henry and Moose (so called because Luis Ginglo from Canada had named his boat *Moose on the Move*) were all solo rowers. As a group we were the only ones still out at sea.

getting the timing just right was a logistical nightmare. There were tales of rowers arriving 'early' and so having to meet their families at the airport, and of friends spending two glorious weeks in Barbados but the rowers arriving the day after they had to fly home.

There were so many ways Dad could bugger it up. When he first read our April Fool's Day email he totally believed what we'd written. I can just imagine the colour draining from his face with the thought of Mum wandering off across the Pacific by herself. How would he cope? Gran told me later that on his visits he would just sit and stare into space.

Which brings me to this point. Why is it that when a woman's abandoned at home she's pretty much left to get on with it, whereas deserted men practically have the community rallying around to support them?

'Oh Steve, you must miss Sarah terribly, here, have this casserole!'

'Oh Steve, you must be so lonely without Sarah, how about you come round for dinner?'

Dad's diet had no chance whatsoever!

It didn't help when Malcolm called Dad, saying we were 'lost at sea'. Malcolm had received a call from Kenneth in the middle of the night saying our Argos beacon had 'gone off' and they couldn't get hold of us. I think he misinterpreted 'gone off' as being 'set off': we were in trouble and we'd pushed the button. In fact, the battery had died and therefore the beacon had stopped transmitting and with no outward sign of this predicament Mum and I had no idea our beacon wasn't bleeping any more.

All the boats in the regatta had been given a second beacon just in case the battery ran out or they experienced some unforeseen difficulties. They were only supposed to transmit for approximately eighty days but unfortunately ours just happened to fail a few days shy, so poor Malcolm had understandably feared the worst, especially as we'd been hit by bad weather and were now going in the wrong direction. Having taken the call so late at night he and Jane must have been frantic. I know Dad was extremely grateful that they didn't break the news to him until the next morning.

Although Mum didn't like the idea, I was still turning the phone on between 12.00 and 1.00 pm, as promised, and you can imagine my surprise when Malcolm rang just after 12.00 one afternoon and, with audible relief, said: 'Are you ok? Where have you been? We've been worried! I've been trying to call you all morning.'

'Why did you try calling this morning? You know we don't have the phone on till twelve,' I replied uncharitably. I was beginning to think that we should have thrown the sat phone overboard. We didn't realise that the team at home was convinced we'd died at sea, we thought they were overreacting, which in turn felt like a criticism of our ability to look after ourselves. Mum and I were quite selfishly thinking Dad and Malcolm needed to stop worrying about us – it was driving us crazy! Anyway, we had enough on our plates. We were going backwards, and if we did eventually get across the likelihood of hitting Barbados was fairly slim.

~

Skipper's Log

04.04.04   Big moon, warm night. Saved fish but fed him
             straight to tuna - whoops! Beeper again from 4.00
             am till morning. Thought I saw Hare. Found squid
             on board. Where did he come from? Changed routine
             to include break at hottest part of day, 3.00-5.00
             pm. Rowed better together in evening/night. Wind
             strong, therefore great progress. V. happy.

06.04.04   We're going in right direction! We're making
             tracks S - slowly. Which is great. Not huge
             distance, but enough. Hope it holds.

08.04.04   V. hot today. Spent time sweating in cabin
             sending diary. Two frigatebirds & mating tropical
             bird pair came to visit. Tried dark choc.

From: Sally
To: Jane
Date: 8 April 2004
Re: *Calderdale* Calling: The Three-Quarters of the
Way There Issue

Lactugal
Glycerin suppositories
Regulose
Duphalae

Anusol
Anusplat

I've found I've been a bit stubborn of late and Mum keeps telling me it's the high caloric/highly processed food and lack of fresh fruit and veg. I thought the cress would sort it out but Mum said it doesn't make up your five portions.

'Not even five stems?'

'Not even ten stems!'

The chilli con carne was doing its job a few weeks ago but now it's wholly inadequate and I'm rummaging through the medi-cupboard looking for a solution, hence the list above. When Challenge Business put the medical kit list together they were definitely on to something, otherwise why would there be six different types of constipation relief? Still, variety is the spice of life!

By the way, Mum insisted I write about this, although I'm completely happy not to tell you about the inner workings of my intestines. She obviously thought it would get me back for all the horrible things I've said about her over the last few weeks. She knows it will do nothing for my glamorous, feminine image!

In the cupboard (approximately six feet long, two feet high, tapering from four to one-and-a-half feet wide!)

Our cupboard is our refuge, our bedroom, our office and very occasionally our bathroom. I'm going to guide you through on a virtual tour ... here goes.

The ceiling is painted white and spilt into four panels, one section is covered in the names of all our Diamond Donors. Unfortunately our sweaty heads have acted as mops, obliterating many of them; although they still remain with us in spirit. You'll probably find 'Tracy Young (Berkhamstead)', amongst others, printed backwards on our scalps. On the other three panels there's a mixture of good luck messages from friends and family and a few pictures I've drawn during the journey. There are other scrawlings but the one I look at before I go to bed is the bar-gate markings of the days as they go by – eleven weeks so far and more to come.

We've shoved an emergency can opener in the insulating piping that criss-crosses the roof of the cabin just in case we have a 'can't open the can of fruit salad' disaster. We've also stuffed good luck cards and a couple of Christmas cards (from the last attempt) in there too. Farley has found a snug little spot up behind the VHF radio - or the walkie-talkie, as Mum likes to call it.

There are two net baskets along one side of the wall overflowing with bits and bobs. One contains flares, a foghorn, torches and other technical stuff; the other sun creams, painkillers, cotton buds, tweezers ... It's basically a typical girls' bathroom. With every delving into the medi-cupboard, out comes another pill or potion to cure our sunburnt, spotty flesh or our aching knees and bums.

I lie on a Canary Islands towel and Mum has decided to turn her orange grub inside out. We're constantly finding fish scales either in our bedding or stuck to various parts of our bodies, and salt crystals make their way into the soft cotton. We're just like two princesses with our respective peas.

We have a very sophisticated weather station up on the wall beside the cupboard door, which has automatically changed its time setting six times now. It currently says 18.29 when it's actually 16.29, but tomorrow it could say pretty much any time it likes. It also shows various weather conditions, which tend to be nothing like the weather we have, will have or are experiencing. We suspect it's confused by the microclimate inside the cabin; needless to say it will be cloudy with rain in the cupboard by tomorrow evening. The flashing pictures are pretty cool though.

The electric boxes with their many buttons are mounted on the wall opposite the nets and our GPS is stuck with gaffer to the top of one of them. This outdoor piece of kit began to corrode just three weeks into the trip so we brought it indoors and we like it where it is now. We can watch the minutes tick away even whilst we're in bed.

The pelicase containing the laptop is mounted on the same side as the electrics. This huge yellow case is bombproof, floats, is pressurised and will basically arrive in Venezuela well before we do if the boat ever sunk, which is quite reassuring really.

Underneath our mattresses are our 'understairs cupboards'. A long one runs practically the length of the cabin and hides an abundance of chilli con carne, extra drinking water and our canned treats. Two other waterproof hatches contain our medi-kit and our electrical items: cables, batteries, chargers, that sort of thing. Two other hatches contain personal odds and sods like books, T-shirts and the other pair of 100 per cent-cotton men's boxer shorts from M&S (large), ready to come out and wreak havoc on the boat.

All in all, our cupboard has the spaciousness of a three-bed semi and the mod cons of a modern naval submarine. What more could two girlies want on their Atlantic safari? Thank God we're only small!

Notes from the arboretum
Oh dear, we're not happy. The second batch of cress has died. Unfortunately we left it out in the sun too long and it cooked. Mum's sown the new batch of seeds for go number three and hopefully we'll be able to give you a glowing report in the next issue.

Tales from the aquarium

Well, no new fish to report I'm afraid, although we were visited very briefly by five dolphins. As soon as I dived in for the camera they had gone. Such has been the experience with practically every animal so far. I think the only creatures I have successfully captured on film are the barnacles currently hitching a ride on our rudder.

We have had an abundance of bird life, though. The usual petrels dart about amongst the waves and the glorious white tropical birds with their long feathery tails soar high above us, taking a quick look to see what we're up to. Now the Magnificent Frigate has joined them, a fantastic if somewhat frightening-looking black bird with a huge wingspan. The wings are shaped like a bat's, angular and vampiresque. We looked them up in our book, they frighten smaller birds into regurgitating their kill and then the scary bird eats the vomit. Grim! Andy and Faye on *Bluebell* (from the last race) described them as pterodactyls and they do look just like them, black dinosaur birds.

Right, going to end here if that's ok? Somewhat abrupt I know but I fear I may lose all my body fluids through sweating it's so hot in here … 36° today! Mum may find a big puddle rather than her eldest daughter, and that wouldn't make for a successful trip, would it?

S & S

~

To help with the organisation of the 'welcome party' Dad was talking to his brother, Paul, on a daily basis. My uncle worked rather conveniently as a travel agent in Manchester and recommended they reserve seats on different flights, according to our progress. We'd slow down, they'd change the reservations; we'd speed up, and they'd rebook.

Dad had also spoken to Kenneth at the ORS and he'd recommended a self-catering complex just up the road from Port St Charles. There'd be enough room, and all he had to do was book it when we were approximately 250 miles from land. At last everything was beginning to go to plan. All Mum and I needed to do was keep rowing.

As news of our journey spread – we'd now featured in *The Times*, on local radio and television news – family members we hadn't heard from for years were popping out of the woodwork. Mum and I were surprised by emails from long-lost cousins and Mum's brothers and sisters on a weekly basis. As one of nine, Mum has a huge family, many of whom she'd lost contact with and some I hadn't seen since I was a toddler.

The row was certainly having some unexpected outcomes. Mum and I were closer than we'd ever been and in fact the communication problems we were having with the team only served to strengthen the bond between us. It was Mum and me against the world! Here we were, bonding, connecting with long-lost family and slowly conquering misconceptions about mother–daughter relationships. It's a shame that Dad innocently managed to say something completely stupid and all hell broke loose.

It was Good Friday and we were enjoying our regular Sunday afternoon chat a couple of days early. Dad was calling from my Gran's and after I'd had a quick chat with her he updated me on the arrangements for the trip to Barbados. I'd even compiled a list of clothes he needed to pack for us. Mum's list read 'Safe in beige': all Dad needed to do was gather all her beige-coloured clothes and shove them in a suitcase – job done. There's no way he could get that wrong and piss her off. My requirements were just as easy: everything was in the suitcase he'd taken home from La Gomera, and he needed to add a book on how to write a kick-ass CV and a pair of my favourite high heels. Having confirmed all this we discussed the flights to Barbados, and it was at this point when Dad tentatively made the following suggestion:

'Sal, if the worst happened and we couldn't get the right flight, would you and Mum mind putting your para-anchor out until we arrived?'

'Yeah, Dad, no problem. Obviously, we'd prefer it if we didn't have to, but I'd rather you be there than not. Anyway, it would only be another day, right?'

We said our goodbyes.

I hung up.

I told Mum.

'Stay out longer? … Stay out fucking longer? You have got to be kidding me. He wants us sit on our anchor because he can't get his act together? That's so fucking typical of your father. This has absolutely nothing to do with getting the right flight. He's just trying to get a cheaper deal!'

I've seen Mum angry, but this was beyond fury. Dad's

suggestion had unlocked emotions that left her weeping uncontrollably at the oars. Essentially, I just couldn't understand it. Why was she behaving so irrationally about this? It wasn't a big deal, we'd sat on our anchor for days and one more night wouldn't hurt. Surely knowing everyone would be there to welcome us would be compensation enough for another night at sea? Anyway, this was only a contingency plan.

'It's money, Sal, that's all he thinks about – how much he can save. He's not thinking about us at all.'

I knew this just wasn't true. Admittedly, Dad was a bit tight, but that's not surprising: by twenty he had a wife and three small children to support. This is not to say that Mum wasn't entitled to be angry. I didn't know the full extent of these surfacing problems between them, and why should I? I'm not their friend, I'm their daughter, but now their relationship issues had been unceremoniously dumped into our boat. I feared this argument would seriously damage their marriage.

'Give me the phone. I'm calling your father.'

Mum disappeared into the cabin. I sheepishly took to the oars, straining my ears above the wind and waves to try and hear what she was saying. There was no need; they could probably hear her in Barbados. The latch turned and out stepped Mum.

'You've still got half an hour's break. You can speak to your Dad if you want but I'm never going to talk to him again.'

I had to call Dad; he needed to know that I didn't blame him, that Mum was tired, angry, missing him and I'd try to talk to her, make things right. He was choking on the other end of the phone, pleading with me that he didn't mean what he'd said: it wasn't the money; he was just trying to get it right.

'We're not meeting you at the airport.' That's what you said, Sal. I just don't know when you're going to arrive. What do you want me to do? Please tell me,' he sobbed.

'Dad, don't worry. Please, just talk to Kenneth, he'll let you know what to do. Mum doesn't want to talk to you but I promise I'll ring you as often as I can. Just do what you're doing. It'll be ok,' I sobbed back.

It wasn't such a Good Friday after all.

~

Skipper's Log

09.04.04   Two flyers saved, Mum screaming as they flapped. Worst day yet (Good Friday!).

12.04.04   Sleepless. Making no headway at all. Put para-anchor out 1.30 pm. Called Kilcullen for weather. Improving to ENE. Must go S. (Opened letters from friends last night – happy new book!)

14.03.04   Sat on anchor all night. Fish carnage – 27!! Disheartened this morning to find still S-ly wind & starting to turn. Hoping it does v. soon. V. sad. Nav light switch broken – still dodgy but gaffered. On anchor all day. Wind v. slowly moving round. Richard (on Najojo) called – v. depressed. 30 flying fish on boat. Watermaker not working. Going backwards. FANTASTIC.

From: Sally
To: Jane
Date: Wednesday 14 April 2004
Re: *Calderdale* Calling: The Hangin' On In There Issue

TRUE BRITS

Atlantic Girls Complain about Weather

Skipper Sally says, 'I knew we were in trouble the moment our knickers, which are pegged to the mast, started flapping in completely the wrong direction. The irony is it happened on April Fool's Day!'

The last week has been awful, the wind and waves are coming from the south or south east, sending us north. To compensate we're having to broach the boat, the oars barely scoop the water, it's wet, tiring and makes for very little progress. We're feeling exhausted mentally and physically. With only ten degrees to go to get to Barbados it's depressing when the only distance we're making in a day is ten minutes, and we're in the best position! *Najojo*, Kenneth C. and Moose must be struggling. We have to row together twenty-four hours a day to stay in the same place, so the solo rowers must be finding it really tough.

I'm writing this in the cabin as the rain hits the roof and it sounds like the inside of a tent on a typical British summer's day. We're on our para-anchor drifting very slowly backwards, it seems the Great Peg Sacrifice of 2004 didn't have the desired effect.

The tuna can sense the smell of despondency and are flocking around the boat. We counted fifteen at one point, all hoping we make a mistake or decide we've had enough and take the plunge.

Mum and I have been talking a lot, analysing our feelings. Why am I so upset when we don't do a good distance? Why are we so concerned that people at home will think we're doing something wrong? Even out in the ocean the demons get you. Anxieties and worries magnify like the vastness of the sky and the never-ending view of the sea.

We've concluded whatever happens we made the right decision at the right time. We've done our best and that's all we can do. We're NOT GIVING UP! We WILL cross this ocean, even if the weather doesn't change and we end up in Florida, having eaten the stuffing from our sleeping bags.

This is the first day off from rowing for two months so there is a silver lining to every cloud. It's given us the opportunity to read some of the letters and cards from friends. They have lifted our spirits and provided me with another book to read. What more could you ask for? Although my friends Kris and Liz are no longer in our good books, as they have sent us a menu from their favourite Balti restaurant in Essex!

Maybe next week we'll have better and cheerier news.

Sally 'Claw Hands' and Sarah 'Pain in the $*&^'
Kettle x (Mum chose her own name, by the way.)

~

IT WAS A few days before Mum decided it was time to take action. Her nemesis the laptop would be her weapon of choice. I wasn't keen on a confrontation but Mum convinced me that it was time to deal with this situation head on. Using a page from my battered exercise book she'd hand-written a letter to Jane, Malcolm and my Dad. It was a mass of crossings out and corrections, the indentations of the pencil passing through several sheets, identifying the firmer points Mum wanted to make.

'Type that up,' she said. 'And don't change anything.'

I dutifully disappeared to the cabin, set the laptop on my knees and one-finger typed whilst sweat trickled down the backs of my legs. After I'd finished I read the email back to her so that she knew I'd left everything in.

I plugged in the sat phone and lay there waiting for connection, my heart in my throat. It took several minutes before the email disappeared off into the ether ...

From: Sally
To: Malcolm; Jane; Stephen
Date: 13 April 2004
Re: From Sarah

Malcolm, Jane and Stephen,

I am fed up with hearing about your worries, sleepless nights, difficulties with websites, accommodation cock-ups and thoughtless ideas to get the best deals on flights.

We kept our bargain with 'yes, we're fine, everything's great' and Sally's 'Oh what a lovely time we're having out in the mid-Atlantic' diaries.

I think you have forgotten we are on what is described as 'one of the world's toughest endurance events'.

We ARE enjoying ourselves and getting past each test as it comes. We are doing our job. We are not on some sort of holiday. In the comfort of your front rooms please get on with your jobs and don't keep telling us we don't understand the stress you're going through. If you can't handle it, tough! Get on with it. Stop offloading on to us.

I just hope none of the rest of my family or friends have got knowledge of this mess and has had it spoiled for them. Don't spoil it for us.

Sarah

As soon as it was sent Mum became herself again. She'd spoken her mind and now it was time to move on. After a day or two it was obvious that Jane, Malcolm and Dad had decided it was best not to call us. I was very grateful for that.

With 600 miles still to row we needed to concentrate on our progress to Barbados. We were way off course and it was now time to do the 'man' thing: dig deep, row hard and row together. The pain would only be temporary ... just the weakness leaving our bodies!

Skipper's Log

17.04.04   Two fat ladies' day.[16] 50 flying fish this morning. Drifting N still. Glad no para-anchor to pull in. Row together today, see what we can do. April showers! Big waves & strong winds, rain. Good rowing though. Dark clouds from NE approaching could change weather? Too much chocolate. Mum ran final inventory - enough food for 40 days! Spoke to Kenneth C. about plan.

18.04.04   Didn't save v. large flying fish, felt v. guilty. Morning comes later every day. Sun doesn't rise till just after 9.00 am. Going S quicker than I thought. Steered on rudder for half day. Waves near on drowned us several times. Adjusted course to slow track S. Wonderful black bird on boat. Eats our flying fish? Is he night-time raider? I didn't feel well all day - tiffin cake?[17]

19.04.04   Martinique (our bird) stayed with us for some time during the night. Skidding on the back window. Rain howling down with plenty of bangs & crashes. On choc hype!!

20.04.04   Mum's sinuses started - thinks it's bed bugs.

21.04.04   Woke up in night in agony - back killing me. Slightly concerned, was in pain during day also.

---

[16] Eighty-eight days – ideally this is when we wanted to come in – a fitting irony since we'd lost so much weight

[17] These deliciously sickly rich fruit cake pieces had been sweating in the hatches for seven months! Whoops.

Full rainbow. Could be only two weeks away!

22.04.04   *Mum snored after taking anti-histamine tablet. Back still painful. Pygmy sperm whales. Pilot whales & dolphin. Birds catching fish. Days getting even hotter, relief when rain came. Computer's a pain!*

23.04.04   *Ship off port side. Nav light playing up still. Saved a fish, only to be eaten by tuna. Dreamt about 70's bikinis. Up most of night. Ocean emerald green. Quite amazing. Loads of birds - gulls? Tuna leaping & hunting. Hit several tuna with oar. Made awning.*

From: Sally

To: Jane

Date: 23 April 2004

Re: *Calderdale* **Calling: The Back in the Saddle Issue**

It's been a funny couple of weeks and through our shared experiences I've come to some conclusions. I have found the answer, the Holy Grail, the meaning of life!

Now, I wouldn't want to spoil your search for the answer to the ultimate question, but I will certainly help you with a pondering I've been having. In life you need a little bit of hope but also a good dollop of reality.

In the last week Mum and I have been struggling

with the reality that if the weather didn't change (as it hadn't for nearly a month!) then we would not make it to Barbados. No amount of hope was going to turn the wind and the waves. We put a call through to *Kilcullen* and Kenneth Crutchlow answered.

'Hi Kenneth, this is not an emergency, we just wanted to tell you our plan. We WILL cross the finish line whatever the weather brings but we may not make it to Barbados. We have forty days' food left and we're both fit and well. Just thought I'd keep you informed.'

Kenneth promised to fetch us from wherever we ended up, at our current trajectory, Martinique, but if it got worse we were off to the Florida Keys. (Unfortunately not Brazil and our gorgeous Frenchman.)

Mum had spent some time on her hands and knees calling out our food supplies. It boiled down to the following:

- If the watermaker and the cooker continued to work effectively (as usual) we had enough food and gas for nearly sixty days-ish (if we really eked it out)
- Without our cooker we could live on our forty-day supply of chocolate mousse, blueberry soup, chocolate bars, chocolate tiffin cake and various other treats
- Without the watermaker and the cooker we had enough ballast for thirty days, and I'd be happy to spoon the chocolate mousse powder straight in. So even if it all went completely tits up

we'll still come home so fat from our glorious chocolate gorging that nobody would believe we'd been down to a waif-like eight stone

We gave Richard on *Najojo* a call telling him our grand plan to make it for the finish line. He's much further north than we are and the struggle to maintain course has been getting him down too. But the weather has turned and we're now hurtling towards Barbados like chocolate mousse towards our tastebuds. We haven't heard from Richard so Mum and I are hoping he's out on the oars on a new course south.

So I'm making no promises, no predictions, no dates, just swallowing this good dollop of reality and saying we'll take every day as it comes. So don't ask us … ok!!!! x

Notes from the arboretum
Batch three is a corker! We've taken extra special care of our growing greens, keeping them out of the sun, watering them regularly and they have rewarded us with a flourish of succulent stems!

Recipe to Cut Out and Keep

CRESS CON CHILLI CON CARNE

Ingredients

Packet of dried chilli con carne
Cress to taste
Water

Method

1. Boil water (more soupy, less for gloopy)
2. Add chilli. Stir and cook until kidney beans are edible (spoon out a couple of beef chunks to chew on whilst cooking)
3. Add snipped cress as desired
4. Eat straight from the pan
(Helpful hint: burn the chilli slightly, tastes divine)

Tales from the aquarium

Well, the fish are happily swimming along; they seem more content now that we're moving a bit quicker. No end of bird life has visited us. We were amazed when a gorgeous brown bird came. We've called him 'Little Noddy' because he is just that - a brown noddy. He pottered about the deck and the cabin roof, skidding on his webbed feet. Mum was very excited. After sitting quietly for some time with her arm out, he came and stood right on it without a care in the world. Mum was grinning like a mad thing, speaking between gritted teeth, desperate not to frighten him away. We think he's discovered our potential for flying fish, which are dying in their hundreds on our deck.

Two enormous flappy fish are regulars around the hull, we've named them Barry White and James

Brown.

I've just been out to row and we've seen WHALES
- three of them, two adults and one calf! Mum and I
thought the same thing: we brought our oars in as
quickly as possible, both concerned these twenty-
ton mammals might hurt themselves on the cocktail
sticks that are our blades. They didn't stay very
long but they have brightened our day no end. One
eyeballed us for about ten minutes, Mum splashing
the water to see if they would come any closer. They
weren't having any of it. But WHALES! How utterly
amazing. We've both had a quick butchers through the
Offshore Wildlife book and agree they were probably
pygmy sperm whales and they're quite rarely sighted.

So, here's to good winds and thanks to all those who
took part in the peg sacrifice, at last it seems to
be working.

Lots of love,

Sally 'aching all over' & Sarah 'desperate not to
burn' Kettle

I think Mum and I were as amazed as everybody else at how
well we actually got on. It was certainly one in the eye for
the psychologists who'd predicted disaster. We worked well
together because we gave each other space, we respected our
idiosyncrasies and, most importantly, we were kind to each
other – this really was a lesson worth learning and I can thank
Mum for teaching me it.

It started on the first day. Mum would lay out my sleeping

bag ready for me to jump into as soon as my shift was over. I followed her lead and did the same for her. We made each other's chocolate mousse exactly as we liked it. Mum preferred a milkshake consistency whereas I loved it so thick you could actually stand your spoon up in the bowl.

It was these little things that made us a great team. We would always put the other first. We were also silly ... we did stupid things, like name our fish. We really did try to have fun, but I can't lie and say there weren't darker times when we just didn't see eye to eye, and in the light of recent events stress levels on board had escalated. Yet we'd remained friends.

In any expedition arguments are seen as par for the course and for us there were plenty of minor grievances to sort out, although once aired these were soon sorted. I lost my new watch in the first week and then insisted on asking Mum for the time every five minutes. A quick blast, and we decided it was best to leave all time-keeping equipment in the cabin – including Mum's watch, a small digital alarm clock and the GPS. It became the 'off-duty' oarswoman's responsibility to keep an eye on the time. Problem solved.

Unfortunately now, after days of frustration due to the unfavourable winds, I was finding it difficult to stay positive and became increasingly irritable. Every night I'd moan tearfully, having worked out just how little we'd rowed during the day. To try and ease the disappointment I decided to chart our progress on the map every few days. That didn't work quite so well when we started going backwards! Our speed, or lack of it, was really beginning to grate on me. I sat in the cabin watching the minutes on the GPS tick by slowly ... so ... incredibly ... slowly ... I was a real bundle of laughs!

Eventually Mum lost it with me. We were about to swap places; I'd just been in the cabin lamenting our lack of progress, again, and I probably came out on deck looking like a wet weekend. I can't remember what I said to trigger it, maybe something along the lines of 'We've hardly done shit again today,' or something equally eloquent – I had a mouth like a swamp by this point.

Mum wailed, out of the blue, 'You're just like your Dad, you're both trying to force me to go at your pace. Every time we go cycling your Dad races ahead of me, expecting me to keep up. I hate it. Stop going on about the bloody mileage! I'm doing my best!'

She must have been worrying that I was blaming her for our lack of progress. But why didn't she just talk to me about it? Why did she have to lose her temper? I wasn't prepared to put up with it.

'Don't you dare say I'm like Dad!' I screamed back at her. 'I've never told you to row harder, I've never judged you! Do you expect me to be happy with this situation? Well I'm not, and I'm sorry! It's not your fault, nor mine. It's just shit!'

I leapt into the cabin and tried to slam the door shut behind me, unfortunately the sealant around the doorframe didn't allow it to slam properly. So I pulled it to, as furiously as possible. I did feel surprisingly proud of myself. Not because I'd upset Mum, but because it was the first time I'd defended myself without fear of her reprisal.

Once I'd sheepishly stepped back out on deck it didn't take us long to come up with a plan to make life on board a little easier. I promised not to talk mileage and we both resolved to spend our break times out on deck to keep each other company.

We were both so lonely out on the oars. It gave us too much time to think and negative thoughts had a tendency to circulate. Mum disappeared into the front cabin and fished out a sarong I'd stowed, although I have no idea why I'd packed it– maybe I thought it would be great to wear during Sunday lunch. She then delved deeper into the cabin for some string and the knife. Together we tied the sarong to a cleat on the side of the cabin, stretched it across to the fully extended boat hook, which we'd lashed out at an angle from the footwell, and pegged the flappy edges to string pulled taut between the oars that ran along the side of the boat. Our creation – an awning, providing a shaded glen fit for one. With knees tucked up to our chests we could squeeze into the footwell on our 'off' hour, enjoy the cool breeze and a chinwag whilst listening to the minidisc player, which we'd shoved into a poly bag because the on-deck speakers had died over a month before.

Although cramped, with pins and needles from the waist down, we were happy again – it saved us from the sauna cabin and the GPS and we looked instead at the ocean, the endless sky and the occasional happy-flappy fish. The phone rarely rang and, as I could now finger type at 100 wpm, there was no need to spend too much time away from Mum. Having realised how lonely it can get out on the boat, we'd found a solution – we'd just have to ignore the fact that we'd broken another regatta rule. No awnings![18]

[18] For safety reasons awnings were discouraged because they could potentially affect the boat self-righting. We took the risk because the weather was so good. I certainly wouldn't recommend it to other rowers.

Skipper's Log

24.04.04   Started going backwards after rudder set! V. strange
            & upsetting, hardly went anywhere at one point.
            Worried GPS not working: because we were
            stationary! New flying fish species, one with v.
            long point from head. Both pissed off at slowness
            again. Struggle to keep speed. Rowed together half
            day. Ocean even greener. More birds. Strange
            choppy areas. Sea goes mad, then quiet. Dad
            & family flying out 3 May.

27.04.04   Horrendous night, stormy, wet & v. rolling. Mum
            suffering with allergies, me with leg. Hardly slept,
            both of us. Door blind falling off, v. annoying. Went
            N in night, losing ground there - promise of NE by
            Friday. Breaking a record with 30 mins in a day!!
            Lost to the N though. Strong winds, lots of rain.
            Ruddered all day. Ate too much chocolate. Zooming
            along! Little Noddy & friend on roof, hundreds
            of birds & frigates. Long day.

28.04.04   V. sore bums from sitting on rudder. Tommo arrives
            in Barbados tomorrow!

29.04.04   Big winds & waves. Impossible to row, only ran
            watermaker for hr because clouds & power. Noddy
            came & sat on my head / foot! Much pain in legs.
            Made absolutely no distance S. Might not get there.

30.04.04   Noddy on boat all day. Only 134 miles to Big B!! I was v. sick after chilli, both took ProPlus to stay out later, made it till 12.00 am!!

02.05.04   Zooming along. Held course. Hoping tonight does the same. So close now. V. dull day, final shower & shave! Still feeling dodgy & so no dinner. Hopefully tomorrow will be last full day. Tony should be in Big B by now. Both nervous & excited!

03.05.04   Really pleased with track during night. V. gentle seas as well. Didn't drift too far N. Steady progress W. Almost there! Noddies galore! Three on boat today! Amazing sunset. Both v. excited. Good distance, should see land tomorrow morning. Mum desperate to see red light! Haven't decided whether to stay up all night yet. Sam, Dad, Lines arrived today!

04.04.04   Mum saw land 9.40 am!! Time to get out there & get home!

From: Sally
To: Jane
Date: 4 May 2004
Re: *Calderdale* Calling

WE DID IT!!
N14.18
W59.29

Lots of love
Sally & Sarah x

TEN

Dug Deep, Rowed Hard and Rowed Together

From: Sally
To: Jane
Date: 17 May 2004
Re: *Calderdale* Calling: The Final Chapter

I'm sitting in my bedroom, on a bed that doesn't move. I can stretch my legs and dive to the fridge for food I actually enjoy eating, and I'm feeling good!

It's been nearly two weeks since we rowed into Port St Charles and everything we've been told about the elation, the relief and the briefest feelings of sadness that the journey has come to the end are all true. And now it feels like a dream. After staying the night tied to a quarantine buoy after an arduous row around the island, our families and friends were on the harbour ready to see us in. What more can you want after 105 days at sea?

The last few days of our row were so exciting. We thought we'd see the red light blinking from the tallest tower on Barbados, but we were disappointed. The Caribbean is in the midst of the rainy season and the island was covered with a thick layer of grey cloud. So the last few days went something like this …

Saturday (Mum)	'I can't see the light.'
Sunday	'I'm looking and I still can't see it.'
Monday	'Nope, nothing there!'
Tuesday	'AAARRRRRR … ARRRR … [gasping for air] … I can see land, I can see land!'

Mum was flapping like an over-excited goose! She was pointing like a mad woman towards the horizon, at a distinct line just millimetres above the sea. If I'd known Mum's morning wee would be so eventful I would have tried to beat her to it.

We were twenty-six miles away from 'the line' and what baffled me was the fact that I'd run the London marathon in five hours fifteen minutes, but the twenty-six miles ahead of us would take us nearly two days. How did that happen? I have to admit I'm a runner built for comfort, not for speed, so my pace was pretty much that of a hip-wiggling speed walker, yet our rowing pace was even slower than that.

We went to the oars with newfound vigour, the birds guiding us in as we desperately tried to stay on course. I'd been panicking that the boat would suddenly drift and we'd not hit Barbados. But we'd managed to make an excellent track towards the island, the 'cone of success' being between 13°15 and 13°18, and we were heading for 13°17.

We snailed (a new word(?), but quite apt I think) ever closer to the line. But it's not unusual for Mum and me to make fools of ourselves and even at the eleventh hour we managed to get ourselves into an embarrassing situation. We were told by someone in La Gomera that the finish line passed through the most easterly tip of Barbados, so as we crossed this longitude Mum and I danced around the boat, excited to the point of hysteria! We'd done it! By ourselves across the ocean, mother and daughter … FANTASTIC! Two hours later *Kilcullen* called. Mum answered …

'We're coming to get you.'

'Are you? Why?'

'Oh … well … We were expecting a call from you.'

'Were you?'

'Who is this?'

'Sarah! Who are you?'

'It's Phil! Well, we'll just come and see you in then!'

'Ok.'

Mum was perplexed to say the least. They were coming to tow us in, she told me. We hadn't asked for a tow. We didn't think we needed one. But they were coming. We would just have to make it very clear that they were coming nowhere near our boat with a towing line. Not so much as a shoelace would pass between us until we'd made it safely into Port St Charles.

Having decided we'd probably not make it to port before dark, we pottered along, grinning, and wondering whether our family were looking out for us.

Kilcullen's mast soon appeared on the horizon.

'Right, Mum, look busy!'

As they drew up beside us, we were happily told that the line was only half a mile away. WHAT?

'Act cool, Sal, and don't say anything,' Mum said.

I was straight on the blower …

'So, just to clarify, the line is half a mile away, so we haven't crossed it yet? [Not that we didn't know where the finish line was!] Just making sure … you know how it is … too many days at sea and so on.'

Bugger. We'd got it wrong … how embarrassing. Oh well, we could celebrate with an audience this time. Five hours later, with *Kilcullen* by our side, her crew constantly shouting at us, having had a brief visit from the BBC on another yacht, Mum and I tied up for the night just outside Port St Charles.

Battling headwinds and desperately trying to stay as close to land as possible, we rowed non-stop, digging deep, rowing hard and rowing together in the pitch black with only the mast lights of *Kilcullen* and the dark silhouettes of the cement factory on the shoreline to guide us. From our quarantine buoy we heard distant shouts from the harbour wall. Breaking a few rules of the sea I lit a white collision flare to signal our arrival. We'd made it, unsupported, by ourselves, across an ocean, 3,000 miles, and now we were just metres from land and the people we loved. We slept well that night!

We spent two glorious weeks in Barbados, getting our legs working again, enjoying being clean and strutting around in bikinis, having dealt with the hair issue! Being skinny wasn't going to last long, so we definitely made the most of it.

Now to a different life and different challenges. We're nervous but excited, I'm planning to write a book on the entire experience, and maybe if you've enjoyed reading these diaries you'll enjoy reading that. Mum's back to gardening and not planning her solo trip across the Pacific. It's amazing how many people fell for that April Fool's trick! Anyway, I suppose this is it. The Challenge will tie up in the next couple of months. Our major sponsor the Mayor will soon be coming to the end of her term so there'll be a few events to celebrate her year and her support for the row. I'll be revisiting the schools I went to see last year, showing them how the boat has stood up to the ocean and how we have too. It's going to be great. Maybe we will get to see you, the readers, soon too.

WOW, what an adventure xx

Lots of love,

Sally & Sarah

~

IT TOOK ME ages to write about this final part of the journey and I seem to have left a lot out. At this point, I really couldn't be bothered to write anymore. On land, with so much to do and see, I didn't feel the need to fill my days with thoughts of witty prose. But, remembering it now, our arrival in Barbados was pretty incredible. Of all the teams only three managed to make it into harbour without a tow or a rescue. Mum and I were one of those three! Also, with the conditions the way they had been, sending us north then sending us backwards, it still amazes me that we made it to the island at all.

Unless you've spent a long time at sea, or maybe in the desert, you may not appreciate the dramatic impact the sight of land can have – that lush greenness that surrounds us every day is something we can often take for granted. But you can imagine our awe as the island slowly spread across our horizon, its features sharpening – trees, houses, cars, then people and birds. We were totally captivated by its sounds and smells. It was a sensation ten times that of any I'd ever experienced before. After four months at sea nothing could compare to the beauty of Barbados.

As the sun set and the stars slowly filled the sky we stared up into the heavens knowing this would probably be the last time we would see them looking quite so stunning, uninterrupted by buildings and not drowned out by an orange haze of artificial lights. I think we were both surprised to feel an almost overwhelming sense of sadness. I had spent so much time wishing myself home and now, so close to stepping off the boat, I wished it would never end.

We rowed along in the dark and revelled in the distant hum of cars, the mixed babble of people enjoying dinner in the beachfront restaurants and the chattering tickerty-tick of insects. The air was full of the organic sweetness of freshly cut grass. This was 'land'.

From our buoy, we heard voices calling from the harbour wall. It was so dark we couldn't even see shadows, just a torchlight waving about in mid air. We instantly recognised my Dad as he called over and Mum couldn't contain her excitement. I felt so relieved: Mum's promise never to talk to him again had been an 'in-the-moment' thing, but I suspected my Dad was still going to get a rollocking! There was a voice we didn't recognise (Tony's?) and my brother's — all three were tripping over themselves to shout out.

'We love you both!'

'We missed you so much!'

'We're so proud of you!'

Tearful and laughing, we called back, promising to see them in the morning, telling them to be up at dawn because we weren't going to wait for them!

As the torchlight disappeared, I turned to Mum and said, 'Shall we put the kettle on?' And with a cup of tea and some chocolate mousse we jumped into the cabin for the last time.

From our experiences in La Gomera we knew all too well that ocean rowing boats are fantastic in the vast expanse of the ocean but they're absolutely useless in confined spaces. At 5.00 am, as we began to steer ourselves carefully into Port St Charles, I was ordering Mum as she sat at the oars. 'Right a bit. Pull a bit harder. Left. No, the other left!' We meandered within a hair's breadth of several multi-million-pound yachts: we were somewhat magnetically pulled towards their glossy white hulls, drifting ever nearer to an insurance nightmare, whilst a crowd of spectators cheered from the pontoon.

We pulled up to our mooring beautifully. Who says women can't parallel park? It was an odd experience, nobody wanted to come close to us, there was a strange 'respectable distance' being kept. Maybe they'd heard we'd been on the quarantine buoy for the night and thought we'd caught something contagious – the dreaded 'rowers' bottom', perhaps?

Mum didn't get off the boat for ages, in fact my Dad had to step aboard and collect her! He clung to her for a long time and they whispered to each other in their embrace. Tommo was there for me on the pontoon, a welcome sight of curly dark hair and tortoise shell glasses. He swelled with pride as I clambered overboard to wrap my arms around him.

I could hear Malcolm behind me. 'They've kept the boat nice and tidy!' he exclaimed. Releasing myself from Tommo I went over and squeezed him hard.

'Well done. We're so proud of you.'

'Thank you for everything. Jane, you too,' I replied and I meant it. I most certainly would have loved Jane to be there. I think she would have enjoyed the experience. Perhaps it would have healed a few wounds.

My nephew Lincoln couldn't contain his relief and, as Mum grabbed him close, he sobbed. So many faces and so many hugs, and with a rum and coke in my hand and the virgin version in Mum's, we finally wobbled off the pontoon and on to dry land.

We knew my Gran had also been watching us in. My Uncle Paul had logged on to the Internet and found the webcam feed that 'beamed' footage straight from the harbour. I still find it incredible how technology allows these things, and although my Gran probably didn't know how to turn the computer on, she had, in fact, become a silver surfer at the age of seventy! We spoke to her on my brother's mobile, waving frantically.

The voice that we hadn't recognised soon identified itself and Mum couldn't believe her eyes. With a double take, she questioned, 'Brian?' Her elder brother (and, I later found out, her comrade, confidant and partner in crime when they were children), who she hadn't seen for almost twenty years, had been lurking in the background waiting for the penny to drop. My Dad had co-ordinated his arrival. It's a long and complicated story as to why he had disappeared, to the Bahamas in fact, and maybe it's one only my mother should tell. Either way, my Dad most certainly scored some Brownie points there!

Kenneth Crutchlow grabbed hold of us before we had a chance to say hello to him. Arms aloft, he boomed to the gathering: 'Sally and Sarah Kettle, the first mother and daughter team to row the Atlantic! Go on, give them a clap!' And with that he whisked us off to passport control. I say whisked, I mean wobbled, the land legs had not yet kicked in and because our calf and thigh muscles had atrophied we weren't able to support ourselves properly. What a perfect excuse to grab hold of a couple of men!

With passports stamped, the words '*Calderdale: The Yorkshire Challenger*' handwritten around the inky mark, and a quick trip to the loo made (porcelain heaven!), my brother led us round to a yacht we narrowly missed. Looking slightly perplexed, the cricketers Ian Botham and David Gower greeted us from the decks. A quick photo of Ian, Mum and me in a pleasant clinch and it was off to ORS HQ to talk to the press, and then to the hotel, where beds were ready and waiting to cocoon us within their clean cotton sheets and soft fluffy pillows. The shower was also beckoning …

~

I COULDN'T SLEEP. After a hectic day unpacking, settling into the hotel and having our first and surprisingly ordinary meal (there was no firework display on our taste buds – it was just food, like food we had every day at home, it didn't taste any better or any worse) I remember feeling very jealous that my family were now enjoying time with Mum.

Having laid awake for over an hour, my body gently swaying as if I was slung in a hammock, I decided to go for a swim. It was 4.00 am as I sneaked out of my room, leaving Tommo half in and half out of the sheets. Padding silently across the still-warm tiles towards the pool, I thought I'd go and see if Mum was up. I found both my parents sitting on their porch looking out to the sparking sea. Having spotted me skulking in the bushes below them they called me up and we sat together and talked until the sun rose.

We had two weeks of family holiday bliss with Tommo, Tony, Malcolm, two of my sister's friends and Andrew, our new man from the BBC, tagging along. We regularly nipped down to ORS HQ to see how Henry Dale[19] and *Moose on the Move* were doing ... they were still out there battling with the weather.

We took trips around the island, Dad's 'no-expense-spared' way of saying how proud he was of us. I even bought a bright orange summer dress that I knew would probably never fit me again and a pair of high heels. For all the festering, I did miss that little bit of glamour.

Mum and I did go to Villa Nova in the end. We called them and asked if they would be happy to have us for a couple of days and they were all too pleased to look after us. With that, we made arrangements to stay on after everyone had caught their flights home. I'm glad we didn't stay there for the duration: it was a luxurious tranquil paradise, not a place where Lincoln and his friend could divebomb into the pool.

We were alone, together again, sharing a room and the same bed! We were well looked after, although the tea-making facilities left a lot to be desired. There weren't any. Mum had to order a cuppa from room service and it arrived on a big silver tray with every cup, saucer and sugar bowl hidden dramatically under its own individual silver lid. I have to admit it was a little bit posh for us. We tried not to spend anything, eating the biscuits from the tea tray for dinner because we hadn't the guts to ask if hospitality included any meals!

I struck up a conversation with a very wealthy American

---

[19] Henry's friends had come over especially to see him in, having travelled around the world from Australia, but their flights left before he had arrived so they missed each other.

businessman – quintessentially groomed, his teeth gleamed with a set of rather overpowering da Vinci veneers. I truly believed he was interested in the row, he asked to see my etchings (sorry, pictures!) and he promised to talk to his 'contacts' about the publication of a coffee-table book and accompanying tour of the States. It seemed too good to be true … and it was. We met for dinner in London some six months later – to discuss the book, I thought – but as his hand edged across the table, clasping mine in a vice-like grip, I sensed he wanted to go further than my contents page. He promised me ski-ing trips in Colorado, a beach-front villa in Barbados. I could stay in his penthouse apartment in downtown Manhattan. I could bring Mum! All were fabulous offers … if only he wasn't in his sixties.

'What would it feel like if you kissed me now?' he crooned in my ear at the end of the evening.

Like kissing my Grandad! I thought, before swerving the da Vincis.

During the next year I would have my slightly unexpected fair share of proposals from the affluent Saga generation. Can I put that down as one of the benefits of the row? Erm … perhaps not!

ELEVEN

'Don't You Know Who I Am?'

WE RETURNED HOME feeling like heroes returning from a bloody battle, the jubilation of our achievement carrying our tired and scrawny bodies through the decorated front door of my parents' house. Dad and the neighbours, the Stumpies, had made a 'Welcome Home' banner and surrounded it with a multicoloured array of balloons.

The house was exactly the same as we'd left it four months earlier, except we'd missed spring and the garden was practically in full bloom. Pip, Mum's Yorkshire terrier, skidded about on the laminate floor, leaping up our legs to greet us. The rest of the animals were frankly non-plussed!

I placed my heavy suitcase on the bed and looked out at the flourishing back garden. Being home again felt as comfortable as an old cardigan. I'd saved the exercise book I had so studiously scribbled in, I'd been sure to pick it up from the boat, which had been packed up in Barbados and was now sitting in a container aboard a banana boat bound for Falmouth. Leafing through it I found lists of things I intended to do upon my return. There was so much to do, but the cold reality of life back home soon became apparent as I found out that I'd be living at my parents' pleasure for a little longer. After the fiasco of evicting my tenant before Christmas I'd decided to put my Brighton flat on the market, asking Dad to keep an eye on the 'guaranteed sale' (or so the estate agents said). It had been on the market the entire time we were away but hadn't sold. In fact, there was a pile of demand letters from the mortgage company gathered on the mantelpiece, as my savings hadn't been able to cover the outstanding payments. I was in a bit of a predicament.

Having not worked since August the previous year I was already well over my overdraft limit, and with my savings spent, the debt was beginning to spiral out of control. By now I had already defaulted a month's mortgage payment. It was time for a trip to the bank and the job centre. Hardly the glamorous life of a triumphantly returning ocean explorer.

As I sat in the dining room fretting over final demand letters, I wished myself back on the boat, where deciding whether to eat chilli con carne or chicken curry was the most taxing decision you had to make.

~

THE PROJECT 'PROPER' didn't end until late 2005. There were schools to revisit, parties to attend and after-dinner speeches to give. Jane, Malcolm and Geraldine were up to their eyeballs tying off the loose ends, gathering the final donations and thanking thousands of sponsors and supporters. Together the team raised an incredible £268,000, an absolutely remarkable sum. Not quite £1,000,000, but close! I can only imagine the outcome if I'd called The Fund for Epilepsy and said we'd raise £20,000 instead. I'm so glad we set our sights so high.

Mum and I enjoyed our fifteen minutes of fame. We were invited to appear on BBC breakfast news, we took part in studio chats with presenters on all the local news programmes – in fact, our story had been syndicated around the globe by The Press Association, people had heard about our adventure from Pakistan to Kuala Lumpur. We were asked for an interview by CNN in the States, which was very exciting, but it was a shame they didn't invite us over – we spoke on the telephone!

We even stood on the lawns outside Parliament, nipping along for an interview with the BBC before heading off to the ORS presentation party where we picked up our certificate of completion, along with the other rowers from the regatta. What a privilege it was to see them all again. Although every single one of us had had a very different experience it really did feel like we'd all been there together.

For Mum and me our media experience was all very Z-list celebrity stuff, until we were catapulted into the limelight (ok, on to the Y-list) with a stint on the cult daytime television show

Ready, Steady, Cook!

During our twilight rows I'd joke with Mum about the programmes we'd love to go on. We'd rate them out of twenty and row the number of strokes they'd scored. For example, *Parkinson* scored a twenty, and so off I'd row at a blistering pace imagining us sitting on the black leather seats. *Richard and Judy* scored a good fifteen, whilst Jonathan Ross only a modest ten. *Ready, Steady, Cook!* – well, we rowed all night for *Ready, Steady, Cook!*

I downloaded the application form for the show and, to our surprise, they loved our story and invited us on. Mum was a red tomato and I was a green pepper. Mum cooked with the chef Nick Nairn and I had Brian Turner. And you'll never guess what we had to cook with? Bloody rice! (Oh, and some pineapple chunks.) I lost by one vote, which meant that Mum walked away with £100 and I went home with a hamper, containing a knife to stab her in the back with. She spent her hard-earned winnings on an ottoman for the landing at the top of the stairs – how disappointing!

Soon after the show went to air people stopped Mum in the streets of Northampton – we put it down to her distinctive ginger hair. She'd gained a loyal fan club at La Fontana's, my parents' favourite Saturday morning greasy spoon cafe. (Their staff had got to know my Dad pretty well – he was often in there drowning his sorrows with a full English breakfast.)

But Mum soon tired of the 'celebrity lifestyle' and decided that after *Ready, Steady, Cook!* she wouldn't do any more interviews, although she did agree to come with me to an audition for *Deal Or No Deal*. She was definitely relieved when she wasn't called to take part.

~

WITH SO MANY exciting things happening I was very conscious
of not wasting the opportunity to change my own life. After
all, that had been the point of the row: to learn new skills, gain
some confidence and eventually find a career that suited me.
So, although I didn't have a penny to my name, I decided not
to find work as a waitress, refused a job as a barmaid and was
resolute about not wanting to work in a factory again (much to
my mother's disappointment!). Instead I signed on for the first
time in my life and volunteered at the local BBC radio station,
with the intention of learning the ropes and applying for any
upcoming jobs. It had been an ambition of mine for as long as I
can remember to work the BBC. I had visited radio stations on a
number of occasions and found the medium incredibly exciting,
so I reluctantly stayed on benefit whilst voluntarily learning the
tricks of the DJ's trade.

Anyway, financially I had a fallback plan. Tommo and I had
signed a contract with Jane and Malcolm, giving us a modest
recompense for the money we'd raised for the charity. It would
only be paid out if we raised a substantial sum, so there wouldn't
be huge monetary gains for the team. It was more a goodwill
gesture for two years' hard work.

I called Jane and Malcolm to ask them about this. A brief
email from Jane explained the situation. It seemed the trustees
hadn't actually approved the contract. It had been hellishly busy
before we left so Jane and Malcolm probably didn't think to
mention it, and anyway, who could foresee the catalogue of
disasters that would lead to my financial demise? I lamented

the fact that, if the contract had been honoured, there would have been just enough to get me out of this tight spot with the mortgage company. So, I was back with my parents and on the dole and I have to admit I was pissed off. I mean I was *really* pissed off!

Perhaps unrealistically, I'd expected Jane and Malcolm to empathise with the situation. After all, it was also their hard work that had enabled the project to get off the ground so they must have been feeling the pinch too. But my worries were brushed off with the stress of pulling the project to a close.

I soon realised the only way I would be able cope with the disappointment of my predicament was to move on from Epic Challenge entirely — no more fund-raising, no more events. Contact with Jane and Malcolm slowly fizzled out and life went on.

Part of the 'moving on' process included Tommo. The physical distance between us became a natural barrier to any ongoing relationship. Also, having made the decision before we left, four months at sea had only given me more time to think about it and I had come to the same conclusion — our relationship was over.

I drove down to Brighton, and over a very brief and tearful meeting we parted ways, ending a five-year loving but essentially tempestuous relationship. I returned to Northampton single but relieved.

I never thought our return to the UK would be so fraught with difficulties but I did learn two very important lessons that summer ...

- We should have considered the project as a business – the stress related to such an incredibly expensive financial and emotional undertaking would probably have been better handled if we had approached it in a more professional and businesslike fashion
- Don't ever row with your boyfriend/girlfriend unless you are prepared for it to make or break your relationship

A month after my first benefit cheque came through, BBC Radio Northampton asked me to apply for a job as a producer – and I got it!

Part Three

The Rowgirls Family Tree

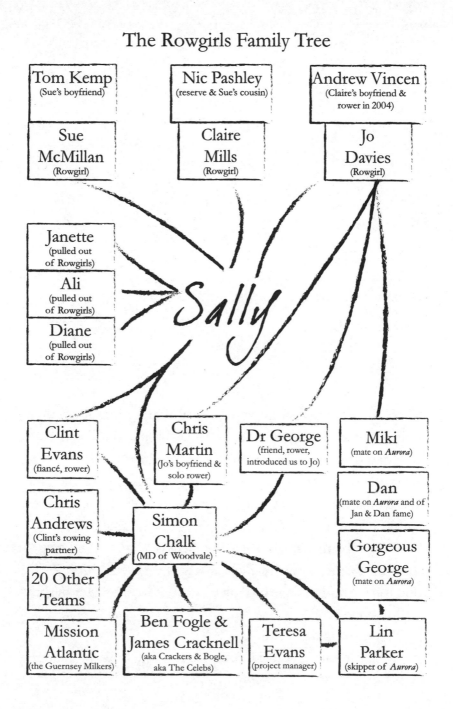

Tom Kemp (Sue's boyfriend)

Nic Pashley (reserve & Sue's cousin)

Andrew Vincen (Claire's boyfriend & rower in 2004)

Sue McMillan (Rowgirl)

Claire Mills (Rowgirl)

Jo Davies (Rowgirl)

Janette (pulled out of Rowgirls)

Ali (pulled out of Rowgirls)

Diane (pulled out of Rowgirls)

Sally

Clint Evans (fiancé, rower)

Chris Martin (Jo's boyfriend & solo rower)

Dr George (friend, rower, introduced us to Jo)

Miki (mate on *Aurora*)

Chris Andrews (Clint's rowing partner)

Simon Chalk (MD of Woodvale)

Dan (mate on *Aurora* and of Jan & Dan fame)

20 Other Teams

Gorgeous George (mate on *Aurora*)

Mission Atlantic (the Guernsey Milkers)

Ben Fogle & James Cracknell (aka Crackers & Bogle, aka The Celebs)

Teresa Evans (project manager)

Lin Parker (skipper of *Aurora*)

TWELVE

Go Go Rowgirls

'Don't be so stupid, Sally, you'll never skipper a women's four,' Mum spat as we sat out on deck discussing the April Fool's Day diary entry I'd been composing. I'd already decided to tell everyone that Mum would be rowing across the Pacific alone and to make it sound more realistic I thought I'd juxtapose it with my own seemingly improbable plans for adventure.

The problem was I'd started to believe that I could skipper the first women's four, which is why I'd asked Mum for her opinion on it, thinking she'd give her full backing. Her negative reply stunned me.

'Why not?' I replied, hurt.

'Well, for a start, you like your bed too much. Would you row through the night?'

'Erm, yeah, I would if we were racing.'

Mum's eyebrows raised. End of conversation.

I harrumphed around the boat for a bit, arrogantly reassuring myself that Mum had no idea what she was talking about. I couldn't believe she doubted my capabilities, even now, after two months at sea! She'd been all too happy to nominate me skipper for this trip. So what the hell did she know?

An email arrived a day or two after I'd sent the Fool's Day diary. It was from a young woman called Claire Mills. She reminded me that we'd met in Northampton. She was a pretty strawberry blonde, with a toned, sporty physique and an even, confident demeanour. I specifically remembered her because, rather unnervingly, my Dad's eyes began to twinkle when she came to talk to us! Dad and I had been shaking buckets and she'd come over to take a look at the boat. His obvious attraction to this young woman was only amplified when she told him she played women's rugby! She'd also mentioned her own plans to row the Atlantic as a pair, and what a coincidence that we were there with an ocean rowing boat just days after that decision. Her email went on to say: 'If you decide to go as the first women's four, I'd love to do it. Would you consider me for the team?'

~

DIANE, A TALL, feisty, dark-haired woman in her late thirties collared me at one of the Fund's final fund-raising dos.

'I read your diary about going as a women's four. I want to do

243

it. I've competed in indoor rowing championships, but I can't row properly. I mean, I've been on the river, but that doesn't matter, right?'

With everything that was going on I hadn't really given it too much thought.

'I haven't decided yet, but if I do, yeah, you can definitely come!'

I took her card and said I'd call her.

~

WHEN ALI EMAILED I realised someone was trying to tell me something! Ali's husband, Matt, had taken part in the regatta as one of the solo rowers. It had been his fourth and probably final attempt to make it across. Previously prevented from doing so by a series of unfortunate mishaps, he found himself all the more determined to succeed. He built his own boat – he found the twenty-four-foot design wouldn't fit into his garage, so he built one that did. All sixteen feet of it! Ali had become an ocean rowing widow, and after so many years of supporting her husband's seagoing exploits it was her turn to give it a go.

I now had my first women's four!

~

TO GIVE YOU a little bit of background ... Chay Blyth decided to sell the ocean rowing race side of Challenge Business, having probably discovered that, as a race organiser, you can never ever please all of the people all of the time. Tommo and I hadn't been party to any of the political infighting because we weren't racing, but it had become a tradition that the pontoons would become white hot with contention, rowers complaining that other boats weren't rule compliant, skegs were too low, rudders too long or too short … accusations of cheating abounded. So Chay offered it to Woodvale Events soon after the completion of the race in 2003.

Woodvale – managed by ex-ocean rower Simon Chalk – kept the overall format, promising to continue running biennial races from the Canaries. The next event would take place in December 2005. Leaving from La Gomera, crews would this time head for English Harbour, Antigua, and not Port St Charles, Barbados. This was as good an excuse as any to take part – why go to Barbados twice?

I spoke to Simon about my plans to enter and he was keen to offer me first dibs on a newly designed ocean fours' boat. At thirty feet long, the structure was a moulded polycarbonate kevlar sandwich instead of laser-cut plywood. The cabins at both ends of the boat were big enough to accommodate all four rowers and, according to Simon, it would beat all known speed records as it was sleeker, faster and more robust than any rowing boat ever built.

Well, I needed a boat, and *Calderdale* had been sold to an American, so I placed my order with the caveat that I would only buy it (when the sponsors had come on board of course!) if he painted it lip-gloss pink. The deal was done.

~

The First of the First Women's Fours

My decision to go was primarily to prove to myself that I could run a successful project without being financially screwed. Secondly, there were way too many men in the sport and something had to be done about it! Only fifteen women had ever attempted an ocean row before Mum and me, compared to around a hundred men. Finally, I had to prove to my mother that I could skipper a winning team and, although I do like my bed, when the chips are down I'd be out there at 3.00 am, digging deep and rowing hard!

I spoke to the three women, confirming their keenness to participate and, having felt reassured that they were 100 per cent behind the project, Team Rowgirls was tentatively born.

Logistically, project management was a nightmare. The team really couldn't have been more spread out. Diane was based in Halifax, Ali in Norfolk, Claire in Dunstable and I was in Northampton. The only positive side was the potential to target several local media centres at once. If we were able to talk all the local press into supporting us the likelihood of generating sponsorship would be greatly increased.

It seemed to take us forever to organise anything. Months passed by incredibly quickly with very little progress made at all. Scheduling team meetings had been nigh-on impossible – Ali and Di had children, making their schedules a lot less flexible than Claire's and mine. With two little ones, Ali found it very difficult to get to any meetings outside of Norfolk, and although Di's kids were in their teens her demanding job as a sales executive left her with little time to spare.

Claire and I were regularly getting together to lay the foundations for the project, although she'd long planned a year-long trip to Australia after university. However, the row was important to her and she reduced the length of her stay to six months. But without her, the team felt increasingly disparate.

Team Rowgirls #1 was, perhaps inevitably, doomed to failure and with less than a year to the start of the Woodvale Ocean Race 2005 it looked like this particular project was never going to get off the ground.

On December 26 2004 an earthquake triggered one of the most devastating tsunamis in recent history. Thailand was amongst the worst-hit places, and hundreds of thousands of people lost their lives. Claire was out there on her way back from Australia. Her parents were away over Christmas and New Year and I'd promised to pick her up from the airport on New Year's Eve.

Sick with worry, I sat at my desk at Radio Northampton checking my emails for any news. I just hoped that Claire knew we would be desperate to hear from her, that she'd be able to find a telephone or an Internet connection and reassure us that she was safe. I sobbed as I sat in the silent offices. I turned on the TVs so I could follow the news in the hope of seeing a message from Claire amongst those scrolling along the bottom of the screens.

Three days passed, the death toll rising. The devastation was almost beyond belief, towns completely destroyed, everything gone.

Claire's email arrived on 30 December and I wept as I read it. She was safe, well and amazed that she hadn't been caught up in the disaster. When she arrived in Bangkok her plan was to catch a bus to Phuket, but everything was booked solid, so instead she caught a bus and travelled north, missing the tsunami entirely.

I travelled with my Dad to Heathrow to pick her up. When she finally emerged I gave her a huge hug, which I hoped would convey the relief of not only myself but of all her family and friends. Only days later I found out that a friend from Brighton, Jez Stephens, had died in Phuket. His friends had returned to their hotel after the waves had subsided only to find him missing. He was probably washed out of the window, having drowned in his sleep – they later found his body in a temple and were able to bring him home to his family. He died leaving a three-year-old daughter and a pregnant girlfriend.

~

WE MET UP for a bonding weekend at Di's house at the end of January. We thought it would be a good idea to spend some time together and talk through a plan of action for the next twelve months. Claire had recently introduced us to her friend Nic, a slender blonde, who I instantly got on with. Her background was river rowing and running, so when she expressed an interest in being our reserve rower both Claire and I thought she'd be the ideal candidate. So we invited her to along too. Mum had jokingly agreed to be our second reserve.

Di had a small study at the back of her house, with an adjoining bathroom. We decided it would be a fantastic idea to lock ourselves in for the entire forty-eight hours, in an inspired attempt to replicate the confined space of the boat. Di also had a rowing machine we could jump on. So, armed with sleeping bags, pens, paper, loo roll, gym kit and more humus than we could possibly eat we dived in and locked the door.

We made a pact not to leave the room under any circumstances and Claire proposed we row ten kilometres each before we left. I also installed a camcorder in the toilet (loo-cam) just in case any of us wanted to record our own personal thoughts during our confinement. Welcome to hell!

Day one in the Little Sister house

The planning went rather well. We brainstormed sponsors, discussed the pros and cons of supporting a charity and stressed over the amount of money we needed to raise. It was an eye opener for the girls. I don't think they realised quite how expensive it would be. I made it clear we would have to put the time in and find enough sponsors to pay for every aspect of our challenge.

Having struggled to support four ocean rowing attempts Ali was naturally cynical about our chances of success. Claire and Di looked worried, but I reminded them that other teams had been in the same position and had made it to the start – it was entirely achievable, we just had to cast our nets far and wide and work bloody hard at pulling them back in again.

After chatting into the small hours, we found our way into our pyjamas and sleeping bags. It felt like a proper girly sleepover!

Day two in the Little Sister house

Di looked terrible. She hadn't slept. She looked so stressed and anxious we were naturally concerned, but she brushed us off and took to the rowing machine for her final stint. Ali was also very quiet; in fact she hadn't contributed much to our discussions. We put it down to her shy nature and the fact that she was probably missing her children. There was definitely a change in mood, a shift in the team's enthusiasm. Perhaps forty-eight hours had been too intense?

Diaries out, we booked dates for the coming weeks and began to gather our belongings. Released, we set off to a Chinese restaurant for lunch. Halfway into our main course Di dropped her bombshell – she wasn't coming. She'd been battling to make a decision all night. She'd realised she probably wouldn't be able to cope with the discomfort, was also worried about raising enough sponsorship, plus with her job and kids it would be too stressful for her and her family.

We were gob-smacked. Di had been so enthusiastic: from the moment she had asked to be part of the team she had told all and sundry about her plans to row an ocean. But I knew this had been an incredibly difficult decision to make, especially because she had been so vocal about her involvement. We all knew it would be unfair to try and talk her into staying. We understood her predicament but it was just a little ironic that the 'bonding weekend' had had the very opposite effect!

I turned to Nic.

'Looks like you're in the team, then!'

The First of the First Women's Threes

Claire and I had sensed it was coming, and within days we'd heard from Ali: she'd also decided it wasn't her time to commit. Within a week we'd lost half our team: not great news. Then Claire got an unexpected call from Nic, who'd decided not to come as well. Did we smell, or something?

Truth was, Nic had agreed to be reserve because she would be just that – a 'reserve'. She thought she'd be training in the background just in case, and she'd be there ready to jump on the boat at the last minute, after all the fund-raising had been done, the boat bought and kitted out. Suddenly being in the team had taken her by surprise and she wasn't ready for it. Having just moved in with her boyfriend and settled into a career that she enjoyed, taking a significant portion of time out to row the Atlantic wasn't what she really wanted.

Within a week we were a very lonely pair and there was absolutely no way I was going to ask Mum to come. There would be no 'make-your-own-tea and-row' mentality on this boat.

Nic was really struggling with her decision not to come along, she felt she'd really let us down. The fact was it was far better for Claire and me that she had done it now rather than 500 miles from land! From now on whoever joined the boat had to be there to the finish – full stop.

Nic was on the lookout for potential replacements. She'd told her cousin, Sue, that we were looking for crew. They occasionally rowed in a pair out on the Thames and Nic thought she might be up for the challenge. Also, Sue had already met Claire on a yachting holiday a year or two ago, so she wouldn't be joining a group of strangers on this 3,000-mile adventure.

So Sue McMillan – slender, auburn and elegantly dressed – came along to meet us, and it didn't take long to persuade her to join Team Rowgirls.

From four, to three, to two and back to three again – we just needed Rowgirl #4 and we'd have a team set to challenge the faster-ever ocean rowing crossing. We hoped.

~

BEFORE WE HAD a chance to find our last lady our luck took an unexpected turn for the better when I decided to follow up something Di had suggested at the doomed bonding weekend. Claire and I had been to-ing and fro-ing over a charity for some time. At first I was keen not to support anyone, because although I knew there were benefits to having a charity on board, I just didn't want to get into a similar situation a second time. But Di had mentioned a Rotary charity called Shelterbox. Based in Helston, in deepest, darkest Cornwall, this relatively small charity had played an important role in the humanitarian aid rollout to the tsunami-hit countries in Asia. A gentleman called Tom Henderson had seen a gap in the humanitarian aid structure and had come up with an idea. Having watched footage of refugees sheltering under plastic sheets and old blankets he thought it would be a far better solution to put these very needy people under canvas. Shelterbox was born.

A ten-person tent, a multi-fuel stove, ten sleeping bags and basically enough equipment to enable a group of ten people to 'camp' for six months would be packed into a big green crate and shipped off to anyone who needed it. With the backing of fund-raisers all over Cornwall and the national Rotary network hundreds of boxes had been sent to Asia to 'home' families affected by the tsunami.

We could 'extreme camp' to help other people camp, I thought to myself. What a fantastic idea! Also it would be a positive way for me to remember my friend Jez.

The day before my birthday I drove the six hours down to Cornwall, spoke to the Rotary Club of Helston Lizard about my adventures with Mum and asked permission to approach Shelterbox with a proposal of support. With their blessing I went to meet Tom Henderson the following day.

I was absolutely overwhelmed by the operation. The warehouse was overflowing with green crates ready to be packed. Volunteers were filling them with equipment – pliers, bundles of rope, stoves, latrine shovels, pots and pans. Tents were stacked to the ceiling. On the walls were maps of all the countries the boxes had been sent to, figures detailing the thousands of people accommodated. It was such a simple and effective idea I just couldn't believe that I hadn't heard of it and that it hadn't been done before.

I was so excited. I couldn't wait to tell Tom all about the row. He seemed keen to reassure me that he believed we could do it and he certainly didn't have any problem at all with our proposal to raise funds for Shelterbox. I made it clear that we would have to put sponsorship for the entire event first and anything made over that would straight to the charity. In fact, if Shelterbox was happy to involve its own supporters in the fund-raising, it could stand to raise a significant sum of money.

I also waxed lyrical about the press an all-girl crew in a bright pink boat could generate. With the contacts I'd accumulated from Epic Challenge I promised to do everything I could to promote Shelterbox to a wider audience. As far as I could see the charity was only well known in Cornwall. Tom saw PR as a terrific bonus; in fact he gave me the impression that the charity was more interested in PR than any fund-raising potential, as it had already been spectacularly successful in its own fund-raising achievements.

'Now, what can we do for you?' he asked.

'Erm ...' (thinking on my feet, a little alarmed by the unexpected question ...) 'You could buy our boat?'

If you could get grades for cheekiness I think I probably would have scored an A. I have to admit I really didn't think he would actually say yes, but when he did, well, you can imagine how I felt.

'Yep, that shouldn't be a problem.'

'Oh!'

'Does it have any resale value?'

'Well, yes, especially when we pack it full of equipment, you can pretty much sell it for more than you paid, even though it's second hand.'

'Well give us an idea as to how much and who we should buy this boat from and we'll get to it straight away. Oh, we'll need to pass it by the trustees, but that shouldn't be a problem.'

I drove home completely shell-shocked. What a fantastic and unexpected birthday treat – we now had an incredible charity to support and we would soon have our lip-gloss-pink boat.

The Final First Women's Four!

Word of our rower-less predicament spread through the ocean rowing community and you wouldn't believe the number of men who were offering themselves as up as Rowgirl #4. Although tempted, Claire, Sue and I thought we'd probably go topless whilst wearing a G-string for decency, and we felt a thong just wouldn't contain a man's attributes. Plus, quite frankly, nobody wants to see that – not even 1,500 miles from land!

But remember Janette, who I'd asked to join me if Mum decided not to come along on the first trip? Well, I called her again, and asked her if she'd like to join the team. Of course, she said yes, but another girl gave me a call out of the blue to ask if she could come along too. Jo Davies had met another rower from our race, the somewhat infamous Dr George Simpson,[20] at Reading Rowing Club. She'd been training there as a novice and had tried desperately to talk her way on to George's all-male fours' team. He wasn't having it, but recommended she rang us instead.

We decided to conduct an *X-Factor*-style row-off. Claire used her contacts at her old university in Birmingham to organise a test, conducted in the sport science lab. Somewhere along the line communication must have broken down because Claire set it up so that we all had to do it! Surely that wasn't the plan? Sue and I were already on the team and the last thing we, I mean I, wanted to do was a test! It involved rowing at increasing speeds until we fainted, threw up or died, whichever came first. But as skipper I had to show willing.

When Jo and Janette arrived, it was instantly obvious who would come away the victor. Jo, in her mid-twenties, was tall,

[20] The 'Dr' has one of those personalities one doesn't easily forget. His qualification is in laser beam technology.

broad through the shoulders, had thighs like tree trunks and essentially 'looked' the part. She also had a competitive nature, and at first seemed a bit 'full on'. Janette, on the other hand, was short, in her late thirties, didn't have the figure of an athlete, but possessed a gentle, caring nature I took to immediately. I didn't want her obvious lack of athleticism to affect our choice but as soon as we hit the machines Jo rowed her under the table. If we were intending to go for a record Jo would have to be on the team.

The following day I decided to call Janette first – I felt awful. It was the second time I had let her down, but she took the news well, even saying she knew she didn't have a chance having seen Jo. I tried to reassure her that Claire, Sue and I hadn't taken the decision on face value but, unfortunately, the results did speak for themselves.

When I called Jo she sounded like a completely different person. Her ultra-competitive front was replaced by a fragile and slightly under-confident tone. She cried when I gave her the news, and it dawned on me that our decision would ultimately change Jo's life. It was a frightening power to possess, but the joy and excitement in her voice was infectious and I came off the phone feeling equally joyful and excited.

I looked upon my new team like a proud mother – we were strong, fit, competitive and committed, and if anybody dropped out I would personally throttle her. Oh, and if any team could set a women's record, well damn it, we could!

The Long (But Short) Slog to the Start Line

As far as packing our boat with equipment was concerned, well, sponsorship was late in coming. In fact, until Shelterbox came aboard in March, only eight months before the start day, we had absolutely no money at all. It took all my powers of persuasion to reassure Claire, Sue and Jo that we were actually going to make it, fully financed, to the start of the race. Admittedly my resolve was beginning to waver and it didn't help that I'd asked an accountant friend, Brian, to come along to one of our meetings – a moot point really, as we had nothing to account for. But setting up a limited company did make us feel like we were doing something constructive.

We weren't completely useless, though – we did find our feminine charms worked very well when it came to sponsorship in kind. After a visit to the Outdoor Show[21] we returned with the promise of a full compliment of up-to-date comms kit from another fours' rowing team called Vivaldi (after the potato company), an all-male crew who were preparing for a northern Transatlantic row that summer. It was an amazing gesture – the two sat phones, a PDA (personal digital assistant) and associated software would allow us to send email updates directly to a website. We wouldn't need a 'Jane' to download them and I wouldn't have to balance a heavy laptop on my sweaty knees. It would save us thousands of pounds. The only problem would be if the potato boys turned turtle during their attempt – there'd be no comms kit for us!

So a comms kit here, reduced-rate dehydrated chicken curry there, and we were very slowly building a compliment of

---

[21] The show is the biggest showcase for outdoor sports in the country. It was very same one Tommo and I had shaken a bucket at a couple of years before. Always a great place to blag equipment and money!

equipment for the boat, but bugger us if we could find a major sponsor.

We shook buckets at Women's Henley and took the boat down to the Maritime Museum in Falmouth, where the girls popped in to see Shelterbox for the first time, and were as impressed as I was with the charity's set-up. Whilst there they joined hundreds of runners in the annual Helston 10k (these sporty types, honestly, I don't know where they get the energy). I got out of it by citing my old war wound – my marathon-knackered knee!

We raised £1.10 and a bacon sandwich at a dragonboat race organised by Northampton Rotary Club. I'd decided to join, having seen the organisation supporting charities like Shelterbox. I thought it would be good fun and perhaps offer some excellent networking opportunities. As the youngest member and a woman to boot I did prove to be a bit of a novelty.

Unfortunately, the dragonboat race was a complete washout. A torrential downpour started just before the first boat launched and didn't end until the fund-raising stalls had been pulled down. We lost every race, even after my Dad jumped in as a late substitute when one of the team cried off injured!

Claire and I took part in the Northampton Carnival. We'd borrowed a Land Rover (and you know how excited I get about those!) to help us tow the boat. With Dad at the helm we trundled through the streets of the town centre, grinning wildly and waving frantically. We raised a few pounds, nothing mind blowing, but the experience was one to remember.

Aside from raising money the girls were keen to get some experience in the boat. A choppy day in Chichester harbour, although pleasurable, wasn't going to cut it. So we lined up a few events that would test their skills in relative safety. We took part in a sprint across the bay at Torquay organised by Woodvale, open to all the crews taking part in the challenge. Over four-and-a-half miles the men's teams unfortunately left us floundering in their wake. We did try to reassure ourselves that Ben Johnson probably wouldn't beat Paula Radcliffe in a marathon, so with that in mind we decided we'd definitely 'ave 'em over 3,000 miles.

Claire, Sue and Jo also took part in the Eddystone Lighthouse Rowing Race – a twenty-six-mile round trip from Plymouth Harbour to the Eddystone Rocks, just south of the harbour entrance, and back again. By this time I had become very conscious of my constant references to my previous attempt: 'Well, Mum and I did it like this ... Mum and I did it like that.' It must have been incredibly irritating; fortunately I had to work on Saturday mornings producing the weekend radio output, which meant I wasn't able to join them, so perhaps the weekend would prove to be a welcome break from my 'know-it-all' attitude.

The trip would give the girls the opportunity to see what rowing conditions were really like out at sea but I have to admit I did feel a bit nervous. Knowing how dangerous the English Channel can be I was worried they'd not only lose control of the boat but more worryingly they'd realise how futile ocean rowing can be. What if they didn't enjoy it and decided not to be in the team anymore?

As soon as they were out of the harbour the wind did take hold of the boat and they weren't able to control her. Off they went to Cornwall before cool-headed Jo finally persuaded Claire and Sue that no amount of rowing was going to get them back to port again. They called the race organisers and requested a tow to shore having not made it anywhere near the lighthouse.

Tired and grumpy, they took their defeat on the chin and no one decided to leave the team. With hindsight it was a fantastic training session, as they'd faced what we would probably be facing every day for at least a couple of months out in the ocean. The weather and water will be what they want to be and there's absolutely nothing you can do about it.

Whilst the girls were off to the gym every day and taking the boat out on to the high seas, my training regime was somewhat more relaxed. Unfortunately the experience of having done it before was starting to work against me. I knew that hours at the gym wouldn't really prepare me for the row – nothing you do on land can simulate the experience – so I reached the point where I just couldn't be arsed! I had completely lost my motivation for physical training. Working long hours at Radio Northampton, I barely made it to the gym, and when I did, the very thought of sitting on a rowing machine made my bum cheeks sore.

I was subject to an internal power struggle that I only really remember feeling as a child: I knew I had to do my homework, but there was something really good on the telly, so I'd watch it even though I knew I'd get into trouble. Same here: time was running out and if I didn't train properly I would, almost certainly, face the wrath of the other girls for my lack of commitment. With that in mind I decided to try alternative training methods in the hope that I could claim I was maintaining a core fitness which would at least see me through the first couple of weeks of the row.

I flung myself off upturned crash mats in an attempt to learn parkour, aka free running, but instead of going over them I found myself ploughing into them and as they were there to simulate brick walls I decided rather quickly that this white girl can't jump!

I strapped myself to a wake board and tossed myself into a lake, clinging to a rope tied to the back of a jetski. I should have known it wasn't the sport for me when I got myself into a knotted pickle secreting myself into a wetsuit in the back of some bloke's van, but it still took a dozen attempts to stand up and falling face-first into the concrete-hard water before I came to that rather obvious conclusion!

Mum suggested I join her, my sister and Nic (of the Stumpies) in the Moonwalk, a twenty-six-mile walk around the streets of London in the middle of the night, raising awareness of breast cancer and funds for the many charities that support women with the disease. Thousands of women took part and as we arrived at Hyde Park we didn't feel quite so stupid in our DD-decorated white lacy bras, an obligatory addition to your training kit that every competitor had to wear. Starting at midnight, we marched for eight hours through the dark streets of the capital, past Buckingham Palace, the Houses of Parliament and along the Embankment. This was more like it – no sweaty gyms or fancy 'extreme' sports, just a good old-fashioned walk with the girls. Arriving back in Hyde Park blistered and sore, I split from the group to go and meet my new boyfriend for breakfast.

I met Clint Evans on an astro-navigation course in Devon. Yep, another astro-navigation course, in fact my third. It's complicated stuff and if you don't use it every day everything goes pear shaped!

Jo had arranged for us to stay in a caravan just a few miles from Woodvale HQ, where a series of courses for team entrants, namely first aid, astro-navigation and sea survival, were being held. Once the girls had rescued each other in life rafts and I'd gatecrashed the first aid course, we retired to the classroom, charts and sextant in hand. There, sat across the table, were Clint and Chris, studiously plotting away on their charts. They were a pair's team, calling themselves C^2, were also very tall (neither shy of 6'5") and forty-something. Claire and I chatted casually to them during the lunch break and they agreed to become our study buddies. We invited them round to our caravan that evening so we could copy, I mean, help each other with our homework.

Clint isn't regularly handsome, but his attractiveness was in his eyes – an inner wisdom and gentleness. His voice is so deep its bass audibly resonates and we soon found ourselves seated together at the dining table. After a few beers, Claire asked the boys what attributes they looked for in a woman. I tried to convey the full extent of my horror by twitching my eyebrows at her wildly. Although I wasn't in a relationship and she was, the last thing I needed was a rather obvious match-making attempt whilst sitting in a caravan in Devon doing complicated long division with two blokes almost twice our age!

Not unsurprisingly, they both liked women in good physical shape, but Clint went on to describe his perfect match ...

- Curly auburn hair
- An athletic figure
- Big eyes

- Full lips
  Oh shit, he's describing me!
- Intelligent
  Oh, no he's not!
- Slightly quirky
  Here we go again!
- And creative
  This man is dangerous. If I don't end up going out with him I'll probably do something naughty!

And I did! The last night of the course, all the rowers went for a celebratory drink at the local pub. Clint and I were left alone at the table. It was an awkward moment, made worse by the fact that an alien took over my brain. I looked Clint straight in the eye and said, 'I just thought I'd let you know that I fancy you.'

'I know you do,' he replied.

'Good!' I said. *You arrogant bugger.*

Thankfully people started to return to their seats, we broke our stare and barely spoke to each other for the rest of the evening. The knowledge of our secret conversation had created electricity between us.

A couple of weeks later, I found myself at a loose end on a Saturday evening. My parents were out and I had the place to myself. Debating what I should do, I landed upon the idea of inviting Clint round for dinner, and called him. Yes, we did exchange numbers!

'Would you like to come over for dinner this evening? Oh and by the way this isn't an invitation for sex!' I proposed bluntly, feeling ever so slightly mischievous for mentioning the word sex whilst standing outside the bastion of British conservatism – Marks & Sparks in Northampton.

Clint turned up with a fine bottle of red wine and I cooked a magnificent spaghetti bolognese, although to this day he still insists that he did the lion's share of the work. Quite frankly, pouring dry pasta into a pot of boiling water is not cooking!

Although we had to build our relationship on stolen moments at hotels and one-nighters at Henley Management College – a residential institution where Clint worked as marketing director – it made such a difference that we were going through the same experience together, training, raising money and worrying about the row.

Within the same six months, by some strange coincidence, all the Rowgirls had boyfriends who were in some way connected to the Atlantic. I'd intentionally introduced Claire to a lad called Andrew who I'd met during the Challenge Business race. I knew they'd be a match made in heaven and after a few hours together they were also cooking spaghetti bolognese!

Sue also found herself a man, a guy called Tom who'd sailed across the Atlantic on many occasions and had been the skipper on the sailing trip where Claire and Sue first met. And Jo? Well, she was as bad as me! A solo rower, Chris Martin, was also attending the courses in Devon, and within a week they were also stirring dried pasta into a pan.

~

PAIRED UP BUT still short of money, we set to work on the boat. Through Shelterbox we were able to find a spot in Falmouth Marina to store her, and we proceeded to tinker away under the watchful eye of a professional rigger and friend of the charity, Mel. He'd promised to help us design the rudder system. My limited expertise only really stretched to drilling holes and sticking or screwing things on, so complicated gearing mechanisms were not my thing at all.

Jo posted herself in Falmouth for August, setting up camp at a local site and spending days pottering around the boat. Because of our work commitments, Sue, Claire and I took it in turns to stay for a week and help out. As testament to Jo's organisation skills, by September we had an incredible-looking boat. Everything from screw-down hatch covers to bright pink fluffy sheepskin-covered seats had been fitted. She'd also managed to persuade a boat builder to design and build a unit for the electrical equipment inside the cabin. A local electrician had also been persuaded to fit LED lights all the way down the roof of the main cabin, half white (for when we needed bright daytime lighting) and half red (for during the night, when we didn't want to affect our night vision). With both sets on at the same time it created this fabulous pink glow.

I'd made a big deal about comfort on the boat. With so little in the way of luxuries I'd harped on and on about the cushions in the back cabin needing to be the best we could possibly get our hands on. Our sheepskin sponsor Easi-Rider came up trumps by providing the most professional-looking mattresses I have ever seen on an ocean rowing boat! Covered with waterproof fabric, these super-firm cushions were the business, but bloody hell they were heavy!

'Do we have to take them?' Sue asked more than once.

I did agree that the added weight was an issue, and we were racing so anything we had to carry would affect our speed, but with sore limbs and blistered bottoms these mattresses would be our saviour, so I over-ruled Sue.

Over this stressful and uncertain period leading up to the race each Rowgirl was proving her worth in spades. We all had individual strengths and it worked in our favour that we were all completely different people. Jo was incredibly organised, fearless and hardworking. If we needed to be somewhere or do something Jo would sort out the logistics and make sure everyone arrived in the right place, and on time. She was also a brilliant cook, conjuring up meals that would be the envy of a Michelin-starred restaurant.

Claire had boundless enthusiasm. Her ability to bring the team together emotionally was an invaluable asset. She often bridged the gap between all our personalities, offering a mature, balanced opinion when tension occasionally threatened to overflow into argument.

Sue questioned everything we did – she double-checked what we bought, queried every event we organised. She forced us to stop and think about our decisions and kept us grounded, especially when it came to our financial situation. She was particularly good at keeping an eye on my often over-optimistic view of our monetary situation!

Also, what Sue lacked in time she made up for with money. Her job was very demanding and she told us from the moment she signed up that she wouldn't always be able to join us on training weekends and fund-raising trips. But with great generosity she contributed her own money to pay for much-needed equipment when we hadn't yet raised enough to buy it.

As for me – well, I brought experience. I knew what worked and what didn't, saving us time and money. Over the coming months I also became the reluctant queen of sponsorship, in fact I found it relatively easy to extract cash from the tightest of wallets. You see, unlike the girls, I wasn't scared to come straight out and ask for sponsorship whatever the situation, and in the end it did pay off. In fact some of my fund-raising networking allowed me to meet many new and interesting contacts, but I have to admit that a few of the men were definitely more interested in what I had to offer in the missionary position rather than the Rowgirls' mission. I'd like to think I deployed my feminine charms sparingly and kept what little virtue I have left firmly intact. Anyway, for the fun of the chase I probably attracted some sponsorship income that might not have come my way otherwise. No hearts or homes were broken, and besides, I would never kiss and tell!

To ensure we were all singing from the same hymn sheet, Claire organised a session with a trainee sport physiologist. A natural sceptic, particularly after my experience with the 'psychos' in the regatta, I was reluctant to believe that these sessions would be helpful. I completely underestimated how enlightening they would prove to be.

At our first meeting Sanna asked us to fill out sheets on our perception of the overall goal, and it was remarkable how different our individual responses were. Admittedly I thought I'd sold the trip as an opportunity to become the first women's four, but looking at it now this was an entirely ambiguous goal. When we first came together as the finalised team we were the only female four in the race so just by stepping on the boat and getting across we had completed that goal. But circumstances had since changed: another girls' team from Guernsey had entered.

So I was surprised when the girls put 'Getting across safely' or 'Rowing an ocean' at the top of their list. Both are, of course, realistic and sensible goals, but Sanna made it clear that our attitude and motivation on the boat would be very different if half the team were focused on rowing an ocean whilst the other half were trying to win. 'When times get tough, how will the team respond if your goals are not the same?' Sanna asked, before sitting back and letting us wrestle with the question.

We had to make some tough decisions. Were we all prepared to focus on winning or were we happy just to get across? We talked for some time before finally agreeing we were going out there to win. The Guernsey girls, aka Mission Atlantic (aka the Guernsey Milkers) would have to fight hard to beat us. There was no way they were going to get to Antigua before us!

~

I HAD A lot to learn during the lead up to the race. I made plenty of bad decisions, some of which I would later regret. I have to admit I wasn't the greatest skipper in the world and I often felt doubtful about my ability to lead the team. In fact, I didn't feel like I was leading the team at all. Its momentum was driven not by me personally but by us all and I really never expected it to be like that. My ego wouldn't allow me to feel good about the way we were working. I wanted to be able to take credit for our successes, to be the celebrated captain of our ship! But I later found out that that isn't what makes a great leader.

I know now that I sometimes let things go when I should have been firmer and stuck by my own opinion, or that I stubbornly held on to decisions when I should have let them go. For example, the rudder mechanism wasn't good enough, the whole system was too flimsy and complicated, but because the build had been sponsored I was loathe to go back to Mel and tell him it needed to be replaced.

I also regret holding on to a gimmicky idea for a PR stunt. The girls really didn't want to do it but I thought a *Calendar Girl*-style picture of the four of us sat on our boat would be a great way to publicise our team in the tabloids, namely the *Daily Mail*. I contacted a local photographer and journalist in Falmouth who came out with us whilst we rowed around a secluded harbour. We went topless, covering our modesty with our oars, and he took the pictures promising that he would approach the *Daily Mail* and write a suitable article to promote the charity and us. Instead he sold the photos to the *Sunday Sport* and we found ourselves stuck between adverts for sex lines and prostitutes, emblazoned with the headline 'We're rowing the Atlan-TIT'.[22] The girls felt cheap and ashamed, as did I. The only saving grace was the fact that we didn't add to their daily nipple count!

But for all my leadership doubts, together we did make it to the start of the Woodvale Race 2005. Sue had secured a major sponsor in GE; she'd worked for them for a couple of years and although they'd been keen to support her with time off, they took a little longer to see the sponsorship potential. She managed to convince them that through her achievement

---

[22] I've seen some interesting row-related puns in my time and this one was most definitely the worst. The best featured in the *Daily Express*, a very short paragraph summarising our attempt entitled 'Coxless Phw-oars'.

they could, in turn, inspire their workforce to go out there and achieve great things.

It was with huge excitement and great pride that we were able to decorate our boat with the logos of our two major sponsors – Shelterbox and GE. My dream that we would get to the start fully financed, as strong as any other team, had now been realised. All we needed to do was get out into that ocean and win!

THIRTEEN

The Exits are Here, Here and Here

SEVEN PEOPLE ON Tenerife died when one of the worst tropical storms in fifty years hit the Canary Islands. We were a week and a half into our final preparations in La Gomera and I suddenly felt an overwhelming sense of dread – the sort that's fabled to stop people boarding planes that go on to crash.

It didn't help that I was ill from the moment I stepped off the plane. Stress has a nasty habit of sneaking up on you when you're not expecting it and the cumulative effects of full-time work and full-time fund-raising had taken their toll just when being fit and well was most important. I had a persistent, sleep-depriving cough; I lost my voice and generally felt like shit.

~

THE START OF this race wasn't as exciting as my two previous attempts. The rose-tinted glasses had suddenly dropped away, opening my eyes to the true nature of the task ahead. This was going to be hard, harder than anything I'd ever done before. It was also going to be painful, nauseating, exhausting and emotionally challenging.

For the first week Jo and I shared an apartment, Sue and Claire shared another. We worked hard to finish the boat. There were hundreds of little tasks we'd left to sort out in Gomera. Because of the cumbersome size and shape of our boat we were separated from the other teams, unable to trundle her around on a cradle. The pairs' teams were working together in a compound closer to San Sebastian town centre. The distance between us and the rest of the crews, in particular the Guernsey Milkers, enabled us to focus on our own goal, and we developed a one-track mind for the task ahead.

Twenty-six teams were entered in the race, and about a third of the crew members were women, an encouraging statistic when you consider how few had attempted an ocean row before Mum and me. A celebrity crew had also entered, TV presenter and housewives' favourite Ben Fogle and Olympic rower/blonde-haired pin-up James Cracknell. Their presence did change the atmosphere amongst the teams but they kept themselves to themselves and were barely seen as they desperately worked on their wholly inadequately prepared boat. They had also struggled with sponsorship and with their hectic work schedules they were unable to get the boat shipshape for the start.

It became a hot topic of conversation that they would be disqualified from the race because they were so unprepared. Crackers and Bogle, as they were often affectionately referred to, had their work cut out for them, but many teams pitched in to help them and I have to admit I felt a little star-struck when I went over to show James how to use the para-anchor.

Rumours had also spread that a tropical storm was heading our way, and it would hit the Canaries the day before the race start. Once this was confirmed Woodvale could do nothing but postpone the race for three days, only heightening the agony of the wait. Tenerife would face the worst of it, but as the winds hit the island palm trees bent double as the storm whipped through the streets of San Sebastian, while anxious-looking rowers braved the torrential rain to continue work on their boats. The storm didn't last long, the winds died quickly, the sun found its way out and the ocean settled down. Woodvale organised the first 'Gomera Cup' – a sprint race out to sea, round one of the support yachts and back again.

With three extra days in port many rowers' friends and family would have to leave the island to catch their pre-booked flights home, and the Gomera Cup would give them the opportunity to watch the teams go out to sea, although they'd be back again within half an hour!

Claire, Sue, Jo and I donned our Lycra all-in-ones (not a pretty sight when you're packing a few extra pounds), rowed to the start lie, threw a few evil glares at the Guernsey Milkers and on the whistle shot off towards the horizon. The men's pairs and the two men's fours overtook us almost immediately, but we were cranking out the nautical miles like women possessed.

The Milkers were close behind us – the staggered start made it difficult to estimate their relative speed, but as we took to the oars two at a time, the two that weren't rowing were screaming encouragement instead. It was going to be a close race, and what we gained in youth, the Milkers made up for in muscle. They looked incredibly strong and as gig rowers they certainly had more experience at sea. We knew they would be formidable opponents, which only drove us to row even harder.

Rounding the support yacht, *Sula*, we decided it was time for our own powerhouses to take to the oars. Sue and I came off, Jo and Claire jumped on. The screaming became so high pitched I'm surprised dolphins weren't attracted from miles around. As we crossed the finish line, just inside the harbour entrance, it was difficult to see whether the Milkers had gained on us.

Exhausted, but happier for our excursion, the mood at base camp had been successfully lifted. That evening we all squeezed into the Blue Marlin for the race results. As the names and times were read off, the girls and I clung to each other in anticipation.

'And in tenth place ... Mission Atlantic ... in one hour, thirty-seven minutes and twenty-four seconds, and only one minute behind them ... The Rowgirls, in one hour, thirty-eight minutes and twenty-five seconds!'

'Oh, bollocks!'

Disappointed but happy, we went over and congratulated the girls – Cathy, Lois, Sarah and Paula – because in any other circumstances it would have been a pleasure to spend time with them.

I'd moved into a hotel with Clint for those final three days, as almost all the rowers had to find new accommodation. Claire and Sue were sharing an apartment with Andrew and Tom, and Jo had moved in with Chris.

Up until this point I'd purposely avoided spending too much time with Clint, one, because he had his own boat to prepare, and two, because the Rowgirls were a united force, working, sleeping and training together, and, quite frankly, there was no time for boyfriends. But now, with nothing else to do but wait for the start, we took the opportunity to enjoy each other's company whilst we still had the chance.

It was in the pub after the Gomera Cup that the circumstances between us changed. For the first time in two weeks I was feeling well enough to go out and have a drink or three and so took to the bar with renewed vigour, dragging the exhausted Clint along with me. My voice had also come back so I no longer had to squeak in tones only audible to dogs. Making the most of it, I launched into a long and convoluted conversation with Simon (we were discussing the idiosyncrasies of our boat design). One moment Clint was standing with me, the next he'd disappeared. It seemed he'd had too much to drink and so decided to go back to the hotel room without me. Exasperated, I hoofed it round to the hotel to find out why he'd left without telling me.

We bumped into each on my way back, and after a brief, heated exchange I escorted him back to our room. Laid out on the bed, he looked up at me with his 'come-to-bed' blue eyes and whispered, 'Miss Kettle, will you marry me?'

'You are joking, aren't you?' I scoffed. It wasn't the ideal reply, but as shocked as I was I couldn't think of anything else to say!

'No, I'm not,' he retorted, looking rather hurt.

'Well … Yes! Of course I will!' A grin spread all over my face.

Within minutes I'd sent a text to all the girls, their congratulatory replies buzzing back just as quickly.

Peaceful but fearful we held each other in bed, a newly engaged couple soon to be separated by a race that I dreaded would kill us all.

~

Feeling the Fear and Doing it Anyway

So, why did I get on the boat when every part of my being was telling me something was going to go terribly wrong? At the end of the day I had nothing to prove – I had done it before. I got on the boat because, ironically, I was too frightened to pull out of the race. It sounds so ridiculous, but the shame of abandoning the girls would have been too much to bear. I realised you have to be an incredibly brave person to turn round and say, 'No, something's wrong, I'm not going,' especially when that decision is entirely based on a gut feeling.

So, I jumped on the plane, and although it didn't crash the flight sure was bumpy!

~

I BROKE THE news of our engagement to my parents on the pontoon just hours before the starter whistle. They were very excited, after recovering from the initial shock. Up until this point they'd only really met Clint on the odd occasion when he came to the door, before we disappeared off for the night. With only a couple of years between my Mum and Clint, I was a little jittery about their reaction.

When we first starting seeing each other I did frighten myself with the thought that my boyfriend could just have easily have been my dad, but I got over it relatively quickly. Now my family had to face the fact that my 'older' man was going to be a permanent feature, and all credit to them: they took it very well, even if they were harbouring thoughts that I'd probably change my mind halfway across the ocean!

I'd promised myself that I wouldn't cry, but I just couldn't stop the tears trickling down as I paced impatiently beside the boat waiting for instructions from Woodvale to make our way to the start line. Why does this always take so long? Why couldn't we just get up at dawn, get into the boat and go?

I hate race days, I always find myself crippled by my emotions whereas Jo, Sue and Claire were practically buoyant. You'd think that I'd have got used to it by now, this was my third start, but I had to stick my sunglasses on before I wandered down to Clint's cow-print-painted boat. Although I'd only left the hotel with him a couple of hours before, I grabbed hold of him, buried my head into his chest and hugged him tightly, blubbing into his soft, Lycra-clad tummy. We said our goodbyes quickly, not wanting to prolong the agony.

The ocean was calm, the weather warm and the sun determined to burn my shoulders. In our matching pink and black Lycra we set to the oars. The girls' excitement was infectious; as soon as I was on the boat my heart was racing, not with nerves or dread but with the exhilaration of the moment.

Again hundreds stood on the harbour wall to see us off. Sue and I stood holding on to the cabin roof and A-frame whilst our powerhouses Claire and Jo heaved us out in front of the Milkers and away towards the horizon, where we had a cup of tea before swapping places.

This was it, our lives defined by our shift pattern – an hour and a half on, an hour and a half off during the day and three hours on, three hours off between 12.00 and 6.00 am for at least the next two months.

Skipper's Log

30.11.05   Race start 12.05 pm. Weather calm & sunny, hit choppy outside La Gomera. Winds NE-ly, 20kt, but died & changed direction to SW-ly, calmed overnight.

From: Rowgirls
To: Newsdesk
Date: 1 December 2005
Re: Rowgirls' Diary

```
Weight lost ... 2 pounds at least
Alcohol drunk ... 4 G&Ts, jug of Pimms
Wildlife spotted ... 2 shearwaters
Vomited ... Claire 5, Sue 1 (she thinks she should
get double points for full-on chunks!)
Miles rowed ... 65.4
```

```
The enormity of the challenge is just sinking in.
Only two days in and bums, knees and stomachs are
already aching. It's flat as a pancake out here,
great for easing you into ocean life but it's slow
and really, really boring! And guess what? According
to the weather report it's going to be like this for
the next few days! Hurrah.
```

```
Bored, burnt and whinging,
```

```
The Rowgirls x
```

We were making fantastic progress, we'd already passed many of the other crews and Gomera was disappearing quickly. With music blaring through the on-deck speakers we were actually enjoying the ride, even if our backsides weren't! Also, I wasn't sick. I couldn't believe it. Clint – a qualified pharmacologist, amongst other things – had recommended a combination of anti-sickness drugs. So with patch and pills I bounced about the deck with the legs of a seasoned sailor.

Two days in and our rowing schedule was working really well, in fact much of our early success was down to getting it right early on, although, having settled into the pattern, we did tweak it a little bit. In order to combat the potential boredom of rowing in permanent pairs we changed partners every two days.

The days were fantastic. One of the girls, I think it might have been Sue, had instigated the 'push for ten' policy which, when accompanied by the Abba *Gold* album, would have the boat powering along rather nicely. It wasn't really my cup of tea, all this macho ultra-competitiveness, but I kept reminding myself why we were out here, and with blood pumping and heart pounding I actually started to enjoy this rowing lark. But then the sun would set and the darkness would envelop the boat, bringing with it the nasty reality of the three-hour shift. They were bloody awful!

The first night wasn't bad. The girls were anxious about rowing blind, so it took a little while for them to settle into the rhythm of the night-time sea. As twilight turned the sky an ever-deepening blue the heavens put on a display that didn't disappoint, and I think Claire, Sue and Jo spent much of the night staring at the stars.

For me, the second night was just dire. Sue and I sat out in the dark, and I sobbed silently, mourning my lack of sleep and wallowing in the agony caused by sciatica pain running from my right bum cheek to my ankle, which flared with every push and pull. It hadn't hurt this much on the first row. Having put a brave face on it during the day, I sat hoping the darkness and the wind would disguise my tears and Sue wouldn't know my misery.

Skipper's Log

03.12.05   Monstrous night, Jo & Sally had run-in with powerful painkiller. Sally passed out & both left vomiting & disorientated. Sue & Claire pulled together to keep boat moving whilst the other two remained on deck having been told by Lin Parker to remain awake. Tramadol; Jo had four during day at 4-5 hr intervals; Sally two - one at 5.00 pm, one at midnight. Both experienced no side effects until midnight. Weather picked up - more wind & bigger, rougher waves. Sula visited to check on team. Sally & Jo slowly recovering, Sue & Claire in good spirits.
155 miles

04.12.05   Broken rudder - 20 mins to fix. Visit from Sula, 5.30 am.
213 miles

From: Rowgirls
To: Newsdesk
Date: 4 December 2005
Re: Rowgirls' Diary: Sickness and Sore Bums ...

Yesterday proved to be a great day. We made some good progress and spirits were high. However, at night Sal and Jo came down with a bout of sickness. Sue and Claire took to the oars at midnight and haven't moved since. We're talking serious bum ache.

Sal and Jo are making a good recovery and we're
looking forward to seeing them on their pink fluffy
seats later today. We've got a reasonable easterly
wind helping us along. Must get back to the oars!

The Rowgirls x

~

IT'S AMAZING HOW one relatively small 'overdose' incident defined
our characters for the rest of the trip. If Claire and Sue were in
pain they barely mentioned it. Jo, on the other hand, dived for
the pharmaceuticals at the first sign of discomfort. This is why
I enjoyed rowing with Jo – we could openly share our anguish!
Cocooned inside the cabin, we talked about it, agreeing that
there was an unspoken pressure not to 'fail' in front of Claire
and Sue. They rarely complained or grumbled about anything
and we both found it almost impossible to keep up with their
unrelenting enthusiasm. Together Jo and I would weep openly,
but these tears soon turned to giggles once we realised we'd
spent a good half an hour complaining about some such pain
or other, a half hour often punctuated by my cries of 'Oh, my
ARSE!'

Where Jo and I wore our hearts on our sleeves, Claire and Sue
were more emotionally restrained. We were just different, but it
did create an undercurrent of tension between us. I coveted
their restraint, feeling resentful of my own weaknesses, and
after three days of excruciating pain I foolishly decided to take
the Tramadol.

It's an incredibly strong drug and just two tablets dramatically lowered my blood pressure. After a few minutes on the oars I couldn't keep my arms up or stop myself from swaying wildly before blacking out. My thoughts were still coherent and I remember telling myself to stop pretending to be ill, but my body just wasn't responding.

I could see the looks of terror on the girls' faces as they lifted my dead weight into the cabin and called the support yacht. I couldn't believe it, it was Tommo all over again, and this time I was jeopardising the trip.

Under orders to keep me awake all night, Claire and Sue sat me out on deck under a cold wet sleeping bag, Jo was sitting opposite me having also experienced a similar but milder reaction to the drug. Vomiting over the side and feverish from dipping in and out of sleep, I remember berating myself for being so pathetic. I wanted to be strong, but I'd let myself down in front of the girls.

These feelings only got worse when Claire and Sue related the conversation they'd had with Lin Parker, the skipper of the support yacht *Aurora*: she'd questioned why we had been stupid enough to take the drug in the first place. *Well, you put it in our medical supplies!* I thought, defensively. Anyway, we had read through the information leaflet and followed the instructions to the letter … it's just unfortunate lowered blood pressure was one of the side effects.

Claire and Sue rowed non-stop for six hours, singing, laughing and chatting away to try and keep Jo and me awake. I felt ashamed that I'd put them in this situation. I prayed that the effects were only temporary and I wouldn't have to be taken off the boat.

When the support yacht, *Sula*, arrived the next morning I jumped out on deck, having struggled into a red bobble hat and T-shirt. Looking a bit of a state, my T-shirt inside out and back to front, I grinned and waved whilst shouting over to the support crew that I was completely fine and happy to keep going. They sailed off satisfied all was well and, still weakened from vomiting all night, I returned to the oars and rowed for three hours to demonstrate to Claire and Sue that I hadn't been beaten. Jo, on the other hand, remained in bed having complained that she still felt too ill to return to the oars. From their looks I could tell that this didn't go down well. They were not at all impressed by her lack of motivation, especially as they had sacrificed their entire night to keep the boat moving. Whilst I rowed they took it in turns to jump into the cabin for some much-needed sleep.

Skipper's Log

01.12.05   Encounter with small tanker, 10.30 pm. Used parachute flare & hand-held. No response from ship on VHF. Also spoke to Dan on Aurora.
320 miles

From: Rowgirls
To: Newsdesk
Date: 6 December 2005
Re: Rowgirls' Diary: All at Sea ... and Our Saviour is Tea

It's day seven on the pink beast and she's doing us proud. She's sitting happy on the swells and surfing the waves, which are starting to show themselves.

With 345 miles in the bag our bodies are throwing their arms up in disgust – fingers have doubled in size, blisters[23] are multiplying at a rate of knots and tubi-grips have become the latest fashion accessory on board. After several zombie like night shifts Jo and Sue have now found the secret to surviving the three-hour pitch-black endurance test ... a good old cup of Yorkshire Tea followed by some dehydrated choc mousse. What more could a girl ask for?

Signing off to clock off a few more miles,

The Rowgirls x

~

NIGHT-TIME ROWING was not working. We physically couldn't stop ourselves from falling asleep at the oars. Our eyes ached from trying to keep them open and nausea set in because we were so exhausted. Our morale took a nosedive as soon as the sun set and we all started to feel depressed.

Jo and I were again desperate not to show any weakness so we tried to row non-stop for those three long hours, not daring to take a break unless we needed a wee. So, you can imagine our elation when super-competitive Sue decided to treat herself to a tea halfway through the shift. It was a revelation and gave us all an excuse to stop, just for fifteen minutes, have a drink, maybe even make up some chocolate mousse before returning to the oars again. This one break not only staved off the nausea that hits you straight in the sternum half an hour in, but also made

[23] I had two huge blisters on my hands, I called them Frank and Bruno. They were so large they were beginning to spread from my palm, round my fingers and down the other side.

us feel human again. Our morale shot up and we actually started to look forward to that simple mid-shift treat.

The Evolutionary Cycle of the Genus Rowgirl

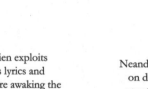
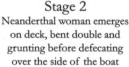

Stage 1
The amoeba awakes unable to co-ordinate or speak

Stage 4
The modern day homo-sapien exploits a wide vocabulary of songs lyrics and shares tales of family life, before awaking the sleeping amoeba with the following call: 'Ten minutes, chica'

Stage 2
Neanderthal woman emerges on deck, bent double and grunting before defecating over the side of the boat

Stage 3
Limited language skills develop, short sentences are constructed, homo-erectus woman begins to socialise. She also discovers fire, tea is made and the final stage in development accomplished ...

Skipper's Log

07.12.05   *Visit from yacht, Les Oiseaux.*
             378 miles

From: Rowgirls
To: Newsdesk
Date: 7 December 2005
Re: Rowgirls' Diary: Drama at Sea!

Oh it's been a dramatic last few hours! Last night Claire and Sally saw some lights on the horizon and half an hour later all the girls were on deck preparing to launch the collision flares!

Yep, it's always a bit of a risk with shipping but we know what to do and we were ready when a small tanker made a beeline for our little boat at 10.30 pm. We were on the blower, but no reply ... Jo, in full-on white Lycra, leapt to the middle of the boat and shot a parachute flare into the air, shortly followed by a hand-held.

Well, as you can probably tell, we weren't hit, but it was rather an exciting night had by all. Amongst the furore we gained our first fish on deck, but to much distress lost our poo bucket. There'll be a service some time today.

Also spotted a pod of pilot whales this morning. They didn't stick around for long, but the smiles on our faces did!

Thanks to all for text messages and emails.

Still sore,

S, S, C & J x

PS Also cracking weather at moment.

The loss of that bloody poo bucket was a relief to all of us expect Jo. It didn't matter how many times we said it, her grunting and groaning whilst perched precariously atop of it was putting us off our food, but she stubbornly refused to stop using it. I was biding my time though: she'd tied a rope to the flimsy handle and not around the main part of the bucket. I knew it would only take a week or so of constant use before it broke and disappeared into the drink! With bucket overboard she joined us, bums dangling over the edge.

Skipper's Log

08.12.05 First flying fish hit Sally. One on deck. 439 miles

From: Rowgirls
To: Newsdesk
Date: 8 December 2005
Re: Rowgirls' Diary: 458 Miles and Still Smiling!

Oh yes! Surf's up! Sue and Sally scored a magnificent 5.8 knots on the waves today, in fact Jo and Claire are out on the oars right now trying to beat it.

The seas are huge, a bit of a struggle last night but the fact that Sally's got an ocean row already in the bag means we've found it a breeze handling the strongest winds yet.

Sally also got hit on the head by a flying fish at 4.00 am but saved it from floundering on the deck by tossing it, flapping, back into the waves.

Still being plagued by other ocean users. Yesterday a large yacht came over to say hi. We promised Jorgen on *Les Oiseaux* that we'd pop along to St Vincent for a rum and coke! Last night another nav light on the horizon. We can't wait to get into the middle of the Atlantic, maybe then we'll get some peace and quiet!

Happy Birthday to the mother of all ocean rowers, Sally's mum Sarah. 'Mum, I'm having a cakey right now!' Love you and see you in Antigua, Sally x

Off to surf some more,

S, S, C & J

Skipper's Log

10.12.05   Sluggish sea, no winds. Still, happy we're reducing distance to waypoint.
549 miles

From: Rowgirls
To: Newsdesk
Date: 10 December 2005
Re: Rowgirls' Diary: Wrong Wind!

Oh no! It's the wrong wind and we've had to put our para-anchor out for the first time. After valiantly attempting to row into the south-westerly wind we threw in the towel, made a cup of tea and had a piece of fruitcake!

On the positive side it has given us the opportunity to make some running repairs and get a full night's sleep. Let's just hope those Milkers are stuck in the same weather front and aren't making up the miles!

It's been a funny old day really. It started with a flat calm where we felt we were rowing the ocean one nautical inch at a time. Sal said 'It's fantastic whale-watching weather' and within half an hour a pod of pilots sauntered past!

As the wind picked up about fifteen dolphins came alongside. They must have known we needed cheering up, the smell of burning just minutes before told us the iPod charging cable was caput ... so no more music. What's worse is we all have Robbie Williams in our heads!

Also we heard yesterday that Fogle and Cracknell are making waves with their naked rowing ... well, we've been wearing just sun cream for days now and we can tell you it's a far better sight! No wonder all the male crews behind us are trying so hard to catch up!

Much love,

S, S, C & J

Taking the decision to go on the para-anchor is one it's almost impossible to be happy about. It's basically an admission of defeat in the face of overwhelming evidence that there is absolutely no way you're going to be able to row in the current weather conditions. Again, this situation only emphasised the differences between us. Where I saw an opportunity to bed down, get some sleep and recover, Sue saw failure and a lack of commitment. In fact, I recognised myself from the first row in her. I imagine the same thoughts must have been going through her head: 'Why can't we row? Surely if we sat out there and kept going we'd make some distance, even if it is only a mile!' She questioned my decision to stop rowing and sit out the weather, and even when we were going backwards she struggled to cope with the situation. In fact we rowed far longer than we should have, losing distance with every stroke, just because I didn't want her to think I was happy to up sticks when the going got tough. But, like Mum and I quickly discovered, you cannot control the weather or the ocean. They control you, and once you learn this invaluable lesson the happier and more accepting of the situation you will be.

We all bedded down in the cabin for some much-needed but uncomfortable sleep, but Sue still climbed out of the cabin on the hour, every hour, to check the flag was still flapping in the wrong direction. In fact I don't think Sue ever got used to the lack of control on the boat and at the time I was selfishly unsympathetic to her distress. The constant 'Has the wind changed? Can we row now?' attitude wound me up, probably as much as my 'Let's stop' attitude wound her up. Although Sue and I were at polar opposites, we never argued. We just didn't always understand each other. But we tried, and that took considerable patience on both sides.

Skipper's Log

11.12.05   *On para-anchor with v. strong SW winds all night. V. choppy – had started flat calm – wind moved, predicted to remain till Tuesday.*

519 miles

13.12.05   *Glad to be off anchor – making back some miles.*
Wind not changed but fighting it. Steady SW.
107 miles

From: Rowgirls
To: Newsdesk
Date: 13 December 2005
Re: Rowgirls' Diary: Michael Fish — When Weather
Reports Go Wrong!

Now you'd think, after three reports stating that
we'd wake up to a fresh north-easterly, that we'd
spring out of our cabin to find our flag merrily
flapping in the right direction. Alas, no! So, being
typical Brits we obsessed about the weather and
rowed eagerly for the entire day hoping that our
flag would in fact stop flapping with the south-east
breeze. Unfortunately it's been a headwind all day
with little sign of changing; also you can imagine
our horror as we stare towards the horizon at the
thunderstorm that will probably drench us throughout
the night. We shouldn't complain though ... at least
it's not cold!

Further developments on the boat include the
discovery of more teabags! For two distressing days
we thought we were down to our final ninety bags (do
the maths ... that's no way near enough!). We had
a flood in the kitchen and it turned into a giant
hatch full of tea. The girls recommended Sue suck
it up using the bilge pump (aka Simon Snake) but the

team stuck together knowing Sue would not make it across without her cuppa and so sacrificed their own daily brew. But more bags were discovered and much celebrating was had. We even sang a few Christmas carols and argued over the lyrics for 'Fairytale of New York'. What is Shane MacGowan singing?

Here's to a wet night and better weather tomorrow, perhaps?

Much love,

The ever-shrinking Rowgirls x

Skipper's Log

16.12.05   *Another bloody awful day. Started pretty flat but picked up with v. strong S wind, driving rain. Para-anchor from 1.00 pm till 1.00 am. Came off to steady NW.*
714 miles

From: Rowgirls
To: Newsdesk
Date: 16 December 2005
Re: Rowgirls' Diary: B*ll*cks to This!

Where's the elusive north-easterly?
   Ever tried walking up the street in gale-force winds with someone chucking buckets of water at you while someone sings out-of-tune Dolly Parton in your ear? Then you pause to catch your breath and

realise you are actually going backwards? Welcome to the world of ocean rowing!

Our patience has taken a battering these past few days. If anyone has any top tips for staying chirpy during such frustrating times, please send them in. Any jokes, news from home, funny stories would be most appreciated ... there's only so much happiness a girl can get from a bar of Dairy Milk!

As I write this from the cabin, Sue and Sally are singing 'Go West' by the Pet Shop Boys ... well, if the oars won't do the job maybe the voices will!

Signing off from camp Rowgirl,

C, J, S & S x

The updates we sent home were always upbeat and positively dripping with a saccharine 'stiff-upper-lip' attitude. Understandably the girls didn't want their parents to worry, so were really keen to paint a picture of courage and harmony on the boat. Their natural 'glass-half-full' outlook influenced everything they wrote. I, on the other hand, wanted to distribute a more honest account of our situation.

Where Claire would write 'It's been a slow day and we're feeling a bit down, but the sunset is beautiful and it makes us feel like it's all been worthwhile' we'd actually be thinking 'God this is awful, no sunset is going make the pain in our arses go away and quite frankly the next fish that looks at us in the wrong way is going to get eaten!'

I just couldn't understand why we were so different. Where the girls would be out in their specialist wet weather gear, I'd be sat in my spotty cagoule from Millets. When the girls drank tea at night I had coffee instead. When I pulled out my pegged packet of cress seeds I think they thought I was from a completely different planet! They went with it though, but we only grew one crop before I realised they really didn't care.

Our relationships were awkward. Where Mum and I only found similarities, on this trip all I discovered were differences. We all made compromises but I think the girls made more for me then I did for them. They had to put up with my idiosyncrasies, my need to stand out, be different. I thought I'd got over that as a teenager, but no, I still wanted to be the only mod in a group of rockers.

Skipper's Log

17.12.05   NW all day. Gentle to brisk. Rowed into it all day. Made good progress though. Made it to 2,000 miles to Antigua & less than 100 miles to waypoint. Saw large whales – about four. Didn't stay long. 751 miles

From: Rowgirls
To: Newsdesk
Date: 17 December 2005
Re: Rowgirls' Diary: A Blistering Mile per Hour

But we're not complaining (that much), we're singing instead! Unfortunately we have floundered somewhat when it comes to the right words. Having forgotten our copies of *Hymns Ancient and Modern* we get halfway through a triumphant 'Jerusalem' before being reduced to a 'la, la, la'.

The same could be said for our regurgitation of Christmas carols (ancient and modern!). Perhaps we could ask for a few emails with the right words to 'White Christmas', 'The Twelve Days of Christmas' (particularly days ten, eleven and twelve), 'We Three Kings', 'Oh Little Town of Bethlehem', 'Silent Night' and 'Oh Come All Ye Faithful' ...

We're making the very best of the final battery blip on our iPod knowing it will die on us in the next couple of days, so please save us with some lyrics if you can!

The Great Peg Sacrifice

Yep, we didn't realise we'd be calling for the great peg sacrifice so early on in the trip but it seems we are now desperate.

All you need is a wooden peg and a body of water (be it a bowl of tap water or a lake). At 6.00 pm tomorrow (Sunday) we will cast our pegs into the water together as a gift to the gods of the wind and waves. If we do it all together it may work! All you need to say as you toss your peg is: 'May you grant the Rowgirls fair winds and waves, particularly on Christmas Day, but not too brisk between 12.00 and 2.00 pm when Jo is cooking dinner.'

Let's get these winds in the right direction TOGETHER!

Still rowing despite the headwinds,

S, S, J & C

296

With our lead slowly diminishing panic started to set in. We'd been doing so well I think we thought we had the race in the bag, but because the weather had been playing havoc with our speed the Milkers were beginning to catch up, and fast.

These were testing times, frustration was evident and we were all becoming a little less patient with each other. Jo and I were on the verge of strangling Sue, who seemed quite incapable of getting out of the cabin on time. We'd call 'Ten minutes, chicas' and fifteen minutes later Sue would climb, disorientated, out of the cabin having not realised that we'd been sat there fuming as we waited for her.

I asked Claire about the best way to broach the subject. As ship mediator her take on the situation would be far less Machiavellian then ours. Jo and I also felt we needed her on side to be sure Sue knew we were all unhappy about the situation. Jo and I were very conscious that we could be quite anal about things, like keeping the cabin tidy, writing in the 'right' place in the Skipper's Log or putting the lighter back in the cupboard so it wouldn't go missing. Claire and Sue, on the other hand, were far more relaxed: it really didn't bother them that clothes were strewn everywhere or that we were on our last lighter because the rest had rusted from being left lying about in the damp cabin.

So, not wanting to come across as the time-keeping police, we pressed Claire for her support, but in her usual even way she said, 'Well, we all come out late occasionally, perhaps you should cut her some slack.' (It was all very petty, but if no one was going to say anything I appreciated the extra five minutes' sleep when paired with Sue. Whilst she was floundering about in the cabin taking ten minutes to put a T-shirt on, I got more shut-eye!)

Skipper's Log

18.12.05   Headwind all day. Steering difficult. No change in wind direction. Reports say it's worse for others. Now ninth.
771 miles

From: Rowgirls
To: Newsdesk
Date: 18 December 2005
Re: Rowgirls' Diary: How to Survive the Graveyard Shift

The three-hour stint of either 12.00 to 3.00 am or 3.00 till 6.00 am has become a source of much amusement onboard. We've started making up games to keep our minds perky and our eyes bright.

Eye spy hastily gave way to the name game, which transformed into the memory trip to the shops and swiftly materialised into a full-blown spelling bee. With little else to occupy our brains, and the fear of them slowly reducing to mush, we upped the stakes from using the standard alphabet to the phonetic alphabet ... but that's not all, folks. We spell backwards! I know, it screams excitement, but when you have the challenge of spelling 'hermetically' phonetically, backwards, it keeps the brain in tiptop condition throughout the wee hours.

It's frightening stuff. But when you've finished talking about babies and shopping it's time to find a new topic of conversation. We are going to know each other very well when we get back! The mind boggles.

So, as you can tell, all's cheery on the good ship Shelterbox. Off to reduce brain pickle-age ...

Much love,

Sierra, lima, romeo, india, golf, whiskey, oscar, romeo.
xray, xray, xray

~

STATISTICS SAY THAT women speak an average of 20,000 words a day[24] (in comparison to men, who only require a rather conservative 7,000), and I can well believe it. Whenever Sue and Claire took to the oars together they talked constantly from the moment they sat on the fluffy cushions to the moment they went to sleep. They talked about family – how what's-his-name had married thingamajig – friends, boyfriends, school days, holidays. Anything and everything about their lives from birth to modern day, and it never stopped!

As I sat in the cabin their muffled conversation, punctuated by laughs and giggles, leaked through the airtight hatch. I have to admit I did feel a twinge of jealousy, they seemed to have so much in common and they got on so well. I checked myself quickly, realising the childishness of my envy – it wasn't

---

[24] A statistic put forward by psychiatrist Dr Louanne Brizendine of the University of California, San Fransisco in her book *The Female Brain*.

as if I couldn't sit with either of them and engage in a similar conversation. The truth was I just didn't want to. I found endless chatting about people I didn't know tiresome and although I tried my hardest to remember the names of brothers, sisters, aunts and uncles I couldn't for the life of me recall who had done what, when. I decided in the end to stop trying and stuck to singing and playing games instead.

Skipper's Log

19.12.05	Headwinds all day. SW-W. Light during day, stronger at night. Only boat moving in fleet! Went swimming, lots of calls from home. 791 miles
21.12.05	Wind's changed! 15kt W. Bit of struggle when broaching waves. Quite a hard night. Now in seventh position. Over-cast day – wind chilly! 879 miles
23.12.05	Moderate S-ly, raining on/off during night. Difficult rowing broadside to wind & waves. Cooker broke – fixed, now stored in front cabin. 960 miles

From: Rowgirls
To: Newsdesk
Date: 23 December 2005
Re: Rowgirls' Diary: Close Calls

You may have noticed that the weather hasn't exactly been in our favour during the last week. We have struggled to row at 90° to the wind, the evenings being particularly rough, causing us to get kitted up in our full-on ocean racer gear. We've had a couple of close calls, the first being our cooker. At the end of a particularly wet shift where the sea had abused us to the limit, Claire and Jo gratefully handed the oars over and retreated inside to cook up some hot water for dinner. To our distress we discovered the cooker wouldn't light. As it was dark and miserable out, we were resigned to eating breakfast cereal for dinner. After many attempts at lighting and several gas bottle changes later we decided that the cooker had drawn its last breath. All was not lost: we were prepared for such an event, spare parts were produced. Much grunting and cursing and beating at the cooker with the axe (we didn't bring a hammer) ensued and finally we dismantled it and replaced the correct parts. Once again we were cooking on gas! We'd be buggered without a cooker.

The other close call involved more tankers in the night.

Anyway, as some of you may well be logging off for the holidays today we want to wish everyone a truly merry Christmas. We will of course be continuing our updates, so if you have access at home, tune in to hear more tales of woe.

Happy Christmas and best wishes for the New Year to our friends and family and all the other avid fans out there! Think of us eating the great meal Jo is going to concoct.

Signing off,

J, C, S & S xxxx

~

Skipper's Log

24.12.05   Christmas Eve. Weather behaved-ish. Steady N-NNE. Made good progress. Wind picked up during night but waves stayed pretty low, Jo fell on changeover, hurt back. Sue, Claire & Sally did extended shifts to cover from 12.00-8.00 am. Called Aurora - advised rest & painkillers. Awaiting further details.
1007 miles

The night before Christmas Eve, whilst changing shifts, Jo slipped on her way to the cabin, slamming herself into the A-frame before falling on to the edge of the overhanging gunnels. She shrieked with pain, clutching her back, before bursting into tears. All of us were out on deck, Sue's eyes rolled as Claire and I asked Jo if she would be able to climb into the cabin. With gasps and groans she lowered herself through the door, tears flooding down her cheeks. 'I can't do it,' Jo spluttered over and over again. 'I can't row anymore!'

For weeks Jo had been complaining about a back injury she'd sustained some months before. She'd been seeing a chiropractor before getting on the boat. We were all sympathetic, but when she first told us we were already at sea and there was nothing we could do to help her. We all tried to reassure her and boost her morale but Claire, Sue and I couldn't help but feel annoyed that she'd put us all in a really difficult position.

'Just do what you can, that's all we ask,' we'd said, conscious that we were all in pain, all struggling to get through each and every minute at the oars. 'Whatever happens, we're all going to get across together!' we reiterated as she sat cringing in pain, clutching her side, weeping as she rowed.

Sue was particularly frustrated, her natural competitiveness meant she found it difficult to sympathise with Jo especially as she'd known she wasn't fit enough to attempt the row. We had all agreed to the goal – to be the first women's four. But what do you do when you know your crewmate was instrumental in getting you to the start, but now she's jeopardising your efforts to finish? You row and you keep rowing, around the clock, until she's fit enough to take to the oars again, and that's what we did for the next three days.

Again we sent back a glowing 'everything's fine' update, totally underplaying the hostility Sue was feeling towards Jo, Jo was feeling towards us all/the entire trip, and what Claire and I were feeling about the entire situation.

```
From: Rowgirls
To: Newsdesk
Date: 24 December 2005
Re: Rowgirls' Diary: Ronan was Right ...
```

```
Life is a rollercoaster, particularly life on an
ocean rowing boat. Physically, surfing the waves is
similar, emotionally, you're up and down all the
time and sometimes you just want to get off but
```

can't. It's funny how things change. Last night the
wind finally spun round to a favourable direction,
only for Jo to take a fall during shift change,
which has left her in severe back pain and unable to
row. So the team has pulled together and is rowing
a gruelling routine of two hours on, one off while
Jo rests up. Needless to say Jo feels awful, but at
least it means she can spend more time preparing us
a sumptuous Christmas meal, following our champagne
breakfast.

We have spotted two massive whales, one of which
swam right under the boat.

Here's wishing everyone out there a very merry
Christmas from the Rowgirls.

J, C, S & S

By Christmas morning there was a general consensus that we
should cancel the day, we were so bloody miserable we just
couldn't face it. Claire, Sue and I had rowed for six hours each
as Jo slept on in the cabin.

My head was filled with thoughts of failure. If Jo decided to
leave the boat we'd be disqualified. As much as I loved her as a
friend I was utterly resentful of both her and the hopelessness
of the situation. We were not in control, this was no longer a
team effort, our fate was in the hands of one person and I can
imagine Jo knew that all too well.

All we could do was row, support Jo and pray that her injuries
would heal. Perhaps we wouldn't have lost too many race places

and maybe we'd be able to make up any lost distance and maintain our strong position in the field.

We could all tell that she wasn't 'seriously' injured, no bones were broken, only muscles pulled and bruised. It would be down to Jo's resolve to get us through to the end together. It was a lot to hope for, especially as she'd been so miserable for so long. But for all my hoping I remember thinking she had probably made the decision to leave the very moment she climbed into the cabin the night before. So as Christmas Day dawned we were all convinced that this was it, we were out of the race.

Ironically, at that moment we were so close to Clint and Chris's boat that families sent us texts, asking if we were planning to meet up with them to exchange presents.

Skipper's Log

25.12.05   Christmas Day!! Continued three up throughout day & night. Two hrs on, one off. Jo rested. Wind E to NE to N. Brisk on occasions up to 15kt. Settling to 5kt.
1047 miles

From: Rowgirls
To: Newsdesk
Date: 25 December 2005
Re: Rowgirls' Diary: The Day Christmas was Saved

Merry Christmas everyone! A cracking Christmas was had aboard the good ship Shelterbox. The events of Christmas Eve nearly had us cancelling the day altogether, but Rowgirl resilience shone through and we chose to celebrate the day in style, champers 'n all!! Wishing all of our friends, family and supporters a fantastic break.

Much love,

C, S, S & J xxxx

Skipper's Log

26.12.05   *Fantastic Christmas Day - salmon pate on toast with champs for breakfast. Coq au vin, potatoes & veg for lunch. Chilled day with pressies. V. calm - light variable wind. V. hard night - no winds - low mileage. Why? Average 1.5kt. Strange! All relatives rang.*
            1083 miles

From: Rowgirls
To: Newsdesk
Date: 26 December 2005
Re: Rowgirls' Diary: The Best Christmas Ever!

As you can probably tell we've had a fantastic Christmas, although at one point we were so miserable that the prospect of spending the day at sea filled us with dread rather than joy.

Sue made a huge difference to all our moods. It had been a long night at the oars without Jo in action, but as our newly employed Cabin Girl prepared our breakfast, Sue emerged dressed as a pirate.[25]   We

---

[25] Sue dressed up in a Jolly Roger flag I'd bought her for her birthday and an eye patch too. A proper sight as she was also topless and wearing just a G-string!

306

couldn't help but fall about laughing! She took command of the sat phone and demanded carols for phone calls.

Jo surprised us with salmon paté on toast for breakfast and we had champagne too! For lunch out came the Harrods' coq au vin, fried potatoes and mixed fresh veg. We ploughed through our presents and cards and for one day we forgot about the race.

Jo tentatively sat on the oars with back brace and 'Sam Splint' in place and it was back to routine again.

How many can say they enjoyed such a sumptuous lunch with such fantastic company? We all got socks too!

Well, it's Boxing Day and we're catching up on sleep. Claire and Sally entertained the boat with their rendition of 'Bohemian Rhapsody' and Jo is doing brilliantly. This morning it felt like we were stuck in the Bermuda Triangle, light winds, good sea but absolutely no speed! Are we towing a whale? It made no sense. Well, as we write, the wind has picked up and the ocean is less gloopy. Here's to our first 1,000 miles!

Bruised and sore like we've gone ten rounds with Tyson,

S, S, C & J x

FOURTEEN

Tis the Season to be Grumpy

CLAIRE'S MUM HAD given her a new pair of scarlet Christmas pants *à la* Bridget Jones and it was a welcome relief for us all when she wore them every day instead of her G-strings. Her poor bottom was so sore, pimpled and red raw with boils I suspect the big pants offered some welcome respite from the coarse salty sheepskin cushions. Although Claire must have been suffering for weeks she never complained, even when her spotty bum was so tender she could barely sit down.

For once our sugared update was true – Christmas Day was wonderful. Together we sang carols, ate, drank and made merry, we forgot the trauma of the previous days and we gave each other time away from the oars, the best gift of all. Sue absolutely refused to let us squander the opportunity to celebrate; if she had I truly believe it would have turned into the worst Christmas ever.

On Boxing Day Jo, powered by painkillers, returned to rowing. All we asked her to do was to try and stay as positive as possible. We were all prepared to get her through each and every day with as much encouragement as she needed as long as she was prepared to commit to the very end. If she could find the courage, we would find the strength to row her to Antigua. But by New Year the weather was starting to turn, and Jo would no longer be the single cause of our problems on the boat.

Skipper's Log

28.12.05   Sticky water all day. V. frustrating. Wind & waves with us but no speed all day. Barely breaking 2kt. Found out we're down to ninth with Milkers on tail - only seven miles behind. 1156 miles

29.12.05   Horrendous day - thunderstorms, driving rain & rough seas. Difficult to get any speed from boat - great in morning but got progressively worse during day. At night wind changed to S, reduced mileage - morale low. Rudder also broken, ongoing repairs needed. 1194 miles

30.12.05   *Wind moved to S. Thunder squall. V. slow. Para-anchor for three hrs during v. heavy rain & winds. Out on oars again. Counting minutes W. Claire fell, smashed her nose. Not broken. Night rowing improving steadily throughout.*
1205 miles

From: Rowgirls
To: Newsdesk
Date: 30 December 2005
Re: Rowgirls' Diary: Kick Up the Bum!

The arrival of the long-awaited easterly has brought with it torrential rain and unruly seas. Rowing in what can only be described as setting cement has left us feeling a tad sorry for ourselves. Whinge!

Over the course of the last couple of days Jo got hit on the head with a knife, *House of Flying Daggers* stylie, and Claire took a blow on the nose. There was a half-decent nosebleed but we're still waiting for the black eyes to emerge. Anyway, when the sun came up this morning we had ourselves a good wash in some emergency beauty products (goodies from Jo) and now we're back to it with increasingly smiley faces! A much-needed kick up the bum.

Much love

S, S, C & J x

Skipper's Log

31.12.05   New Year's Eve. Weather improving! Dry day with SE winds, boat at angle, but got over 2kt - first time in some days. Milkers ahead. Morale low - needed good day to boost it.
1239 miles

From: Rowgirls
To: Newsdesk
Date: 31 December 2005
Re: Rowgirls' Diary: Happy New Year!

As we watch the final sun of 2005 fall into the ocean, we wanted to wish you all a happy New Year from the mid-Atlantic. Have a great evening of fun and frivolities. We will be having a sip of champers to see in the New Year – please have a drink for us.

We've had a busy day today, what with fixing a broken rudder and preparing a trifle (the jelly didn't set but the thought was there!), but we did put some thought into our resolutions for 2006:

- row less
- gain weight
- get out more
- sleep
- shower

Much love to all,

The Rowgirls x

~

AS THE MILKERS zoomed ahead I think we all started to regret having such a lazy Christmas Day. I do believe we all thought it wouldn't be possible for them to catch us, especially as we had been at least a couple of hundred miles ahead for almost a month. In all honesty a certain amount of complacency had set in, and now the competitive glue that had previously brought us together was beginning to come unstuck. Sue vented her frustration by grumbling that we were 'faffing'. She saw everything that wasn't rowing or sleeping as slowing us down. Her criticisms were really beginning to annoy me; certainly she was making no attempt to get out of the cabin on time.

I could tell Jo had reached saturation point. The pain, Sue's condemnations and the Milkers pulling ahead meant she had stopped trying. She came out to the oars late, was more miserable than she had been before and she barely pulled on her blades. Sometimes an hour rowing with Jo was as fruitless as an hour not rowing at all. It was always a little worrying when Jo and Sue were paired. I was half expecting them to get into a blazing row, but they got through their shifts together with grace and humility.

Claire, of course, remained steady. She never criticised, nor did she complain – I was beginning to think she had some super-human ability not to be irritated by anything. Whatever she was taking, I wanted some of it!

We were going slower and slower … and slower. Our weather reports were so off the mark the complete opposite of the predictions would probably be closer to what we were actually experiencing. Without an accurate weather report we were rowing blind into ever-worsening seas. We were also starting to receive messages from home that tropical storms were creating havoc amongst the fleet. If we weren't feeling the full effects now, we certainly would be over the next few days. But with half an ocean still to go there wasn't a lot we could do about it. There'd be no swimming home!

Skipper's Log

01.01.06   Rowing more bearable - SE wind getting lighter. Not fantastic mileage though. Celebrated NY. Champs/sparklers & chocolate! Whales stayed with boat for hr during night. Tropical storm Zeta threatening to bring strong winds, eta unknown, next 48 hrs?
1212 miles

02.01.06   Again another v. slow day. Feedback from home suggested eddies.[26] Rudder broke again this morning. V. hot days. Light S wind & waves.
1280 miles

04.01.06   Lowest day yet. Morale plummeted as speed didn't increase above 0.5kt. Wind direction & waves changed & speed increased incredibly by midnight

---

[26] Using my very limited knowledge of the oceans an eddy is a counter-current – basically the winds and waves are going one way whilst the eddy is dragging the water in the opposite direction. Hence everything looks great on the surface but you're not actually moving anywhere!

*- 2kt average. Mileage increased. Morale higher.
Here's hoping for more!
1311 miles*

From: Rowgirls
To: Newsdesk
Date: 4 January 2006
Re: Rowgirls' Diary: Nightmare on Eddy Street

'What are you doing?' we hear everyone cry? 'Why aren't you going anywhere? Are you dragging an anchor or a sunken fishing trawler? Have you stopped rowing?' Ok, let me take them one at a time.

We're rowing round the clock as hard as we can. Why aren't we going anywhere? That's the million-dollar question … from what we're experiencing and the information we're receiving from home we're caught on the edge of some very localised eddies and have been for a good few days. They're dragging us east, despite favourable winds and waves, and we want to go west! That's our best guess, anyways. We've tried to understand why we're moving soooo slowly, and we've checked we've not got anything tangled in the rudder.

We have most definitely not stopped rowing. We're continuing to row as hard as possible in a desperate attempt to get out of the mess we're in. As you've probably gathered we're finding it extremely challenging to keep going. It's hard work and it hurts to see our competition storming ahead. I guess that's why this is one of the world's toughest endurance races!

Good news though – the on-board greenhouse has sprouted some fine cress.

Until tomorrow,

A United Team of Rowgirls[27]

At one point we rowed for three hours and travelled only one mile! How is that possible? It's against the laws of physics! It would be quite a challenge to walk that slowly.

Skipper's Log

05.01.06   Wow! What a turnaround! Good strong ENE/NE winds, average 2.5kt. Spirits high. Sally almost hit by flying fish. Squalls were pain. Here's to more than 40 miles today! Making good track S to Equatorial current.
1382 miles

From: Rowgirls
To: Newsdesk
Date: 5 January 2006
Re: Rowgirls' Diary: The Only Way is Up!

Yeah, baby! Without the iPod everything we say has turned into a song lyric.

Well, Eddy has decided to go pester someone else for a little while, and we're up and going at a decent pace again. YIPPEE!

It's been pretty miserable at Camp Rowgirl for

---

[27] A reassurance to all at home that we were not planning to throw Jo overboard!

the last few days but now the sun is shining and the weather is sweet. It's also feeling hot, hot, hot. Talk about Sweaty Betties. Eek!

Sally has desperately tried to negotiate some more sleep from the rest of us by agreeing to eat our smoky bacon, mash and peas. Needless to say the rest of us haven't agreed, but she'll probably get the last laugh when we've eaten everything that's nice, leaving fifty packets of the bloody stuff.

Also close encounters of the flying fish kind. Suspect a collision will happen within days. Will let you know if one of the suckers has an eye out.

Bye bye, Miss American Pie,

S, S, C & J x

PS First crop of cress almost ready for the eating.

PPS After much discussion about the animals associated with Chinese New Year, Sally wondered if 2006 could be the Year of the Haddock? Any knowledge would be appreciated.

I'm not going to say I told them so, but godammit I told them so! When we had our discussions about food, I said to the girls 'Take the food you actually like to eat!' There's absolutely nothing worse than having to face 600 packets of chilli con carne when you can't stand the stuff. It may theoretically have enough calories to fuel your sixteen hours of rowing a day, but if you can't put it past your lips then it isn't going to make much of a difference! Shovelling in food with little thought for its texture and flavour is a boy technique, but we women have enough fat on our hips to stop any self-respecting female brain turning off the taste buds even in the direst of circumstances. If there's fuel-loaded thighs to be worked off then the 600 packets of dehydrated chilli con carne will inevitably stay locked away in the hatches. Or in this case, 'Mit Spec', aka smoky bacon, mash and peas.

It seemed no amount of Worcestershire sauce was going make that sloppy bag of vomit and dried peas taste nice, and guess what? The girls decided to pack hundreds of them! In their defence they did like it when they first tried it one lovely summer's evening when the kettle had been boiled with fresh, non-watermaker water and the bag had been left to hydrate fully! Oh well, it's a good thing I actually liked it, and although the bargaining didn't get me more sleep it did add a bit of variety to my own, rather dull, menu. So every morning the haggle would begin, and the auction would continue until each Rowgirl was happy with her three square meals for that day.

'I'll give you two Mit Spec for one of your lamb pilau?' – Jo to Sally.

'How about two Mit Spec and one of my chocolate mousses for your lamb pilau?' Claire would pipe up in the hope that my love for chocolate mousse would sway me towards her offer.

'Ok, two Mit Spec, I'll make your coffee tonight and I'll sing through the entire Robbie Williams album … and you know how much I hate that!' – Jo.

It was a faff, but not even Sue complained: she also hated Mit Spec!

Skipper's Log

07.01.06   *Stonking day - great speeds - good NE wind &*
             waves, lots of splashes though. Still no news on
             Milkers' progress. Here's to more good speeds, Jo
             called Aurora for extra meds - no joy -
             disqualification. Big decisions to be made.
             1440 miles

08.01.06   *Big waves, big winds & lots of rain! Great*
             progress although tough & intense. Rudder broken -
             AGAIN! Cabin flooded.

I was out on deck with Claire when it happened. We'd been
checking the rudder every hour for the past week or so – it had
been clunking strangely and the screws that held the steering
mechanism together needed to be tightened. We took it in turns
to lean out of the back hatch in the main cabin, torch between
teeth and spanner in hand, tinkering and swearing until the clunk
had disappeared. Sue and Jo took the lion's share of the repair
work and found something in common: a mutual fear that the
rudder was going to fall off at any time.

It was in the middle of the night, in particularly rough seas,
when they decided to take another look at the rudder. Exhausted
and worried they opened the hatch without any consideration
for the conditions, and within a matter of moments seawater
was pouring into the cabin. Sheepishly they popped their heads
out on deck and told Claire and me what had happened. The
mattresses were wet, the bedding was wet, our clothes were wet
– our only dry haven was soaked through, and I was livid.

We told the girls we'd sort it out in the morning, they should just do their best to find some dry bedclothes and get some sleep, but my rage increased. Why hadn't they moved the mattresses and the bedding? Why couldn't they have waited until morning? Poor Claire had me whittling in her ear all night.

'Please stop going on about it. Talk to them in the morning before we swap shifts. That's all you can do. It's an accident and accidents happen,' she finally snapped back.

At 6.00 am Sue and Jo emerged from the cabin, and as diplomatically as I could I told them I had something to say.

'I'm really pissed off that the cabin's flooded. I know you were tired and the rudder needed to be looked at, but I think you should have moved everything out of the way first. In fact, I think we all need to do that in future.'

'I'm sorry,' said Sue.

'What did you expect us to do?' spat Jo. 'The rudder had to be fixed!'

'I just wanted you to move the bedding!' I replied in desperation.

'Why does everyone blame me? Why is it always my fault?' Jo flew of the handle.

'It's not your fault! Sue made the decision too!'

'It's a blameocracy on this boat!' Jo screamed.

'Did you or did you not move the fucking mattresses, Jo?' I screamed back.

'I've had enough! That's it. I'm getting off this fucking boat! I'm fed up with you blaming me for everything!'

With this, Jo got up and threw herself back into the cabin. A shocked Sue stared back at me.

'I'm really sorry, I should have thought before I opened the hatch,' she whispered.

'I was angry, I was churning all night and I just needed to tell you. I wasn't trying to blame Jo or you. We just need to move stuff first, that's all,' I said.

I turned to Claire.

'I didn't handle that very well, did I?'

'No, you didn't,' she said, looking just as shocked as the rest of us.

It had all escalated out of control. It was just a stupid little argument, but unfortunately it was the catalyst in Jo's decision to leave the boat. I climbed in the cabin beside Jo as she lay there weeping and ventured an apology, which she accepted and reiterated. Jo tried to explain her position: she told me how difficult it had been for her to deal with the pain day in, day out. She also confessed to not caring about the race anymore, or the fact that the Milkers were ahead – she just didn't have the drive to 'dig deep, row hard'.

She also felt that we didn't believe her when she told us how much pain she was in, and in truth I don't think we did. I explained that we were all suffering, and however much we said that we would support her all the way, neither Claire, Sue nor I could face another day of rowing for six hours non-stop whilst she slept. I left Jo in the cabin having agreed that she should take some time to think about her decision.

It felt like an eternity before she re-emerged. She was going to leave – she didn't want us to carry her to Antigua and she didn't want to be in pain any more. We agreed that if it was her decision, then we would be happy with it. Jo called *Aurora* and asked them to come and collect her.

We were silent on the boat for some time, reflecting on the fact that Jo's decision would disqualify us from the race.

Aurora Arrives

It took a few days before *Aurora* appeared on the horizon. Jo had packed, her modest belongings stuffed into a waterproof sausage-shaped sack. As the sails grew larger, I took to the VHF to help guide the yacht in and Claire and Sue continued rowing. Jo stood clutching the A-frame in anticipation of the swap, but as the yacht drew up beside us, Jo surprised us all.

'I'm not leaving, I going to stay and row this boat to Antigua!' she called across the water.

What?! Claire, Sue and I exchanged looks of horror. Why hadn't she warned us? We sported fake grins as the yacht crew looked on, trying to gauge if we were ok with this revelation.

'It's up to Jo,' we shouted back, united in her decision to stay but secretly wishing she'd decided to go – could we put up with another month of misery?

We made the most of *Aurora* whilst she was there. The watermaker hatch had flooded so often the motor had stopped working, so water supplies on the boat had been vastly reduced. There would be race place penalties for accepting a re-supply but without water we would never make it the end.

We lashed together some empty water bottles and threw them overboard. It took about two hours for the yacht crew to produce enough through their own watermaker to fill them. To reduce the risk of losing the bottles at sea, Dan (of Jan and Dan fame) and Miki (ironically a friend of Jo's from home) jumped aboard an inflatable dinghy, launched into the ocean and paddled across. It had been so stressful over the last few days that seeing their happy, smiley faces left us all a little hysterical. Before we released them Jo shared a moment with Miki, whilst I hugged Dan, whispering into his ear, 'It's been really shit, but we're ok. We'll deal with it.'

'The weather's going to get worse, stay safe,' he whispered back.

With Miki and Dan safely back on board *Aurora*, Lin tacked towards the west. The second they disappeared from sight Jo turned to us in tears.

'Why didn't I get off?' she sobbed. 'I should have got off!'

Skipper's Log

08.01.06

Jo decided to leave boat after visit from Aurora. A difficult decision for us all, after many days of upset. They came past after previous call from Jo two days ago. After they left Jo had change of heart, Lin gave two hrs' grace but she rang them for pick-up within hr. They plan to arrive approx. 3.00 am Monday, pick-up
10.00 am.
1491 miles

By this time it was no longer just Jo's choice as to whether she stayed on the boat or not. During her time on the phone to

Lin, Claire, Sue and I discussed the situation. It couldn't go on, Jo wasn't enjoying it any more and we weren't enjoying having her on the boat either. The constant crying, moaning and complaining was getting us all down. Also, we just didn't want to risk another change of heart.

As she stepped back out of the cabin, we asked her about the conversation with Lin. 'I'm definitely going,' she confirmed.

Claire spoke our minds. 'Please don't take this the wrong way, but we think you should go too, for your sake as well as ours.'

'Don't worry, I won't change my mind again,' she replied.

Exhausted, but smiling weakly, it was easy to see that the weight of the decision had finally lifted. Jo knew there was no turning back.

With Jo's relatively imminent departure the fog of tension dissipated and we all felt happier again. Unfortunately for Jo, Claire, Sue and I launched straight into our plans for after her departure. Without intention, we were already behaving as if she wasn't there. Sensing this growing divide I aligned myself more with Jo, reassuring her that she'd made the right decision. In fact, we drew up a list of promises. The tatty piece of paper she wrote them on read a bit like this:

- Enjoy the time you have left
- Enjoy the time on the yacht
- Remember we still love you
- You made the right decision at the time
- When you get to Antigua give Clint a huge hug
- NO REGRETS

Having 'no regrets' was almost an impossibility. Knowing how Tommo felt when he stepped off *Calderdale* I could pretty much guarantee that the moment Jo stepped on *Aurora* she would regret her decision for the rest of her life.

Skipper's Log

09.01.06   Oh what a lovely day & night! V. rough all day -
            decision to go on anchor 3.00 am. Rudder lever
            snapped. All slept from 3.00-10.00 am. Aurora
            text - pick up Jo today. Starting to get on top of all
            disasters:
            • morale waning
            • watermaker flooded
            • two hatches flooded - food lost
            • rudder broken
            1527 miles

10.01.06   Did some housekeeping to sort boat - came off para-
            anchor. Aurora visited but sea too rough to pick up
            Jo. Maintained two hr on/two hr off shift pattern
            till dawn. Big seas - 35kt winds NE. Adjusted to
            reduce track S. Aurora returns 72 hrs. Digicel
            capsized & saved. Chris capsized[28] - waiting for
            oars.
            1554 miles

Aurora circled us for some hours waiting for the wind to abate, but with no sign of wind or waves calming down we all knew

---

[28] The Irish lads on *Digicel* had the shock of a lifetime when they woke in the night to discover their transom had been pulled clean off. They abandoned to their life raft before a commercial vessel bound for Spain picked them up.

transferring Jo would be ridiculously foolhardy. As she stood up at the A-frame speaking to *Aurora* on the VHF, she looked as excited and hopeful as a puppy with a brand new ball.

Lin made the decision to abandon the transfer; Jo would have to sit it out a while longer. She also told us that Chris had capsized and had lost all his oars. They would go to him and then come back; perhaps the weather would have turned by then.

Skipper's Log

11.01.06 — Waves still big – no sign of weather calming. Now working off ropes to steer. Watermaker faulty. Will dry out when chance.
1592 miles

From: Rowgirls
To: Newsdesk
Date: 11 January 2006
Re: Rowgirls' Diary: Tough Decision

Dear Friends

By now you will all know that I am due to leave the good ship Shelterbox due to my ongoing back injury. After much deliberation and heart searching I made the decision to call in the support yacht. Believe me, it's been the hardest decision I have ever had to make. For three weeks I have tried to row through the pain in my back, the painkillers have run out and there are only so many sessions on the oars that can be spent in tears. My morale has hit rock bottom and that's no good for anyone.

I hope I don't have to emphasise how bad I feel about deserting the girls like this, but I feel that it's the best option. It's going to be with me for a long time.

It has been an amazing experience out here but never underestimate how tough it is.

Just another couple of days till *Aurora* can get back to us, then blessed relief for my back.

Thanks to everyone for all the support throughout the trip, please continue to support my Trojan team mates. They are truly hardcore and I have complete faith that they will get through the next 1,200 miles in style.

Signing off once and for all,

Jo x

~

WORD OF CAPSIZING boats was coming thick and fast, with every passing day another was going over, catapulting terrified crews into the ocean. The whole region was alive with EPIRB emergency signals. It was becoming extremely dangerous and the situation on our own boat was getting worse.

The rudder was performing so badly even concentrated hand steering couldn't stop us from broaching the waves. Walls of water were tumbling towards us and our fear was rising with every mounting wave. I decided it was time to look at the rudder myself, for if it broke at this stage we'd be in serious trouble. Broaching the waves as we were it would only be a matter of time before we went over.

We stopped rowing. Claire and Sue fished out the toolkit and Jo and I disappeared into the cabin. Heaving the mattresses away from the back hatch, Jo held them in position as I angled myself out to get a closer look. Waves were right on our tail, I watched them carefully, following their breaking pattern and ducking every few minutes to pull the hatch shut when one did more than threaten to flood the cabin.

From what I could see the metal plate that lay on the top of the main body of the rudder had come loose and shifted askew whenever we adjusted its direction. The tension had also been too much for the flimsy mechanism; the lack of alignment of rudder and plate had bent the mechanism completely out of shape, rendering it useless. The only way to save it now would be to glue all the bolts in, effectively sticking the plates together. Jo and I set to work.

Blindly, I shoved my finger inside a tubular section on the plate, feeling for the nuts that would have to come off so I could cover the stem of the bolt with Sikaflex – a waterproof adhesive. Annoyingly I just couldn't get to one of the bolts: the one that held the whole bloody thing together! But during my investigation I discovered an unused hole, which presumably should have been used for a third bolt – a bolt that probably would have stopped the plates from moving in the first place!

'Right then girls, we're going to have to line up with the hole, drill through the top, get a bolt through, glue it, get the third bolt through, glue that and, ta da, it should be fixed!'

'How are we going do that?'

'Erm, I'm not sure yet – we have a hand drill, right?'

I'd measured the placement of the hole in the tube using a pencil, marking its approximate position by scoring the wood with my fingernail. If the measurement was wrong, any drilled hole through the top plate would be a complete waste of time. Unfortunately I wouldn't know if I'd got it right until we made it through the five-millimetre steel. With the hand drill precariously balanced on the wet slippery metal I slowly began to pierce the metal plate, ducking into the cabin when the waves hit. The drill bit jammed in the metal, came out of the drill and disappeared into the water.

'Shit! The bit's gone!'

'That was the only eight-millimetre bit we had!' Claire called from the deck, the toolkit stretched out before her.

'Shit!'

'We've only got a six-millimetre left.'

'Oh shit! That isn't going to be big enough for the bolt. Damn it. Right, I'll get the hole done and I'll think about making it bigger later.'

It took Jo and me three hours to drill the hole, taking it in turns until our knees and bellies became too sore from trying to stay upright, our stomachs banging against the hatch frame, our knees scuffing and slipping about on the cabin floor.

When we finally broke through the metal we screamed with joy. I couldn't believe it: the hole was right underneath; my rudimentary measuring system had worked! With the axe and a bradawl I hammered round the edges of the hole to widen it until it was just big enough to poke a bolt through.

'Shit!'

'What now?'

'I've just dropped the bloody bolt!'

'For God's sake! We've only got three left!'

Holding each gluey bolt between my teeth, I'd take them, all fingers and thumbs, and carefully push them through the plate, drawing on the forgotten skills gained from playing Operation as a kid. Sikaflex was getting everywhere: as gloopy as children's snot and as sticky as Superglue it found its way into my hair and all over the cabin. Someone had told us a good coating of spit on the fingers stops it sticking, but you can imagine the mess.

With the tiny nuts stuck to my fingertips, saliva dripping for lubrication, I reached in to attach them to the base of each bolt; then in with the spanner to tighten them up before squirting a meringue-shaped blob of Sikaflex on the top of each bolt. An hour or two later and the glue would harden and the rudder would be shipshape again. Hey presto!

Although we shouldn't have bothered, because a day later the whole bloody thing fell off the back of the boat.

Skipper's Log

13.01.06 Stonking day – 20-25kt wind NE, 12ft swells. Getting a handle on steering & routine. Watermaker running periodically. Made great mileage. Rudder terminal – pintels sheared off completely. Have retained rudder – Claire detached it through back hatch. Fitting on rudder itself has compressed & cracked fabric of rudder. Metal

mount sheared at welded point. Called Aurora -
phoning back. Current situation: on para-anchor
awaiting call from Aurora.
Options:
• Continue to Caribbean using drogues
• Abandon ship - destroy boat
• Continue but locate tanker - ask for rescue & boat
pick-up
Seeking advice from as many different sources as
possible. 9.31 pm - off anchor & rowing.
Experimenting with steering/weight distribution.
Consensus is continue to Caribbean, as close to course
as we can. If safety situation changes, look at rescue
situation then. Possible tanker pick-up before
abandon option. Will sleep & drift tonight to gauge
boat handling & distance.
1870 miles

From: Rowgirls
To: Newsdesk
Date: 13 January 2006
Re: Rowgirls' Diary

It's one catastrophe after another! First we thought
we lost all our teabags when a hatch flooded, then we
despaired when the flapjack tasted of carbon fibre.
Now the rudder has fallen off!! Honestly, will the
trauma never end?

Yep, at 8.00 am, after three days of mastering
the art of hand steering with ropes, we were saving

the rudder before it floated off to Brazil! The irony is Sally and Jo had spent over three hours hand drilling a hole through the top of it in high winds!

So here we all are, feeling a bit sorry for ourselves. We lose a Rowgirl tomorrow, our watermaker is still playing up and the majority of our remaining meals are smoky bacon, mash and peas.

Serious talks took place through some tears this morning. Do we give up? The boat would be blown up. Do we go on? Without a rudder we have to take the ocean as it comes.

We've regularly broached huge waves because Sue's steering leaves much to be desired (hey, we don't have to worry about that any more!), but the boat just takes them on the chin.

Aurora comes tomorrow so we'll be taking as much advice as we can. Rest assured we won't endanger ourselves but we are here to row an ocean and as long as the boat is in good nick and so are we, we're off to the Caribbean. It may just be a bit of a mystery as to where we land. Start your sweepstakes now!

Being the best of true British grit,

The Rowgirls

We sent our report home, glowing with confidence and calm, although we'd spent most of the day panicking.

'That's it, we're done!' I bawled. 'We're definitely out of the race now!'

Instead of remaining cool in a crisis, I let rip, unable to contain my anger. This would be the first time I saw Claire cry. Let's face it – if Claire was upset then we were definitely in trouble! We all sat on deck grieving over the rudder as if it were the dead body of a favourite dog. It was so twisted and shattered by storm-force winds and waves that there was absolutely no way to revive it. The reality was, even if we could somehow repair it, there would be no way to fit it back on to the transom. With over 1,000 miles to go we were up the ocean without a rudder, well and truly scuppered. We called a lot of people for their opinions, because the truth was we didn't know what to do for the best. Quite frankly, our trip was cursed.

We seriously considered calling it a day, not only because the moment the rudder came off our dream had died, but also because we couldn't guarantee our own safety from this point on. How lucky we were that the support yacht would arrive the following day, but how tempting it would be to abandon ship. Nobody would have thought badly of us.

As we deliberated, Sue was so deathly quiet that both Claire and I began to worry that she'd be boarding the yacht along with Jo. Her face was one of pensive torment.

'If Sue does go, we'll row it together, right?' asked Claire.

'Abso-fucking-lutely!' I cursed, determined not to give up. There was no way our boat was going to be blown up at sea when there was still a chance of getting her across.

It took much of the afternoon before we decided once and for all that Claire, Sue and I were going to continue no matter what; but we needed to find a way of steering the boat out of the danger zone. We cobbled together a drogue by tying several T-shirts and a couple of five-litre water bottles to some rope and flinging them over the side in the hope that the drag would pull us round. If we could stay with the waves instead of side-on to them maybe we'd have a chance, maybe if we played about with it a bit – a tug here and a extra T-shirt there – we'd have ourselves a rudimentary steering system. If not, the T-shirts would be a bright, sea-washed white and we'd be swimming the rest of the way home.

Jo was so terrified for our safety that she considered staying on board – we all agreed that she could make that decision in the morning, if we survived the night.

Skipper's Log

14.01.06

Well, we didn't capsize! All slept throughout night to see how we drifted. Total of 20 miles after 6 hrs rowing – 18 hrs drifting. Broached at 180° during the night – lots of water on deck. Looks like squalls & 20-25kt winds again today. Aurora arrived. Continued to row after contact established. They circled the boat for hrs, we threw water canisters overboard for them to refill. Miki & George came across in dinghy to collect Jo. In exchange for Jo they gave us cheese, tortillas & iPod charger from Chris Martin. Eight teams without rudders. Also gave us advice on drogues – recommended lifting out dagger board & moving more kit to stern. V. emotional afternoon.
Two oars broken during the day
1690 miles

After a relatively restful night Jo stuck to the plan and prepared for the pick-up. It was surprisingly low-key. When *Aurora* arrived Lin skilfully circled around our little boat. It took several hours before she felt able to launch crewmates Miki and Gorgeous George (so nicknamed to avoid confusion with Dr George) out in their little rubber dinghy.

I stood with Jo as Claire and Sue rowed, reassuring her as she held on to the A-frame beside me, her face a mixture of terror, apprehension and excitement. I don't think she was quite expecting to jump from a rather small rowing boat to a considerably smaller inflatable one!

Under the cold grey skies, a thousand miles from land in either direction, steely, foam-topped waves whipping up round the boat, we watched the little dinghy as she tipped and tossed about in the water, Miki and Gorgeous George clinging to the side and their paddles. For one small moment we were rather glad we were on our rudderless boat. It goes to show there are always people in worse situations than you!

During our wait two oars snapped almost simultaneously; they'd become caught beneath the hull and the pull of the water and the strength of the catching waves cracked them in half. One pair gone, only two pairs to go!

Miki and George paddled ever closer, Claire and Sue stopped rowing. I set up the camcorder on the A-frame, keen to capture this incredible mid-ocean rescue. Claire and Jo reached out over the side, grabbed the dinghy and pulled it up closer to our gunnels, holding tight, as Miki seized them round the necks. The air was thick with relief and the joyous sounds of laughter and happy weeping. I took my turn, edging down the deck to give Miki a squeeze.

'Eight boats are without rudders,' she whispered. 'But they're all still rowing. Please don't worry.' *Thank God*, I thought. *We're not the only ones.*

Jo manoeuvred herself over the side and tied herself with her harness to a cleat on the dinghy; Miki handed over a giant cheese and some tortillas – cheese sandwiches! Whilst trying to co-ordinate the transfer with *Aurora* on the VHF I'd joked about the prospect of some cheese sandwiches in exchange for Jo, a fantastic trade as she was so talented in the kitchen. Jo had already promised to be the support yacht's galley slave!

The dinghy party released itself from the side of the boat and began paddling off over the mountainous waves towards *Aurora*. We called our goodbyes, and as the paddlers clambered back on board the yacht, Sue, Claire and I watched as Jo's figure disappeared below decks. It was quite surreal really, knowing that within days she would see land again, eat 'proper' food and meet rowers who had already made it across, unlike the three of us, who were facing the prospect of another month at sea.

Aurora turned her sails and tacked off into the distance.

The First Women's Three

That same night Sue and Claire landed on top of me at 2.00 am. Our boat had been hit by a wave so huge we almost turned turtle.

Just hours before we'd decided to treat ourselves to a full night's sleep ready to attack the Atlantic the following day. We were so exhausted but exhilarated by the events of the day that we all squeezed into the cabin and stuffed ourselves with the dinner-plate sized cheese, served between the flour tortillas. We played cards, had a cup of tea and went to bed.

At 2.30 am we lay there in the darkness wondering if we'd see the sun rise again. We figured out our escape route, visualising our every move if the boat turned and didn't self-right.

'Ok, let's go through it. Open the hatch. Cabin fills. Out of hatch. Remember footwell. Feel for A-frame and follow it to gunnels. Remember swim under oars. Hold side. Find girls. Set off EPIRB.'

'Where's the EPIRB?' Claire asked innocently; but we all realised at the same time.

'Oh God, it's still out on deck!'

'Right, I'm going to get it,' Claire bravely volunteered. 'If we go over there's no way we're going to be able to set if off if it's still in the bloody bracket!'

Sue and I helped her into a lifejacket and harness. She disappeared through the door and out on deck. We waited nervously, desperately listening out for Claire above the wind and waves. We both gave an audible sigh of relief when the hatch handles turned and Claire's aggravated, red, sweaty face appeared in the darkness.

'I can't get it out! It won't come out of the bracket!' Tears of frustration trickled down her freckly cheeks.

'You've pressed the button at the back and pulled, right?' I ventured somewhat unhelpfully.

'Yes, I know how it works and I've tried that but I'm telling you, it won't come out!' she snapped back.

'Ok, I'll go and have a look,' I harrumphed.

I struggled into my lifejacket and harness and on my hands and knees worked my way along the deck towards the EPIRB, which of course was as far away from the cabin as we could possibly put it. The deck seemed unusually slimy, and whenever the boat jolted unexpectedly I bashed elbows and hips, caught fingers and banged toes. I inspected the EPIRB. The instructions were simple enough – push the knobble down at the back to release, and then pull the EPIRB out. Easy! I press, I pull, I press, I pull harder. I wiggle, wobble, grab with both hands and heave but there was no way in hell that it was going to come out of its bracket. Damn it!

'Claire!' I called. 'You're right, it won't come out! I'm coming back in.'

It had to come out, so we decided to attack it with an axe.

With EPIRB clutched to Claire's bosom, the deck now littered with the remains of the bracket, our lifejackets tightened firmly around our torsos, and the emergency grab bag serving as Sue's pillow, we tried to make the most of what darkness remained and went back to sleep.

I couldn't help feeling guilty. I had told the girls what a fantastic trip Mum and I had had, how we laughed all the way across, how the sun shone and the ocean twinkled. I had told them about Jan and Dan, the beautiful sunsets and their gin and tonics at bedtime. And here we were, facing the very real prospect of drowning along with an abundance of Mit Spec and half a cheese. It was all starting to look a bit dire!

Skipper's Log

11.01.08   Went back to the oars after night in cabin – seas
huge & confused. Lots of waves coming overboard,
lots of soul searching during day – Sally sorted
cabin for most of morning. Battened down 1.00 pm.
Cheese & tortillas for dinner. Wind E-ENE with E
swell making progress SW again. Another big leak
through back hatch. Sally went to sleep in front cabin
– much more comfortable for all.
1747 miles

By some small miracle we made it through another night, and we
were able to eat the rest of the cheese! But life on the boat was
beginning to feel a little cramped, especially as we hadn't dared
venture out on to the deck at night. So, only a couple of days
into the three-woman row, I thought it was about time I moved
out. Having sandwiched ourselves into the cabin, practically
hallucinating due to lack of oxygen, I decided one of us should
decamp to the front hidey hole and that person had to be me.

I'd watched the relationship between Claire and Sue grow and
I knew I just wasn't as close to them as they were to each other.
Also, I quite enjoyed the prospect of having my own space. The
back cabin had previously been split in two: Jo and I had kept
our half neatly ordered and tidy, unlike Claire and Sue. It was a
constant source of aggravation. So, for the sake of space and
happiness, I grabbed my belongings and spent the morning
making up the front cabin so it would be fit for habitation.

I'd already spent some time in amongst the clutter of boat spares and toolkit; on para-anchor days we'd taken it in turns to hole up in the front, giving the other girls a bit more space in the main cabin. Now, with the broken rudder as bedfellow, I blew up a Therm-a-Rest (Sue's alternative to the heavy mattresses), laid out a wet sleeping bag, shoved tubes of sunscreen, moisturiser and my last four wet wipes into bungies that held the spare bits of boat kit in place, and hung my Christmas socks from a cable that dangled from the ceiling. My little three-by-six-foot space had become my new home from home.

~

ALTHOUGH I HAD become the girl next door, at the oars Sue and I found our own connection – mutual terror. After nights of petrified rowing, having been tossed from our seats and slammed into the gunnels, left bruised and shaken, she and I decided to call a meeting. We put it to Claire that it was time to stop rowing at night. Our makeshift drogue wasn't working as well as we'd wanted it to, we were still broaching and in the darkness we couldn't prepare for the onslaught of the bigger waves.

Sue and I had spent many a gobsmacked moment transfixed by the truly monstrous walls of water that were heading straight for us. All we could do was sit there as a thirty- or forty-foot mountain rolled under us. Claire was less keen to stop. After some long and difficult negotiations we eventually reached a compromise. We rowed until midnight, then battened down and drifted. If we did capsize we would be far safer stowed in the cabin than out on deck in the dark.

As I scuttled into my den and Claire and Sue disappeared into their cabin I felt certain they were cursing my lazy, give-up attitude. I grew more anxious, fretful and paranoid – did they think me weak and pathetic for refusing to row at night? The seeds of self-doubt were sown and the ten-foot deck that lay between us seemed to be growing ever wider.

~

JANUARY CONTINUED TO be one dank, wet day after another. Every morning I peered out of my hatch in the hope that the sky would be cloudless and blue, but every morning bought with it gale-force winds, torrential rain and confused seas. The blacker the day the more difficult it was to brighten our moods, but we sang songs to lift our spirits, told jokes (usually the same three or four over and over again) and spoke of our plans for when we got home. Anything to take our minds off the situation.

By now we had lost a considerable amount of weight, our flesh was taught and brown, stretched over bones that were sticking out at all angles. Our legs were festooned in salt sores, so much so it looked as if we had chicken pox. Ulcers had begun to develop on my shins so I resorted to wrapping my calves in cling film to protect them for the seawater.

Sue refocused her competitive energy on bilging the food hatches two or three times a day. In the morning I'd see her G-stringed white bum cheeks bent over in the rain, a hose in one hand, the pump in the other. She became completely obsessed with the idea that the boat was going slowly because of all the extra water we were carrying. I occasionally made a half-hearted attempt to join her but I have to be honest and say that at this point I didn't care any more.

Skipper's Log

21.01.06   *Conditions remain unchanged. Clint & Chris arrived Antigua!*
1921 miles

From: Rowgirls
To: Newsdesk
Date: 21 January 2006
Re: Rowgirls' Diary: Letting Go of the Ferret!

Hey, it's Kipper here with some words of wisdom! I've decided dreams are like ferrets; sometimes they are difficult to hold on to. The more you grip them the more they wriggle until eventually you squeeze the life out of them. Sometimes it's best just to let them go and see if they come back to you.

Certainly on this trip we've had to let go of a couple of ferrets. We've been at sea for just over fifty days, which would have marked the world record for the women's fastest crossing, something we would love to have taken. Weather conditions scuppered that particular dream many weeks ago.

Before we left Gomera we spent some time talking about our goals for the trip, the biggest one being the first women's four. Again, a dream we can no longer fulfil.

Accepting this has been hard. It feels like it's
been a race of two halves, this second part being
very different from the first. I know none of us
thought we'd be rowing rudderless across the ocean.
We never thought there'd be just three of us either,
and quite frankly that has been tough, but we're
doing brilliantly. We've adjusted, made up a new
schedule and even treated ourselves to a large bowl
of cake, custard and strawberry jam.

  So it seems we have a new ferret to hold, one
which involves making it across the ocean safely.
Let's just hope this one doesn't wriggle too much,
but if it does we'll hold on to it as tight as we
can!

May your ferrets come back to you,

Kipper, Sue & Claire xx

Maybe the lack of vitamins was starting to send me slightly
mad because by this point I had started to pray for a bigger
disaster – spotting tankers on the horizon, I was practically
wishing them to come and run us down! You see, in my mind
all the achievement had gone. Getting home was a triumph in
itself, but I'd already done that. I had formed the Rowgirls to
break records, not potter about drinking tea, and anyway the
watermaker had completely packed up so we were putting every
cup, bowl, pan and basin out on deck to catch enough rainwater
just to make a mug!

  We'd been driven to flaccidity and I just didn't like it. I wanted
adventure, I wanted the race back, I wanted to live off my wits.

It was a bit foolhardy, wishing to be run down by a tanker, but anything, absolutely anything, was better than this everyday humdrum existence. Making a wet wipe last four washes had turned into the highlight of my week.

But all was not lost: the gods of adventure were listening to my pleas …

From: Rowgirls
To: Newsdesk
Date: 23 January 2006
Re:Rowgirls' Diary: Aaaaaarrrrrrrggggggghhhhhhhhh!

That was the sound emanating from the cabin this afternoon! It was the three of us screaming like girls as a huge 'fish' threatened to pull the transom off.

I was on the phone to Clint, Claire had just started her break and Sue was out on the oars at the far end of the boat … then suddenly things didn't sound right.

Sue was shouting, the boat was rocking all over the place and water was cascading over the side. Claire and I were trying to grab Sue as she clambered down the boat, but she was still attached by her harness to the other end. Water was being thrashed over the top of us and into the cabin. With Sue safely inside, we locked the door and sat frightened and shaking as the boat lurched from side to side. Claire said she could see fins flashing through the back hatch. The boat was creaking as the 'fish' (let's call it a shark!) struggled to release itself from our drogue bridle.

I got on the phone to *Aurora* ... line busy! *Sula* ... Bruce answered. I'll maintain I said something along the lines of 'It's Sally on Rowgirls, a shark has got caught in our bridle, we're in a bit of trouble.' I think it may have sounded more like 'Arrrrgggghhh!! Rowgirls ... Arrrrgggghhh ... Shark!'

I totally panicked. Claire took the phone; Sue leapt out the door, grabbed the knife and cut the drogue trip line. The horrendous creaking and splashing stopped and the boat settled into its normal bob.

When people tell tales of their high-sea adventures you always think, 'Yeah right, the fish was that big. Likely.' Brownies' honour, the fish really *was* that big!

If it looks like we've picked up speed this afternoon, you now know why ... Some shark is currently chewing on our makeshift drogue and we're trying to get as far from it as possible!

Shaken but not stirred,

Sally 'panic in a crisis' Kettle
Claire 'I saw the fins' Mills and
Sue 'great with a knife' McMillan

It couldn't get any better than that really — my life flashing before my very eyes! You can't keep a Rowgirl down. A week or so later Claire and I decided to dive into the shark-infested waters ...

From: Rowgirls

To: Newsdesk

Date: 28 January 2006

Re: Rowgirls' Diary: When Ignorance is Bliss!

It's been a beautiful, calm, wind-free, wave-free day. No scary grey wave monsters trying to knock us into the ocean and no rain! We've dried out wet bedding and clothes, cleaned and cleared the boat; everything feels less chaotic all of a sudden.

It has been extraordinarily hot though, so we took the plunge this afternoon. It's the first proper wash we've had in three weeks! We've lost about half a stone in grime.

Claire and I took a wee peek at the transom to look for damage after the 'shark' incident. A few scrapes and scratches in the anti-foul, a chunk out of the corner and a bloody great big hole!

'Erm …' we thought! Well, all we can say is thank God we didn't see it a couple of days ago in the really big seas. Well, we're not sinking, so it can't be too bad. Water has probably leaked through into one of the compartments[29] between the hull and the cabin floor but otherwise we're still here, bobbing about happily. Quite cool to have some war wounds though, something to show off with when we get back.

So off to estimate the size of the gigantic shark,

Kipper, Claireos & Susie xx

---

[29] Compartmentalised hull – just like the *Titanic*! Oh, and I called Dad (who else?) and asked him what to do for the best. He asked if we were sinking, I said no. He said, 'Well don't worry about it then!' although I was absolutely convinced the back of the boat was at a 45° angle – but that was probably the lack of vitamins!

PS Whilst I've been writing this the rain clouds have come in and Sue and Claire are out on the oars getting completely drenched! I can't laugh too long though: I go out there in ten minutes.

PPS the wind has suddenly changed, we're heading south east, i.e. backwards! Another unpredictable day at sea.

Skipper's Log

31.01.06   Moderate seas. V. wet day. Consistent squalls. Back to bilging! Warned by race officer not to travel further S than Antigua - have v. little control over our direction without rudder.
2241 miles

Thin, hungry and desperate for sex and a good curry the three of us decided it was time to ask for another re-supply. Although *Aurora* wouldn't be able to ship the boyfriends out for a conjugal visit they did agree to gathering up some food and dropping it off. Quite frankly they'd got used to coming over for a quick 'hello', so one more visit wasn't going to put them out too much.

Teams who had already finished donated their spare dehydrated meals and Jo promised to visit the local supermarket to pick up some goodies and pack them on the boat. There were treats a-coming and we absolutely could not contain our excitement. Sue and Claire were practically beside themselves imagining the edible delicacies stowed aboard *Aurora*. Sod the whales, waves and spotting land for the first time, I think the arrival of those extra provisions had turned into the highlight of their trip.

When *Aurora* arrived, again, like Santa and his merry elf, Dan and Miki took to the dinghy with several black sacks stuffed with food. They paddled over and threw the bundles aboard. Sue was so giddy she nearly wet herself. We dived in, ripping open the plastic like rabid dogs, allowing the contents to spill all over the deck. There were hundreds of bars of chocolate, Pepperamis and dehydrated sundries that left our eyes as big as saucers: tiger prawns in white wine risotto, 'Sunshine Breakfast' (a combination of wholesome oats and grains, raspberries and sunflower seeds), Marmite, cheese, ham, a loaf of bread. Our days of eke were over: no more Mit Spec, no more cups and buckets on deck to catch rainwater. Take three tablespoons of chocolate mousse for breakfast ... damn it, I was now able to eat the lot. Giggly as six year olds on Christmas morning we set to, dividing our presents as we chumbled on cheese. Dan and Miki drifted off back to the safety of the support yacht and we sat on deck surrounded by enough food and water to feed the entire population of Wales.

~

FEELING FATTER AND happier made the bitter pill of the Guernsey Milkers' success easier to swallow. When they finally made it into Antigua we all felt a huge sense of pride that they had been successful, and as much as we would have loved to beat them it was indeed a fantastic achievement. For the very first time in history a team of four women had rowed across an ocean – it was just a bugger that it wasn't us!

In fact, crews were now overtaking us left, right and centre – even solo rower Chris had now made it across the line. Every day we received text messages telling us the agony of another crew was over. It didn't make me feel any better when I spoke to Clint on the sat phone. I tried my best to hide how jealous I was that he was ashore and we weren't, but with a bit of salacious gossip to share, I was soon distracted from the fact that he had finished and I wouldn't be back in his arms for at least another fortnight!

It seemed word from base camp was that teams were getting a bit angsty because Crackers and Bogle were being promoted by the British press as having won the race, although they had in fact lost race places for drinking their ballast water. If we were lucky we might get into Antigua in time to see the ruckus.

~

THE LAST TWO weeks of the trip went quickly. Against all odds, we were on track for Antigua. If the weather remained as calm as it had been for the previous week or so then we had as good a chance as any of getting into English Harbour without a tow. Could we do it or would fate throw us another curve ball? It's not a surprise, really, that there was one final calamity to come …

FIFTEEN

The Luminous Lights of Land

From: Rowgirls
To: Newsdesk
Date: 14 February 2006
Re: Rowgirls' Diary

Jeepers, we've been waiting to say this for so long ... here goes ... Friends, we're coming home! The countdown is firmly on and only fifty-one miles remain on the clock. The hair has been washed, the last piece of homemade flapjack consumed, the final teabag is waiting patiently for Sue to make her move. We've been vigilantly scanning the skies all day long for signs of the plane carrying Tom,

Clint and Andrew. The thought of finally seeing our families and boyfriends again, closely followed by the thought of wrapping our clawed hands around a cold beer, has become overwhelming. We still have two more days at sea, but that should only make the moment even sweeter when it arrives.

We'll be looking out for our first sighting of shore lights tonight and hope to see land tomorrow if the weather's clear.

We were incredibly lucky yesterday to be visited by two large whales that swam around and under the boat for half an hour. They were at least the full length of our boat and were clearly checking us out; one of them showed us its big white belly whilst spinning under the boat! It was utterly beautiful.

NEWSFLASH! In the time it's taken to write this despatch we have had our closest encounter yet with a tanker! After spotting the vessel on the horizon it took just minutes before it was upon us and headed towards us. For a moment there we thought our row might come to a premature end! After numerous frantic calls on the VHF with no response and a distance of only a couple of hundred metres between us we had no option but to set off flares. After two white fireworks, which lit up the sky, the tanker changed its course and chugged past us with little room to spare.

The Rowgirls x

It's the nightmare that all rowers hope won't happen: arriving on land without your friends and family to see you in, or worse, meeting your family at the airport after getting off the boat. Well, that's almost exactly what we thought we were going to end up doing. There seemed to be difficulties booking flights that would get everyone to Antigua on 14 February, our predicted arrival date. Imagine how lovely that would have been: Valentine's Day, three gorgeous girls, a bright pink boat, their boyfriends waiting with a kiss, their parents with banners and balloons ... But flights were booked for 16 February, and no matter how hard the dads tried there was no way of getting our families to Antigua on time.

We were going to be the first ocean rowing boat in history to try and stay out in the ocean longer than everybody else!

~

SO WE SAT it out. We deployed our para-anchor and drifted; we cleaned the hatches, had a wash, read our books, suntanned our bright-white bum cheeks. We ate, got some sleep, watched whales and bitched about the fact that we couldn't land because the people we loved wouldn't be there.

Unfortunately all our efforts – if you can call doing absolutely nothing an effort – were in vain because the boat was still travelling at over one knot per hour without being rowed. With approximately fifty-five hours until all parents were ready for our arrival, it was fairly obvious that we were going to drift to Antigua too early.

Sue and Claire's emotions had been all over the place before we made our decision to put out the anchor and wait. By this stage Sue was quite prepared to jump out of the boat and swim to land. Claire was really conscious of Sue's distress and was keen to end her misery. They both argued with me when I suggested we wait it out, but I knew how important it was when Mum and I saw our families at the harbour so I tried to talk them round. We had faced worse than a day or two on the para-anchor and there was absolutely no way I was going to meet my parents at the airport. Mum would be livid!

But the decision was taken out of our hands: we would have to row in whether our parents were there to meet us or not.

~

WE CROSSED THE line on 15 February just after 4.00 pm. A RIB carrying Lucy, the Woodvale race officer, hurtled towards us. Having already crossed the line she was keen for us to accept a tow into the mouth of English Harbour. From there we could row the gentle waters of the marina and moor on the pontoon where, we were told, a huge crowd had already gathered.

Perhaps our parents would make it after all?

As the sun set the island was bathed in a deep purple haze, the lights of houses and cars twinkled amongst the lush green palm trees – it was so incredibly beautiful my eyes and brain just couldn't drink it all in. Hitched up to the back of the RIB, we bobbed over the waves towards the safety of the marina. We could hear the cries of Clint, Tom and Andy as they ran out to the very end of the harbour wall to see us in. My heart skipped a beat as I picked out the silhouette of Clint's frame. Having finished his own race a month earlier he had travelled all the way back to Antigua to meet me.

As I looked over at 'my girls' I was consumed with pride and awe, because together, through everything, we, the Rowgirls, Claire, Sue and Sally, had made it across 3,000 miles of ocean. In seventy-seven days, nine hours and twenty-five minutes.

~

OUR PARENTS DIDN'T make it, but we stood before a crowd of locals, holidaymakers and yacht crews and lit our flare, grinning wildly and cheering along as they clapped. When the flare's light finally flickered away Clint, Andy and Tom were there on the pontoon, their arms out ready to grab us.

Clint was so skinny and brown; his tummy striped like a tiger's, his suntan interrupted from bending over at the oars. I threw my face into his chest and stayed there for quite a while. Claire and Sue disappeared into the arms of their men too. Wobbly and giddy with adrenaline the three of us took each other in an embrace and squeezed.

Within half an hour the crowd had dispersed and, supported by the boys, we hobbled up to a hotel where Claire and Sue's parents met us. Banners were erected and balloons inflated. We all went and sat on the loo for the first time in two and a half months, I threw on a pair of high heels and we all gathered in the hotel garden to eat cake Sue's sister had bought from home.

When my parents finally arrived I could tell Mum wasn't happy!

~

JO HAD NOT been there to see us in. She'd wanted to be, but having spent a month in Antigua her finances had finally failed her and she'd had to go home. In fact, she left just hours before we rowed in. Claire and Sue were relieved that she wasn't there, they both still felt a little betrayed by her decision to leave the boat and, perhaps understandably, they were keen not to let this dilute their own achievement.

Jo left a gift for Clint and me, the most gorgeous white woodstain cottage up on the hills around English Harbour. She'd rented it for part of her stay and had asked the owner if we could take it on after her. It was just big enough for the two of us, and as I pranced about in a bikini Clint slept on the clean cotton sheets, his soft, contented snores competing with the buzz of mosquitoes and the rustling of the wind through the palm trees.

SIXTEEN

Epilogue

IT WAS SNOWING when we finally returned to the UK and, not to miss an opportunity to vacate my parents' house, I moved in with Clint the day we flew back. He picked me up from Heathrow and took me straight back to his house in Hampton Court, where I lived out of a suitcase of summer clothes and borrowed his over-sized jumpers whilst I re-introduced myself to normal life – very slowly.

Sue and Claire settled back into work. Sue's achievement won her some much-deserved accolades at GE; in fact she was invited to their international conference in the States where she was given a standing ovation. Her boyfriend Tom converted the loft whilst she was away: she came back to builders' dust, rumble and a brand new bedroom!

Claire started a teacher training course, PE at secondary level. She has recently qualified, giving her the opportunity to encourage disaffected teenage girls to continue participating in sports. She has also moved in with her boyfriend Andrew and their walls are decorated with pictures of their adventures – triathlons, Andrew's trip to the North Pole, their rowing charts!

Jo, on the other hand, landed herself a job as cook on a private super yacht that was set to sail from the Panama Canal to Australia. She has bought a second-hand boat and she plans to attempt the Atlantic again, but as a solo rower!

Mum is back to gardening for her elderly ladies, and they are really pleased to have her back. My relationship with my parents, especially Mum, is now founded on friendship, and is as relaxed and rewarding as any parent–daughter relationship could be. I feel so lucky to have them in my life. Their marriage has also gone from strength to strength and by the time you read this they will have cycled the length of Britain, from Land's End to John o'Groats, celebrating over thirty years together.

And finally, Tommo. Well, I have to admit I'm not really sure what he's up to. I have heard from friends in Brighton that he now lives his girlfriend in Halifax, near his mum. Without Tommo and the summer argument of 2002, much of this adventure might never have happened, and my life would have been the poorer for that.

~

The Epic Challenge for Epilepsy raised a considerable sum of money, £268,000 in all, and within the last couple of years it has been put to good use. A post in Epileptology has been financed and inaugurated at King's College Hospital in London, where efforts are continuing to be made in finding a cure for the condition.

I went to take a look at the facilities and meet the staff at King's having been invited by Jane and Malcolm. After almost two years it really was a pleasure to see them again. Geraldine Carter, the former Mayor of Halifax, also joined us. We really had made a difference and I think we can be truly proud of our achievement.

As for Shelterbox, they kept hold of the boat in the hope that another group of intrepid individuals would take up the gauntlet and row across an ocean for them. The Rowgirls managed to raise approximately £30,000 – enough to buy 60 boxes, which will in turn provide shelter for 600 people. As a charity they continue to grow, which in some ways is entirely unfortunate. With global warming and war many more desperate communities will look to them for accommodation.

~

And me ... Well, I settled back into my rounds of after-dinner talks and signed myself up for background work in films and on the telly – if you're lucky you may even spot my arse on several soaps and commercials, but blink and you'll miss me!

But as I look forward I have found myself in a state of uncertainty, which has surprised me. Even writing this book has not provided many of the answers I sought when I decided to row the Atlantic again.

I thought going again would solidify my new-found confidence, but instead it rocked my self-esteem, all because my ego had been screaming out for some sort of recognition. So, instead of celebrating our monumental achievement, I found myself questioning the meaning of it all.

If I'm honest I was disappointed with the Rowgirl project and that feeling has been very difficult to shift. However hard I've tried to look at it with 'half-full' eyes, I can't help but feel that circumstances dealt us a dud hand.

Why did I go again? Well, it's because I wanted to win – I wanted the record so I could secure the respect of my peers and perhaps even make a name for myself in the public eye. But instead I sat cursing jealously at the television when Ben and James's documentary went to air and not even my arse featured on it.

But with a little perspective and time to think, I have come to realise that the pursuit of recognition is not the best reason to row an ocean, climb a mountain or even go to the moon. Any pursuit driven by ego alone is nearly always an unhealthy one. Although, if there is one thing I have learnt about myself, well, it's that I am not, and will never be, perfect. Also, I really do love my bed!

So what next? Well, a friend did tell me that 'happy people don't climb mountains', and looking ahead at my life with Clint I am very happy and because of this I don't see myself rowing across any more oceans ... Not this year, anyway!

Sally x

Glossary

5'3" (63")	The height of my mum. (NB an inch taller than Rod Stewart and two inches taller than Kylie Minogue and Napoleon Bonaparte)
Anusol	Bum cream. You'll need a nozzle
Argos beacon	A piece of kit that emits a signal reporting your position for tracking purposes. Can also be used for emergency purposes. Similar to EPIRB
Atlantic	An ocean formally known as *oceanis occidentalis*

Awning	A cobbled-together sunshade. Boat hook, string, pegs and sarong required
Backy	To sit two on a bicycle built for one
Bajan	Hailing from Barbados
Bird, Peter	Godfather of modern ocean rowing, first person to row solo across the Pacific in 1983 taking 294 days. Lost at sea in another attempt to cross the same ocean in 1996
Boreham, Stuart	Stuart rowed solo across the Atlantic, leaving just after the Challenge Race in 2003. Although he has cerebral palsy he successfully made it across, becoming the first physically disabled person to row an ocean
Bow	Same as 'forward' and 'aft', front and pointy end
British Rail	Former nationalised rail network provider and employer of Dad. Well known for erratic timekeeping and curled-up bacon sandwiches – that's British Rail, not Dad

Broaching	When the boat is side-on to approaching waves, highly dangerous for smaller boats because of the increased risk of capsize
Bucket shake	Money-raising technique or disposal of effluent at sea
Budd, Zola	Barefooted diminutive South African runner of the 1980s
Budgie smugglers	Very tight men's swimming trucks
Cable knit	A style of knitting that looks like a cable
Calderdale	District around the Halifax area
Canary current	A ubiquitous underwater current that moves south of the Canary Islands
Cava	Reasonably priced sparkling Spanish wine
Challenge Business	Events company set up by Chay Blyth. Principally yacht races until 1997 when he organised the first ocean rowing race, where teams left Tenerife in the hope that they would arrive in Barbados. The ocean rowing arm was sold to Simon Chalk in 2004

Cornish pasty	Parcel of minced lamb and vegetables invented by the wives of Cornish tin miners to prevent metal poisoning
Countdown	Long-running television game show – it's riveting. Featuring Carol Vorderman, a well-known thinking man's Midlander, probably from Tamworth
Crackers and Bogle	aka Ben and Jerry or BJ. Ben Fogle and James Cracknell, celebrity entrants in 2005 race
Da Vinci veneers	Posh false teeth
Drizzle	Not quite rain. The Inuit have twenty words for snow; we have just as many for rain. Also the middle word in lemon drizzle cake
Drogue	Similar to the para-anchor but smaller. Can be deployed to slow or turn the boat. Great as shark bait
EPIRB	Emergency Position Indicating Radio Beacon
Equatorial current	A ubiquitous underwater current that runs from east–west

Faffing	Doing anything that isn't the task in hand, i.e. a welcome break from rowing
Footwell	A well to put your feet in. Located just outside the main cabin door. Fills constantly with festering water where soggy rice crispies float and skin scum accumulates
Galley Puella	Latin for Rowgirl. Sounds a bit like paella
GMT	Greenwich Mean Time
GPS	Global Positioning System, much like a tomtom but on a much bigger scale
Halifax	Birthplace of Tommo (see Yorkshire) and well-known UK financial institution who didn't want me in one of their adverts
Hamill, Rob	Gorgeous New Zealander who'd rowed across the Atlantic in 1997 setting the fastest time for a pair – forty-two days
LT	Local Time
M1	Arterial motorway from London to Leeds. England's first motorway, hence M1

Mango	Exotic fruit and alternative for 'M' in the phonetic alphabet
Mary Rose	Tudor warship where everyone went for a swim and forgot to get back on again. Oh, sorry that's the *Marie Celeste*
Mary Rose	Tudor warship that spent centuries under the water and only a few years on top
Mini coach	Combines the comfort of a coach with the manoeuvrability of a minibus but lacks a toilet and, thankfully, the smell of rugby players' vomit
Northampton	East Midlands market town and home to the first ginger-haired ocean rower. Famous for its extensive motorway network for easy exit
ORS	Ocean Rowing Society. Founded in 1983 by Kenneth Crutchlow in memory of diminutive ocean rower Peter Bird. Set up to support all who attempt to cross an ocean by rowing boat. Motto *nosce te ipsum* (know thy self)
Para-anchor	A large parachute-shaped piece of kit that, once deployed on a long line from

the front of the boat, creates drag and turns the boat into the waves, reducing speed and drift. Used when conditions are pushing the boat in the wrong direction

PDA — Personal Digital Assistant

Portaloo — Trade name for portable latrine

RIB — Rigid Inflatable Boat. Also one component of skeletal array

Rotary — A now-global charitable organisation founded in Chicago around 1912. No secret handshakes or weird religious notions; their members have raised enough money to practically eradicate polio

Rowers' bottom — A flat, spotty and highly unsightly derrière

Seagulls — Brighton FC and the common name for a species of aquatic flying bird

Sea-me — aka the stress-me. A radar reflecting device that allows other vessels to see you

Scotch Corner — Landmark on the road north to Scotland off the A1. Not to be confused with Scotch egg

Securité	Attention all ships!
Stern	Same as 'back', the 'bum bit' or the blunt end
St John Ambulance	Helpful, uniformed volunteer first aid army. Good with Vaseline
Supermarket Sweep	See *Countdown*, but without Carol Vorderman
Swanky	Cool, posh, trendy, stylish, chic
Tacking	A loose sewing stitch/action taken to secure carpets/manoeuvres made by a yacht when attempting to sail against the prevailing wind
Tamworth	Now modest Midlands town but once the mighty capital of Mercia
Tap	The English word for faucet
Therm-a-Rest	A roll-up sleeping mat. Once inflated the honeycombed air pockets prevent heat loss. Surprisingly comfortable
Tiffin cake	A lovely rich fruit cake type cake

Trade winds	Prevailing winds found around the Equator, blowing clockwise in the Northern Hemisphere, anticlockwise in the Southern Hemisphere. Theoretically these winds should blow ocean rowers from east to west. Realistically the winds are all over the place, often blowing them backwards
UT	Universal Time
VHF	Very High Frequency. Portal radio technology, aka the walkie-talkie
Watermaker	A machine that sucks up undrinkable water and makes it nice (something about a reverse osmosis membrane and pumping)
Wellies	Rubber boots named after Arthur Wellesley, Duke of Wellington, military leader of Britain's glorious conquest of the French at Waterloo in 1815
West Pier	Derelict Victorian pier in Brighton. On the left or on the right, depending on which way you're coming

Woodvale	A construction company with Simon Chalk as its MD – the title sponsor of the Atlantic Rowing Race in 2003. Simon took over the event from Challenge Business and currently organise races annually under the company name Woodvale Challenge
Yorkshire	God's own county

Acknowledgements

There is so much to say it's difficult to know where to start, although if there were an opportunity for a group hug then this would be it.

Mum, you won't believe how many women have said they'd never in a million years go rowing with their daughters. Well, I'm so glad you came with me, because when I asked and you said yes we changed our lives. Here's to the 'first ginger-haired woman to row an ocean'! By the way, when you told me you didn't like the front cover, well, I couldn't have had a better endorsement. So there you go: some things never change!

Dad – I can't begin to thank you for everything you've done for me. I hope the feeling of pride I have for you and your achievements is as huge as the pride you feel for me.

Clint, my beautiful fiancé – for keeping me in the manner

that I'm accustomed to and for not losing your temper with me for my constant interruptions about spelling / punctuation / cups of coffee / lurve!

Joe the Toad aka Mike Robinson – my 'myspace'/real space buddy. It goes to show that the person at the other end of the computer isn't always a freaky psychopath, but a kind, gentle person with an offer of help with the book.

A sincere thanks to Jill, for her awesome editing skills.

The extraordinary Epic Challenge Team – Tommo, Jane and Malcolm, Tony, Shoena, Ben and Geraldine, Josephine, Rachel and Robin.

The incredible and inspiring Rowgirls – Claire, Sue and Jo and their families and friends. Sisters are doin' it for themselves. Yeah!

My friends – Zoe, Ruth and Andy, Dr George and Accountant Brian. Thank you for supporting all my daft plans for world domination.

Margaret and Bill for giving me a week in your beautiful villa in Italy – my first three chapters were born there.

My friends in ocean rowing, particularly Jan and Dan, Kenneth Crutchlow, Tatiana and Simon Chalk; in fact all those ocean rowers who offered their advice and stories of terror and arse sores. Ocean rowing is one of those few remaining Corinthian sports where camaraderie and support rate higher than out-and-out competition.

Teresa Page – for help, patience and advice over four years (can you believe it?) of ocean rowing.

Lin Parker – for saving us on more than one occasion! Glug glug glug!

The Fund for Epilepsy and Shelterbox – it has been such a pleasure to work with two incredible charities who continue to support those who really need it. Although it's been rough seas at times we all got through it together.

www.thefundforepilepsy.org

www.shelterbox.org

All those who have helped get the boats ready for action: Ben and Malcolm, Mel and the boys in Falmouth.

The poor buggers along the way who have suffered with me in the gestation of this book, among them many supporting artists (extras to the hoi poloi) that I've worked with whilst getting it written … in particular the crowd in the green room on the set of *Holby Blue*! As I tipped tapped away waiting for my turn to walk past a frosted glass window, the temptation to seek approval from my co-supporting artistes was all too strong – so thanks for the input and encouragement, guys.

All the media outlets who followed our attempts – particularly *The Times*, BBC Radio Northampton, BBC *South Today* and BBC *Look East*. The *Chronicle & Echo* in Northampton, the *Halifax Courier* and the *Yorkshire Post*.

And finally, all the sponsors, supporters and contributors – if I tried to list you all I fear I would miss some of you out, but I hope by reading this book you will understand the huge impact you have made to so many people's lives. Not just my own, but all who have benefited from the money that has been raised.

THANK YOU x